SEASONS OF REVIVAL

Understanding the
Appointed Times
of Spiritual Refreshing

SEASONS OF REVIVAL

Understanding the *Appointed Times* of Spiritual Refreshing

FRANK DAMAZIO

CITYBIBLE
PUBLISHING

Published by City Bible Publishing
9200 NE Fremont
Portland, Oregon 97220

Printed in U.S.A.

City Bible Publishing is a ministry of City Bible Church, and is dedicated to serving the local church and its leaders through the production and distribution of quality restoration materials.

It is our prayer that these materials, proven in the context of the local church, will equip leaders in exalting the Lord and extending His kingdom.

For a free catalog of additional resources from City Bible Publishing please call

1-800-777-6057 or visit our web site at www.CityBiblePublishing.com.

Seasons of Revival
© Copyright 1996 by City Bible Publishing
All Rights Reserved

ISBN 1-886849-04-8

DEDICATION

I wish to dedicate this book to my father-in-law, Kevin J. Conner, who also is a father in the Lord. He has the unique spiritual ability to sense God's seasons of change and make needed adjustments in order to enjoy new showers of God's Spirit. He is a man with a love for the Word and the Spirit, has a unique sense of humor, and is a wonderful example of never becoming fossilized.

Pastor Frank Damazio

FOREWORD

We are living in perhaps one of the most exciting times in the history of the church. There is a culmination of many significant movements that are impacting this day and age. The prayer and spiritual warfare movement is strengthening the church and its focus. The men's movement is rallying literally millions of men to once again take rightful leadership of their marriage, families, homes, churches and cities. The emphasis and fruit of reaching all people groups with the gospel of Christ is yielding an average of 140,000 people a day. The move to reconcile race with race, parents to children, and denomination to denomination, combined with a fresh outpouring of the Holy Spirit, may change the face of Christianity.

With each significant move of the Spirit, comes the potential for great blessing and growth as well as a potential for division and deception. There is no question that such is the case in these days in which we live.

Every river needs banks to guide and direct the waters to their intended destination and to minimize the potential of disaster. The same applies to seasons of revival.

Recently, I had the privilege of viewing the manuscript for this book, and to my delight, I found some very insightful and relevant truths on Revival. Over the past few decades I have been exposed to many books on revival. This book contains many elements that are mandatory to sustain and strengthen season's of God's out-pouring. Here are a few:

- Seasons of Revival is biblical—this book is profuse with scriptural references of both the Old and New Testament to help validate the philosophy and strategies recommended.

- Seasons of Revival is informative—Frank Damazio has pulled in appropriate information drawn from the literature on the entire history of revival and its effects on the church.

- Seasons of Revival is pastoral—the book deals with many issues of revival that are on the hearts of the people in our churches today. It is written by a pastor to impact laypeople as well as leaders.

- Seasons of Revival is contemporary—Pastor Frank deals with today's issues, including the current Renewal movements, college campus revivals, International revivals and he has the advantage of being an insider to such circles.

- Seasons of Revival is wise—Frank Damazio really knows how to walk the fine line between quenching the Spirit and opening up to an "anything goes" type of foolishness.

- Seasons of Revival is safe—after reading the manuscript there is a feeling of safety to enter into an outpouring of God with a clear biblical base, clarity and discernment.

I hope this book is widely distributed to reach the multitudes needing clear direction during seasons of revival. It could become an all-time classic! Seasons of Revival is a must both for charasmatics who seem to feel more comfortable with supernatural phenomena, and also for those of us with a mainline or evangelical background.

As you read on, my prayer is that the Holy Spirit will bring personal renewal to your heart and that it will bear the fruit of true revival in your church and in you community.

C. Peter Wagner
Fuller Theological Seminary

CONTENTS

INTRODUCTION

*M*y upbringing as a Baptist made sitting in the living room with a hundred young people singing choruses and lifting their hands a very uncomfortable experience. I was not familiar with singing in the Spirit, using a different language called "speaking in tongues," or the exuberance that was present in the room. I sat in wonderment that these young people were so free to express their love to God. I wondered what would motivate them to act the way they did and why they spoke about God in such a personal way. At first, it was embarrassing to me.

My dad was a pastor of a mainline denominational church that I had been raised in, but at the time of this meeting I had not totally surrendered my life to Jesus Christ. I had not experienced a divine empowerment of God upon my soul.

I walked to the nearest wall and sat down. I did not know what to do at this meeting, and I did not want to be noticed. I had not come to take part in the worship or to sing choruses with the young people; I had come for a totally different reason. They were there to worship God, but I was not.

It was 1968 and I was a senior in high school, away from God and not attending church. I had been dabbling in the rebellious culture of the '60s. I did not have a belief system that drew me into the environment of the '60s, just a desire to identify with the spirit of that time. There was a spirit of rebellion against "the establishment" in that era, and a radically new vision and dream for a different America and a different way to live.

I was living in a different world than the other teens in the room. I did not understand God or revival. One thing I understood, though, was that there was a void in my heart, a tremendous need for something more than I was living.

Sitting on a stool in the middle of the floor was the man who was leading this meeting. Somehow his eye caught mine as he was asking the young people questions. I was able to understand one of his questions and, for some reason, I blurted out one of the few Scriptures I knew by memory. John 3:16: "For God so loved the world that He gave His only begotten Son, that whosoever should believe in Him should not perish but have everlasting life."

The man I quoted the Scripture to was Albie Pearson, who had played major league baseball for the California Angels before injuring his back sliding into second base. His injury ended his baseball career, and now he was opening his home to the youth of the city.

Albie was not impressed with my response, but simply said to me, "I perceive that you know the Bible, but do you really know God?" The question riveted me to the floor. Of course I did not know God, so I had to answer honestly, "No sir, I do not think I do know God, but I might if somebody would show me."

I left the meeting that night pondering the question Albie had asked me. It was then that I began to slowly turn my heart toward God. Eventually, I surrendered my life to Jesus, was baptized in the Holy Spirit, and began to walk with God in a way that I had never before known.

I had no idea at that time that my life change would put me into the middle of a then-brewing national revival of youth. Nobody had used the phrases "Jesus freak" or "Jesus Movement" at this point. It was just the beginning of the outpouring of the Holy Spirit upon the youth of that day.

During those early days of revival in southern California, with Albie Pearson and the Albie Pearson Youth Foundation that we established, I witnessed literally dozens of absolutely supernatural miracles of God. I watched as blind eyes were made to see and deaf ears to hear. I witnessed tumors disappearing as people received supernatural healing from God.

No one told us that what was happening was a revival. We did not realize then that this movement we were taking part in was actually making history. National magazines, newspapers, and radio and television picked up on the Jesus Movement, but we ourselves did not completely understand what was happening in our midst.

"We did not have any deep theological understanding, or even a practical knowledge of what to do when we met. We just tried to follow the Bible."

We did not understand divine principles. We did not have doctrines of healing or prayer. We did not even have a real understanding of faith. We were not teachers of the Word, nor were we a local church. We were meeting in an ordinary home, baptizing people in an ordinary swimming pool, and serving communion off ordinary plates with ordinary grape juice. We did not have any deep theological understanding, or even a practical knowledge of what to do when we met. We just tried to follow the Bible.

When we read in Scripture that you were to be baptized in water, we took people out and baptized them. When we read that we were to lay hands on the sick and they would be healed, we would do just that. When we read that we were to go into all the world and preach the Gospel, we would pack a brown bag lunch, get onto a highway somewhere, and hitch-hike around southern California, waiting for someone to pick us up so we could witness to that person. We would sleep wherever we would end up that night, hoping that God would open a home for us or that someone would offer us a meal.

We took the Bible so literally that we acted a little strangely at times. But there was such a spirit of revival and expectation in the air when we met, that we believed that God was able to do almost anything.

We saw hundreds of young people bowing their knees to Jesus. But at the same time we saw these people saved, we also lost hundreds of others because we did not know what to do during revival. We knew how to believe God at that point, but we did not know how to build the church. We did not understand the divine principles of pastoring, teaching, caring, and walking in the wisdom of God.

Erroneous doctrines began to surface: extreme doctrines of demonology, doctrines of the coming of Christ, and doctrines concerning the body of Christ.

We saw all these things happening, but we did not have any idea what to do.

At first, witnessing the falling away of the young people during revival made me resentful and bitter toward the leadership—and toward God. I did not trust leaders or pastors or churches, and I did not understand why God would pour out

His Spirit and then allow so many people to fall away with no way to recover them. Miraculously, one of the women in this revival came to my home and counseled me out of the root of bitterness that had begun to grow within me.

It was not until I was introduced to a pastor in a local church that I began to receive teaching and understanding of what it really meant to walk with God and establish divine principles in my life. These things were seared upon my mind and conscience.

I wanted to know how to live and how to seek the kingdom of God. I wanted to know how to have a true Holy Spirit revival, one that wouldn't do the kind of damage to people that I had seen earlier. I wanted to know all these things, yet I had no training at all.

Later, I received that training, first at the local church, then when I went on to Bible college and became a young leader. It was during this time that God began to open my eyes to the things that the body of Christ needs to do in order to maintain balance during a moving of the Holy Spirit.

THE CHARISMATIC RENEWAL

Shortly after that, I was introduced to what was called the "Charismatic Renewal." I was still a young man and a young leader in the church, but I watched again as revival began to spread throughout our nation. People in local churches were empowered by the Holy Spirit, and many of them were baptized in the Spirit. Lifting of hands in worship and praise, receiving of the Holy Spirit with the evidence of speaking in tongues, and moving in the power gifts of healing and deliverance were all part of this movement.

But many churches did not have understanding concerning this kind of Holy Spirit activity, so they did not know what to do with these newly Spirit-baptized believers. Thousands of people left their churches and started prayer meetings and Holy Spirit gatherings in their homes. This caused much confusion and many church splits, but out of this came many hundreds of independent churches that were able to function under charismatic gifts and doctrines. Slowly, the churches began to embrace what was going on. But for many of them it was too late. There was already too much damage done during this renewal.

> "Revival always exposes what is weak and intensifies faulty foundations that are already present."

LEARNING FROM THE PAST

After reading about my experiences and observations in these revivals, you may be asking questions such as, "What can we learn from what happened during these revivals?" or, "If revival is something we should earnestly seek, why are there so many problems?"

I believe the answer to these questions lies in the human factor. Revival always exposes what is weak and intensifies faulty foundations that are already present. Whether it is in the extreme actions of people or in the extreme reactions of leaders, revival causes us to rethink the way we do things or to position ourselves either for or against the changes that revival invariably brings.

Revival is never easy. It brings change, and some of that change can be messy. That is because the moving of the Holy Spirit is always through imperfect channels: people.

SEIZING THE MOMENT OF GOD'S OUTPOURING

Over the past several years, there have been signs in North America—and around the world—of a new moving of the Holy Spirit that is affecting many thousands of people.

A stirring of the Holy Spirit has been reported in Toronto, Canada, where thousands of people have been touched with the Holy Spirit during the more than two years of prayer meetings at the "Toronto Blessing." Revival is also taking place on college campuses across our country. A headline in one recent local newspaper read, "College Students Discover Revivals." The reporter described the wave of revival currently sweeping across our country's college campuses.

As we move into this season of Holy Spirit revival, we face some vitally important questions: Can we learn from the successes and failures of past revivals? Are there scriptural principles that lay a secure foundation on which we can build a platform for greater outpouring?

The answer to each of these questions is an overwhelming, yes! As we enter these seasons of revival, there are principles of wisdom that we can apply that will build a solid foundation for revival in our day.

As you continue to read this book, hopefully you will find spiritual insights that will help you prepare for revival. You will read about past revivals and the lessons we can learn from them. And, of course, you will see what the Word of God has to say about revival in your life and within the whole body of Christ.

PART 1

WHEN GOD COMES DOWN

Chapter 1

OUR NEED FOR REVIVAL

*A*s the children of God, we must pray that God will come down and bring us His deliverance. We must pray that He will rain upon us with His presence, that His fire will come and burn upon us.

Our desire must be to experience individual and corporate revival that has lasting effects. This is God's promise and our hope—our expectation. We must pray that God would grant us a spiritual awakening and open us to receiving a greater outpouring of the Holy Spirit. We must pray that God will renew in us His vision for the world: to reach the nations and make us a missionary people who go out and reap the harvest from the four corners of the earth.

We must pray for a responsiveness to revival, a smoldering of this great fire throughout the land. The desire of the Holy Spirit is to fan the flames into an all-consuming fire that burns hot within us.

THE TIMELY ARRIVAL OF RENEWAL

We need to fervently pray not just for God to give us a spirit of revival, but to send it soon. The church—the world—is in desperate need of a mighty move of the Holy Spirit. Now is the time, we are the people, and this is the place.

Still, you may ask, why is it so important for us to have revival now? Why the urgency? Read on and you will see how very desperately we need this promised renewal.

There is a lukewarmness and traditionalism that is binding the body of Christ today, keeping it from being the culture-changing and devil-confronting church that it is called to be. The church in America has had much activity, but without much growth in the number of new converts.

The church is in desperate need of CPR: A Christ-Prevailing Revival! People of God, particularly the young and the new converts, need a fresh touch of the Holy Spirit upon their lives, just as many of us received in the past.

We, as God's people, need to be delivered from aimlessness and fruitlessness, from drifting away from the purposes of God. We need a new spirit of surrender and willingness—a heart of obedience—to do anything the Holy Spirit asks us to do.

> **"The church is in desperate need of CPR: A Christ-Prevailing Revival!"**

A CULTURE IN DECLINE

Our nation has turned from God and His ways. We have abandoned not just God's Word, but almost all objective standards of right and wrong. As one leader recently stated, "The destruction of Nineveh could easily fit the United States."

This turning away has had frightening consequences. It does not take a cultural analyst to see that we are in serious trouble. Our social problems are staggering.

Our children are not even safe when they get to school in the morning. More than three million crimes occur on or near school campuses every year. One of seven children in the United States is being bullied or are bullies. One in five high school students carries a weapon. One in twenty carries a gun.

The family is becoming an endangered species. During this century, the divorce rate has risen 700 percent.

Thirteen million children under the age of eighteen are growing up with one or both of their parents away from home. Seventy percent of all juveniles in state reform institutions come from fatherless homes.

By 1994 more than 30 million babies in America had been aborted. The United States is the single greatest market on the globe for illegal drugs and leads the world in the export of pornography.

Our turning from God has affected how people of different races relate to one another. Even with all our well-meaning legislation and social reform programs, the nineties has seen a polarization between races in the United States.

Despite all this, it seems that we as a society are willing to turn to anything but God to solve our problems. The supernatural thought structure is shunned as alien in the academic arena. This generation sees Christianity as a grand lie or noble deception. Our culture denigrates God, devalues the Bible as nothing but a book of legends, and rejects eternal things like heaven and hell as myths.

Not only is our nation discarding the notion of God, but in many ways there seems to be hostility toward God. Prayer has been taken from our schools, replaced by the training of our young people in philosophies that are patently anti-God and anti-Bible. In 1980 the U.S. Supreme Court ruled that schools could not post the Ten Commandments because it might prompt the children to read, ponder, revere, or obey the commandments.[1]

We need revival, a touch and a cleansing from Almighty God, if our nation is going to turn toward the cross and away from attempting to solve its own problems.

A RISE IN NEW AGE AND OTHER RELIGIONS IN OUR NATION

Never has there been such an invasion of other gods and god philosophies as we have had in the past fifty years. Millions of people read thousands of different books that espouse anything but Christianity. True biblical Christianity is not "in vogue" at this time in history. New Age religions and other philosophies seem to be shoving authentic Christianity aside.

There is a widespread permeation of New Age religion into every level of society and culture today. New Age-based philosophies have penetrated hospitals, doctors' offices, corporation training seminars, federal agencies, city councils, White House staff, state legislatures, volunteer organizations, universities, and our public school system.

> **"There is a widespread permeation of New Age religion into every level of society and culture today."**

This satanically empowered movement has infiltrated our society by using vehicles such as holistic health centers, Montessori schools, Waldorf education, transcendental meditation, mind-control courses, hunger projects, whole earth catalogs, many health food stores, vegetarian restaurants, and the animal rights movement.

A new vocabulary has risen in our culture from the New Age philosophy. Words and phrases such as holistic, spaceship earth, global village, transformation, crowded planet, god within us, and many others have become part of our belief systems.

New Age has its own priests and gurus, and its own born-again experience, which is called "rebirthing." It has its own spiritual laws and commandments, psychics and prophets.

Mystical experiences and experiential religion with a leaning of orthodox Christianity are sure signs of New Age influence. These philosophies teach that Christianity has much in common with eastern religions, that their basic doctrines are much the same as those in our faith.

There are numerous new books that espouse a merging of New Age philosophy and Christianity. One such book is *The Aquarian Gospel of Jesus Christ*. One quote from one chapter will give you a glimpse into this New Age thinking:

"And as the holy ones have judged, when men have needed added light, a master of the soul has come to earth to give that light. Jesus was not always Christ. Jesus won His Christship by a strenuous life. In ages yet to come man will attain to greater heights, and lights still more intense will come. And then, at least, a mighty master soul will come to earth to light the way up to the house of perfect man."[2]

New Age is only one of many moving and growing religions or philosophies in our culture that are opposed by the Bible. The Scripture says in 1 John 2:22, "Who is a liar but he that denieth that Jesus is the Christ. He is the antichrist that denieth the Father and the Son" (also see 1 John 4:3; 2 Thessalonians 2:2-3).

We need revival right now in our nation in order to counteract and resist the many different religions and philosophies that are coming into our nation through satanic delusions and deceptions.

GOD DESIRES TO "COME DOWN"

When you look at what is happening in our nation—in our churches—is there any question in your mind as to why we need revival? And could there be any question that revival is what God desires for His people?

God desires to visit His people, and His Word gives us a promise of visitation by the Holy Spirit. Our responsibility now is to take God at His word, to believe what the Scriptures have to say about revival:

> "God desires to visit His people, and His Word gives us a promise of visitation by the Holy Spirit."

"You have granted me life and favor, and Your visitation has preserved my spirit" (Job 10:12).

"Having your conduct honorable among the Gentiles, that when they speak against you as evildoers, they may, by your good works which they observe, glorify God in the day of visitation" (1 Peter 2:12).

"Blessed is the Lord God of Israel, for He has visited and redeemed His people" (Luke 1:68).

"Through the tender mercy of our God, with which the Dayspring from on high has visited us" (Luke 1:78).

"If you had known, even you, especially in this your day, the things that make for your peace! But now they are hidden from your eyes. For days will come upon you when your enemies will build an embankment around you, surround you and close you in on every side, and level you, and your children within you, to the ground; and they will not leave in you one stone upon another, because you did not know the time of your visitation" (Luke 19:42-44).

The Bible tells us that God desires to pour out His Spirit on His people. We must believe what God's Word says, and we must actively seek God for fulfillment of His promises. In other words, if we want revival, we must start by asking God for it.

PRAYING FOR DIVINE VISITATION

God did not leave anything out of the written Word that His people need in order to seek Him and His will. The Bible gives us a perfect model for how we should pray for revival in the book of Isaiah, chapters 63 and 64. This is one of the prayer gems of the Old Testament. The cry of this prayer is for divine visitation, a cry that God would actually come down.

Isaiah 63:15 starts with this request of God: "Look down from heaven, and see from Your habitation, holy and glorious. Where are Your zeal and Your strength, the yearning of Your heart and Your mercies toward me? Are they restrained?"

Our prayer for revival starts with us asking God to look down upon us, to consider our situation and see who we are, where we are, and what we need. We must ask God to examine our compassion, our zeal, our deeds, and our motivation. God will honor this prayer because He is our Father God. He is interested in who we are and what state we are in.

Verse 17 of this passage says, "O LORD, why have You made us stray from Your ways, and hardened our heart from Your fear? Return for Your servants' sake, the tribes of Your inheritance."

This verse refers to the condition of the people's hearts. It is a prayer that God would return to save His people from their hardness of heart, to come down and intervene because their adversary has trodden them down. They are being ruled by the enemy, like those who have never even been called by the name of the Lord.

This is a prayer of revival, a prayer that God would help us recognize our immediate needs, that we would recognize our low spiritual state. When we approach God, seeking His visitation, we must begin by recognizing what our needs truly are.

A PRAYER FOR THE HEAVENS TO BE OPENED

Isaiah 64:1 is a passionate prayer for divine intervention: "Oh, that thou wouldst rend the heavens!" The word rend in the Hebrew means to tear upon, to cleave asunder, to divide, to break open, to take by storm, to tear in pieces. One translation reads, "O Lord, tear the covering over the heavens and appear now."

Today's heavens are in need of rending. There is now a dimension of sin and evil that goes beyond that of individual human beings. This is social or corporate sin. We live in a time when our government uses its laws to enforce tolerance toward non-biblical, immoral lifestyles. This will affect every person living under our nation's laws. The heavens may be closed to us unless we as the people of God passionately pray for divine intervention.

This is the cosmic character of sin that brings the need for the heavens to be opened. This dimension of sin is an evil that is beyond that of an individual, an evil that affects all boundary lines, all colors and races, all political systems. This is sin that becomes part of the system in the midst of a nation.

For this reason, today's heavens could be classified in two categories:

Heavens are as Iron

"I will break the pride of your power. I will make your heavens like iron and your earth like bronze" (Leviticus 26:19).

Our nation is moving into spiritual apostasy. The intentional breaking of God's laws and covenants, including disrespect for His house and His people, builds a case for God to make the heavens as iron. The enslavement to sin and flight from the reality of God's laws are signs of apostasy. The continual denial of sin, the self-deceit, the insensitivity, the self-centeredness, the rejection of authority, and the ever-extending sensuality of our day indicate that the heavens are as iron.

God says He will bring seven times punishment upon this kind of nation, with a design to bring it to repentance. In the Scriptures and throughout history, we can see that an apostate nation will encounter multiple calamities because it has invited the enemies to come in and destroy and rape the land. The terror, disease, fever, blindness, confusion, violence, destruction of children, famine, and trouble in the cities of today all testify that the heavens have become as iron.

When we, as the people of God, become apathetic or indifferent toward the divine word of the Lord, when we do not hearken or comply with God's divine standards, when we are contemptuous and rejecting of God's statutes and despise His moral laws, we know that the heavens are as iron.

God desires to bring His people to repentance, to a spiritual reform and revolution that will regenerate our hearts so that He might tear the covering that is over the heavens and appear again in a revival atmosphere.

Heavens are Shut Up

"Lest the Lord's anger be aroused against you and He shut up the heavens so that there be no rain, and the land yield no produce, and you perish quickly from the good land which the Lord is giving you" (Deuteronomy 11:17).

"And the Lord shut up the heavens" is a phrase used over and over in the Bible. We read in Deuteronomy the account of the heavens being shut up because God's people did not heed His words. There was no word from heaven, no glory from heaven, no visitation from heaven because their hearts were taken up and deceived and they worshiped other gods. God did not even look down from heaven to notice the people because of their insensitivity and hard-heartedness.

> "The heavens are shut tight when a people make the tragic decision to build their value system through the world's understanding of truth, meaning, and reality."

The heavens are shut tight when a people make the tragic decision to build their value system through the world's understanding of truth, meaning, and reality. If we are to see the heavens opened to us, we must turn back to God's standards and reject those of the world.

PRAYERS THAT BREAK OPEN THE HEAVENS

Our heavens have become as iron and have been shut up to us. It has long seemed as if God has withdrawn His supernatural presence from us. Yet there is now a cry from the people of God, a prayer that the darkened heavens that hang over us might be rent so that we may see a disclosure of His majestic and saving power.

It is time for a rending, a time for a tearing open, a time for an outpouring of the refreshing presence of God. It is time for revival. We desperately need a moving of the Holy Spirit, and God sees that need and is responding to us. Today's heavens are beginning to open.

When the heavens are torn open, God comes down and everything changes: "When there are open heavens, I will give you rain. I will give you peace. I will look favorably upon you. I will set My tabernacle among you. I will walk among you and be your God. I will remember My covenant with you. I will open the heavens and heal your land and forgive you of your sins" (2 Chronicles 7:1-14).

Yes, God is preparing us for a rending of the heavens. He has given in His Word the prayers of a people who are seeking this tearing open of the heavens.

Prayers of Brokenness

To open the heavens, we must pray a prayer of brokenness. The prayer of a broken people is recorded in 2 Chronicles 12-14 and 1 Kings 18:41. To open the heavens, we need to humble ourselves and recognize that God is sovereign. We must confess our sins and expect God to remember His covenant and come down to us for a mighty visitation.

Prayers to Break the Power of Materialism

We must break the power of materialism that reigns supreme in our land. Malachi 3:10 says, " 'Bring all the tithes into the storehouse, that there may be food in My house, and try Me now in this way,' says the Lord of hosts. 'If I will not open for you the windows of heaven and pour out for you such a blessing that there will not be room enough to receive it.' "

We are praying for open heavens, but money and possessions have become our god, our life purpose. We have made money a measuring rod of our spiritual depth, spiritual life, and maturity. But if we are stingy with our money or if money is our god, then we know that the true God of the Bible is not truly the ruler of our lives.

We must break the bondage of materialism. We need to begin as the people of God to give our tithes and our offerings back to the house of the Lord so that He might open the windows and open heaven and pour out a blessing that we cannot even contain.

Sacrifice of Prayer and Praise

To open the heavens, we also use the key of David as recorded in Isaiah 22:22: "The key of the house of David I will lay on his shoulder; so he shall open, and no one shall shut; and he shall shut, and no one shall open." Revelation 3:7-8 tells us, "And to the angel of the church in

Philadelphia write, "These things says He who is holy, He who is true, "He who has the key of David, He who opens and no one shuts, and shuts and no one opens: I know your works. See, I have set before you an open door, and no one can shut it; for you have a little strength, have kept My word, and have not denied My name." ' "

The key of David speaks of Davidic worship, which is the key to entering into God's presence. It is the sacrifice of prayer and praise, the key that unlocks the mysteries of God and allows God to come down into our midst (also see Hebrews 13:15).

We must pray that our worship and praise are authentic, and not modern-day substitutes. Human hype can be a modern-day substitute for divine anointing. For example, electronic amplification can become a counterfeit for true worship. We must make sure that true worship is not supplanted by the television and Hollywood-style theatrical shows that merely entertain us.

> "We must pray that our worship and praise are authentic, and not modern-day substitutes."

Prayers for Authentic Visitation

We need to pray that the person of divine visitation, which is God Himself, would come down. In Isaiah 64:1 it simply says, "that You would come down." The prayer is for God to appear in the heavens and then go one step further—to come down. The prayer here is to resist the seduction of substitutes. In Exodus 33:2 and 15, as Moses was offered the angel to go with him, he rejected the substitute and asked for God Himself. Moses simply said, "I want You."

The time has come to humble ourselves under God's sovereign hand and focus on who God is. We must look to Him as the true, sovereign source of genuine spiritual awakening. We must forsake all substitutes and ask for God Himself to come down.

Jeremiah 2:13 says, "We have potentially forsaken the fountain of living water and hewn out broken cisterns for ourselves." None of the substitutes that man creates can replace the presence of God or His life-changing, supernatural power. Cisterns can only store water, and eventually it will stagnate. We need to realize the simplicity of God that we have in Christ (2 Corinthians 11:3) and we need to receive the person and work of the Holy Spirit in a fresh and new way (also see Acts 2:1-4, 10:44, 11:15; Isaiah 32:15; Ezekiel 2:2, 8:3, 11:1).

SIGNS OF GOD'S MANIFESTED POWER

It is not business as usual when God comes down. A visitation from the Spirit of God means that things are going to change. There are a number of Scriptures that tell us about what happens when God comes down.

Exodus 3:8 says, "So I have come down to deliver them out of the hand of the Egyptians . . ." This speaks of God's power to deliver and do mighty works when He appears.

Numbers 11:17 says, "Then I will come down and talk with you there. I will take of the spirit that is upon you and will put the same upon them." This tells us that when God comes down there is a communion. There is a ministry of His Spirit upon us.

When God appears there is deliverance, there is the voice of God, and the fire of God. When He comes down, there is the fire for worship, the rain of blessing, the rain of God's word, the sovereign power of God, Holy Spirit activity, and present truth delivered. All of these things happen when God comes down (see Exodus 3:8, 10:20; Numbers 11:17, 11:25, 12:5; 2 Kings 1:12-14; 2 Chronicles 7:1-3; Psalm 72:6; Isaiah 55:10, 31:4; 1 Peter 1:12).

When God comes down, His people will encounter His power and the manifestation of that power. Isaiah 64:1-7 highlights seven things that happen to us when a revival atmosphere takes place and God comes down.

Sign One: God Dissolves Immovable Difficulties

Verse 3 says that, "mountains shook at Your presence." This tells us that mountains of difficulties are leveled into smoothness in God's presence. Difficulties arise from ourselves and our mistakes. Our unfaithfulness or lack of watchfulness creates some of our worst mountains. Yet, by His grace, these mountains will shake at His presence and be dissolved.

Sign Two: God Removes Dead Areas in Our Lives

Verse 2 says that, "fire burns up the brushwood." This speaks of removing needless dead areas in our spiritual lives. During the pruning season, all the dry brushwood is piled and burned. These worthless, dead limbs are removed from the groves of our lives and devoured by the fire of God. When God comes down, all that is evil, all that opposes the progress of truth within us and around us is consumed (see Hebrews 12:29; Luke 12:49; John 15:1-8; Psalm 144:5; Deuteronomy 32:22; Judges 5:4-5; Micah 1:3-4; Habakkuk 1:4).

A typical vine will have about fifty to sixty shoots growing on it prior to pruning. After it is trimmed, the vine will have only about five of these shoots left. These are the shoots that can produce fruit. Likewise, there is a lot more dead brushwood in our lives than there is productive brushwood, so we need to be exposing ourselves continually to the fire of God so that He can prune out and burn the worthless shoots.

Sign Three: God Restores Our Zeal

Verse 2 says that when God comes down, "the fire boils the water." This speaks of God moving us from lukewarmness to spiritual hotness. When God comes down, He burns into our spirits a new love and excitement for Him. A burning zeal and a new enthusiasm surfaces in us when God comes down.

Sign Four: God Brings Victory

Verse 2 tells us that "the name of God is amongst the adversary." When God comes down, there is spiritual victory over our worst enemies. In this passage, the adversaries had come down to trample Israel, and had been largely successful. But when God came down, there was a release from these adversaries and victory over them. God did something for His people that they could not do for themselves.

Sign Five: Vision is Enlarged

Verse 2 says that, "nations tremble." When a nation trembles, its boundaries are shaken and removed. God begins to enlarge our vision, not only for ourselves, but for all the people around us. It is a time of removing the self-imposed boundary lines in our own lives, and for removing vision lines that limit God's people.

> "It is a time of removing the self-imposed boundary lines in our own lives, and for removing vision lines that limit God's people."

Sign Six: The Impossible Becomes Reality

Verse 3 says that, "awesome things are done." The good-ness of God takes place when we least expect it. God begins to do awesome deeds, both in and out of our presence. All things begin to work together as we begin to move in the pur-poses of God. Things that we thought impossible before are now made possible because God has come down and is doing awesome things in our lives and our circumstances.

Sign Seven: God Moves on Behalf of the One Who Waits

Verse 4 says, "He acts for the one who waits." This is a pre-cious promise to the persistent, patient believer. There is none who stirs up himself to take hold of God, but when God moves, we are stirred to take hold of His promises. We wait upon the Lord to renew our strength, and as our strength is renewed, we can take hold of the promises of God that have evaded us, sometimes for long periods of time.

WAITING FOR GOD TO COME DOWN

Yes, things begin to happen when God comes down. Let us not accept any substitutes. Let us not shy away from the promises that have been left us concerning the awesome presence of God.

When God comes down, He comes down to shake up what is there. He comes down to change what already exists. God comes down, not to leave things as they are now, but to change by His miraculous working.

When God comes down, things change. Things happen. Revival is simply this: "God comes."

NOTES

1. Arthur E. Demiss, *Rebirth of America* (Foundation Publishers, 1986), n.a.
2. *The Aquarian Gospel of Jesus Christ.*

Chapter 2

THE PROMISE OF REVIVAL

*W*e live in a time when we as the people of God—as well as the world we live in—desperately need God to come down and touch us with a spirit of revival.

The Bible speaks about the Holy Spirit being poured out upon all flesh, and I believe we can expect this kind of revival in this generation. I believe that revival is indeed a partial fulfillment of biblical prophecy. Why do I believe this? Because I believe what the written Word of God tells us about God's desire to pour out His Spirit on His people.

Here is some biblical passages that tells us of God's desire to revive His people:

"For I will pour water on him who is thirsty, and floods on the dry ground; I will pour My Spirit on your descendants, and My blessing on your offspring; they will spring up among the grass like willows by the watercourses.' One will say, 'I am the Lord's'; another will call himself by the name of Jacob; another will write with his hand, 'The Lord's,' and name himself by the name of Israel" (Isaiah 44:3-5).

"And it shall come to pass afterward that I will pour out My Spirit on all flesh; your sons and your daughters shall prophesy, your old men shall dream dreams, your young men shall see visions." (Joel 2:28-29).

"And it shall come to pass in the last days, says God, that I will pour out of My Spirit on all flesh; your sons and your daughters shall prophesy, your young men shall see visions, your old men shall dream dreams" (Acts 2:17).

"Therefore be patient, brethren, until the coming of the Lord. See how the farmer waits for the precious fruit of the earth, waiting patiently for it until it receives the early and latter rain" (James 5:7).

"Let us know, let us pursue the knowledge of the Lord. His going forth is established as the morning; He will come to us like the rain, like the latter and former rain to the earth" (Hosea 6:3). (Also see Zechariah 4:6, 10:1; Habakkuk 3:2; Isaiah 32:15, 59:19-20; Matthew 3:11.)

"I believe God is responding to the prayers of His people around the world for a promised outpouring of His Holy Spirit upon hungry hearts in our day."

I believe God is responding to the prayers of His people around the world for a promised outpouring of His Holy Spirit upon hungry hearts in our day. And there are many Christian leaders who also believe that renewal and revival are upon our nation and the nations of the world:

Ralph Mahoney, director of World MAP: "Each new move of God is heralded by three momentous signs: (1) some epoch event in the nation of Israel, (2) a parallel counterpart of a spiritual nature in the church, (3) change of leaders from the previous movements with replacement by new leaders. There is a sense in my spirit that we are on the verge of a new visitation of God, right here in North America, that is going to not only affect our continent, but others as well."[1]

Graham Truscott, in his book, *The Power of His Presence:* "The latter rain in prophetic sense is a mighty revival of the church in the last days of the present age. Mighty revival will sweep the world. By comparing Scripture with Scripture we shall see that this glorious restoration is speaking of the great world-wide move of the Spirit of God at the end of the Gospel age, just before the second coming of the Lord Jesus Christ. The revival for which we pray, the revival we so desperately need will be nothing short of a world-wide outpouring of the Holy Spirit."[2]

Dr. Ben Jennings: "Many of us believe a world-wide revival is imminent."[3]

James Robison, evangelist: "I believe the greatest revival in the history of the church is on its way. As I have traveled across the country I have begun to feel it in my bones. Everywhere I go I see new dramatic unmistakable evidence of the awesome work of preparation now being carried out by the Holy Spirit."[4]

Robert Coleman, in his book *The Coming World Revival:* "We go forth with confidence that someday the harvest will be gathered from the end of the earth. This promise certainly accentuates the possibility of a mighty cosmic revival before the end of the age. It is possible to

discern an outline of a future movement or revival that will make anything seen thus far pale by comparison.
- Universal outpouring of the Holy Spirit
- Strange demonstrations of power
- Unprecedented trouble
- Cleansing of the church
- Tremendous ingathering of souls
- United powerful praying."[5]

Billy Graham, at the 1974 Lausanne Congress: "Evil will grow worse, but God will be mightily at work at the same time. I am praying that we will see in the next months and years the 'Latter Rains,' a rain of blessings, showers falling from heaven upon all the continents before the coming of the Lord."[6]

Hudson Taylor, Missionary to Inland China: In one of his furloughs to England in 1855, Taylor was preaching when he suddenly stopped. He stood speechless for a time with his eyes closed. When he began to speak again he explained: "I have seen a vision. I saw in this vision a great war that encompasses the whole world. I saw this war recess and then start again, actually being two wars. After this I saw much unrest and revolts that will affect many nations. I saw in some places spiritual awakening. In Russia, I saw there will come a general all-encompassing, national spiritual awakening so great that there could never be another like it. From Russia, I saw the awakening spread to many European countries. Then I saw an all-out awakening, followed by the coming of Christ."[7]

William Booth, Founder of the Salvation Army: "Six things will dominate the young people at the turn of the century. Religion without the Holy Spirit; forgiveness without repentance; conversion without new birth; Christianity without Christ; politics without God; and heaven without hell. For this will all be turned around with dynamic revivals that will spread throughout the nations."[8]

While I do not necessarily believe that we are living in the "last generation" or even a particularly special one in terms of the fulfillment of prophecies concerning the coming of Christ, it is a hungry generation that is fragmented by the work of the enemy and a culture that is becoming more and more anti-God. Ours is a generation that needs for God to come down.

REVIVALS OF THE PAST

The Bible tells us that God will pour out His Spirit on His people, and many men and women of God believe that revival is imminent, even upon us.

We can read about the promise of revival in the Word of God, and our faith in that promise can be further strengthened by seeing what God has done in past revivals. We can look back and see that God has sent revival to His people before, even in the very recent past.

COLONIAL-ERA REVIVALS

Spiritual awakenings can be seen as three distinct awakenings. The First Great Awakening was from 1740 to about

1750, and was under the ministries of George Whitefield and Jonathan Edwards. The renewal swept the early American colonies from 1740 to 1744. It influenced, enlivened, and refreshed the Protestant church in the still weak and dependent colonies. The revival began with the power preaching of Whitefield, an Englishman who sparked the American revival in early 1739. Whitefield spent forty-five days in America, preaching in forty-five towns from South Carolina to Maine, giving ninety-seven sermons.

The Second Great Awakening was from 1800 to about 1825, under the ministries of Charles Finney and many other leaders during that period. This is when Cane Ridge Revival—the time of the Quakers and Shakers—took place. The Third Great Awakening was from 1857 to 1890 and was more or less under the ministry influence of D.L. Moody.

> "...historical accounts of revival strengthen our hope that God will break in upon our generation and bring a revival spirit."

This is the time when China opened up to missions, and the ministry and prayer revivals swept the United States and many parts of the world.

TWENTIETH CENTURY REVIVALS

The Azusa Street Revival, from which the Assemblies of God and the Pentecostal denominations claim their heritage, took place around 1906 and started in a little church in Los Angeles. This revival moved on and swept through the nations of the world.

Around 1950, there was a renewal that was named the "Latter Rain Revival." More recently—in the '60s and

'70s—was the Charismatic Renewal and the nationally acclaimed Jesus Movement among the youth.

REVIVAL IN OUR DAY

These scriptural and historical accounts of revival strengthen our hope that God will break in upon our generation and bring a revival spirit.

Ask yourself these questions: Since we know that God has moved at many different times in the past, can we have the faith to believe that He will do it again? Could this be another time and another hour as we move into the twenty-first century that God would send us a measure of revival in our nation? The answer to both questions is an overwhelming yes!

Once again, the Holy Spirit is moving upon our nation—and other nations of the world—in a new outpouring. We are seeing revivals in our colleges and in our cities. We are seeing men in our nation touched and we are seeing renewal in our spiritual leaders.

RENEWAL IN THE COLLEGES

Revival has struck college campuses such as Howard Payne University, Houston Baptist University, Olivet Nazarene University, Morehead State University, Murray State University, Louisiana Tech, Criswell College, Sanford University, Wheaton College, Moody Bible Institute, Gordon College, Hope College, and Crown College. Authors John Avant, Malcolm McDow, and Alvin Reid have produced a book documenting, both by testimony and by event, the revivals taking place on college campuses in

America today. This book, entitled *Revival*, gives the reader a window into college revivals.

These colleges have all reported revivals taking place among both charismatics and evangelicals, moving students into repentance, brokenness, weeping, and the seeking of the face of God.

In a memo to his faculty and staff, Chaplain Kellough of Wheaton College wrote of the spiritual awakening occurring on the Wheaton campus.

"You are probably well aware of the movement of God's Spirit on our campus in recent days. We are thankful to our Lord for the outpouring of His love in a dramatic way. Is this something that has been humanly contrived or manufactured? The personal sharing within the body of Christ here at Wheaton College has been spiritually sensitive and biblically grounded. The depth and breadth of the confession, repentance, and reconciliation point to a divine initiative. Every factor seems to confirm the fact that we are experiencing an authentic work of the sovereign Lord who has chosen to visit us in a powerful way. Whether or not you have been able to participate in any of these meetings, you as a faculty or staff person surely will be impacted at a personal level by the events of this week."

The 10:30 a.m. chapel service was abuzz with excitement. Even those who were not at the WCF meeting had heard by now what had taken place. Chaplain Kellough shared with the entire campus community what had happened the night (and early morning) before. His words paint a vivid picture of events, and they offer sound counsel for the follow-up:

"Most of you know that last evening's WCF meeting was an incredible, wonderful time of spiritual refreshment. There were tears and there were smiles. There was crying, there was singing. People confessed their sins to God. People confessed their sins to each other. There was healing. There was worship, there was Scripture, there was prayer, there was the public confession of sin, there was forgiveness. It was biblical, it was Christian, it was orderly, it was sincere, I believe that it honored God. The program last night began at 7:30, but the meeting ended at 6:00 this morning.

In the wake of this remarkable work of God in the hearts of so many people, I would like to share three things to keep in mind this morning.

First, after a time of spiritual refreshment, and I believe that is what we had—a time of spiritual refreshment—we should expect an attack of the enemy. We should expect it! Last night there was a lot of talk about spiritual warfare and many prayers focused on this very issue. At times like these, we should expect the enemy to hammer us, especially this morning I think. The enemy would like nothing more than to give doubts to the legitimacy of spiritual experience in our life with God.

Second, we cannot manufacture spiritual awakening. Last night many people raised the caution of manipulation. Those who were there would certainly testify to the spiritual validity of what happened. And so, be encouraged by the Scripture; be encouraged by your Christian friends; be encouraged by the Holy Spirit, and do not be discouraged by the enemy. Since we cannot manufacture spiritual awakening, periods of spiritual refreshment may be long, or they may be short. We need to acknowledge the work of God that is the work of God—and we cannot bring spiritual awakening by ourselves any more than we can regenerate the heart of an unbeliever. This is the work of God the Holy Spirit.

Third, after a time of spiritual awakening, we need to keep in praying. The experience of some can cause the rest of us to pray for our entire campus and for our world."[9]

From Taylor University came the following report:

"There is something going on at Taylor University that is very similar to the Wheaton College revival of three weeks ago. . . . This morning (Sunday, April 9, 1995) the on-campus worship service was opened for a time of reflection and sharing of what God had been doing recently in people's lives. A couple of people shared on the revival that happened last week at Asbury College. Three people from Wheaton also shared of what God did in their lives through the revival there. These testimonies ignited a time of confession and prayer on Taylor's Campus. The service, which was scheduled to end at 10:15 a.m., did not finish until 2:25 p.m. This service was characterized by confession of sin and support of the body of Christ in prayer around those who confess."

CITY-WIDE REVIVALS

As of late 1995, a city-wide revival was taking place in Melbourne, Florida, as renewal-type meetings were being held six nights a week. This is called the Ecumenical Revival, with emphasis on evangelism and signs and wonders. As of this writing, there had been more than 15,000 people saved at this revival. Most of the Bible-believing churches—charismatic and evangelical alike—in the area are involved, even though most of the meetings have taken place at the Tabernacle, which was originally pioneered by the late Jamie Buckingham. Various churches in the area have provided ministry teams and leadership of all kinds.

Another documented account of a city-wide revival comes from Pensacola, Fla. at the Brownsville Assembly of God. John Kilpatrick, in his book *Feast of Fire — The Father's Day Outpouring*, gives this report:

"Since our initial service on Father's Day 1995 when revival began suddenly and spontaneously and almost every night since thousands of people have come from all over the country and around the world. Dozens of denominations have been represented as we have seen people from all walks of life and from diverse ethnic and economic background come to the fountain, to get a taste of God's presence in these remarkable and extraordinary services. It is a wonder to behold. It is revival, a feast of fire. In a matter of weeks some 97,000 men, women, boys, girls, teenagers, grandparents, friends, neighbors, co-workers, and family members have visited an evening worship service for the first time. Thus far we have recorded more than 10,000 conversions to Jesus Christ."[10]

THE MEN'S MOVEMENT

This revival is also manifesting itself in the men's movement, the restoration of the biblical role of manhood and fatherhood by affirming that true Christianity alone produces real men. We are seeing men being revived and renewed in their love for God, with a new commitment to God, the Bible, the family, church, and personal integrity.

Anyone seeing what is going on the nation would say that the stadiums being filled with up to 100,000 men for the Promise Keepers meetings is truly a supernatural act of the Holy Spirit to gather the men of our nation.

REVIVAL IN LEADERSHIP

Thousands of pastors have testified that the Holy Spirit is renewing them and their ministries. They are seeing revival-type atmospheres of repentance of sin, a new love for the Bible, church attendance, and liberality in giving. They are seeing a new sensitivity to the lost and a new motivation to be involved in serving their communities.

> **"Thousands of pastors have testified that the Holy Spirit is renewing them and their ministries."**

There is a fresh commitment among godly leadership to uniting to create relational bonds and break down long-existing walls between churches and pastors from every denomination.

All of these things are wonderful signs of revival in our land, but the revival is going much further than that. There is also powerful evidence that God is bringing revival worldwide.

GLOBAL REVIVAL

Almost every continent has experienced a massive revival of Christianity in the past three years. Around the world, Christianity is growing at an amazing rate. Every day 178,000 people are being saved worldwide. An estimated

28,000 are coming to Christ daily in China, 20,000 in Africa, and 35,000 in Latin America.

Christianity is the fastest growing movement in the world with a 6.9 percent growth rate. That compared to 2.7 percent for Islam, 2.2 percent for Hinduism and, 1.7 percent for Buddhism.

Here are some examples of the growth of Christianity across the world:

Korea - In 1900 there were no Christians, yet now it is 40 percent Christian.

China - In 1950 it had one million believers. By 1980 there were 40 million believers, and 75 million by 1992.

Iran - More people have been converted in the past ten years than in the previous 1,000 years.

Latin America - Latin Americans are getting saved at a rate that is four times faster than the population growth. In 1900 there were only 50,000 born-again believers in Latin America, but by 1980 there were 20 million. By the year 2000 that number is expected to grow to more than 100 million.

Saudi Arabia - During the Persian Gulf War, more than 100 churches were planted in Saudi Arabia.

Myanmar (formerly Burma) - Thirty-seven of the nation's top Buddhist monks gave their hearts to the Lord during the presentation of the Jesus film.

Algeria - In the village of Bugia in this Muslim nation, every person became a Christian when Jesus appeared to each of them in dreams in the same night.

Nigeria - During the annual Muslim pilgrimage to Mecca in 1991, a number of Nigerian Muslim mullahs were praying inside the Grand Mosque, the holiest place of Muslim people. Jesus appeared to them and declared that He was God, and they were converted to Christianity.[11]

Students around the world are taking the challenge to reach the nations for Christ and record numbers are preparing to go: 60,000 youth in Korea; 50,000 in South Africa; and 50,000 in Brazil.

THE FUTURE OF REVIVAL

Looking at renewals in the past and at the evidence that points toward a new revival spirit being poured out upon the people of God, we are faced with some vital questions: What is the future of revival? How do we respond to revival? How do we sustain revival? How do church leaders wisely lead in seasons of revival?

Only God knows the future of revival. By reading His Word and studying history, we can learn certain principles that sustain or destroy revival. The bottom line is the sovereignty of God. God's will, God's way, and God's purposes are at times beyond our comprehension. It may be that God has hidden His purposes from us, or it may be that we are not in a place to grasp what God is saying or doing.

> "Only God knows the future of revival. By reading His Word and studying history, we can learn certain principles that sustain or destroy revival."

But we know that God is eager to manifest His reviving presence and power on this generation. For that reason, we must take steps to prepare for the release of His fullness in our midst. These steps must be taken personally because nationwide and worldwide revival starts as God moves on each individual heart, one person at a time.

Joshua 3:5 simply says, "Sanctify yourselves for tomorrow the Lord will do wonders among you."

For us to claim the promise of revival—and to sustain it—each of us must be delivered from our hard-heartedness through basic spiritual renewal of the inner man. This is accomplished through repentance, prayer, cleansing, and new habits of spiritual living.

We must grasp the meaning of revival, and we must fully understand what God requires in order for His Spirit to be poured out upon us. God desires to send revival. Read on and see what His Word tells us about how that revival will come and what we must do to take part in the greatest renewal in the history of the church!

NOTES

1. Ralph Mahoney, World MAP.
2. Graham Truscott, *Power of His Presence* (Burbank: World Map Press), n.a.
3. Dr. Ben Jennings, coordinator for the 1984 International Prayer Assembly for World Evangelism.
4. James Robison, James Robison Evangelistic Association.
5. Robert Coleman, *The Coming World Revival* (Wheaton: Crossway Books), 149.
6. The International Congress on World Evangelization (Lausanne, Switzerland), *Let Them Hear His Voice* (Minneapolis, World Wide Publications, 1975), n.a.
7. Hudson Taylor, Missionary to inland China.
8. William Booth, Salvation Army.
9. John Avant, Malcolm McDow, and Alvin Reid, *Revival—The Story of Current Awakening in Brownswood, Ft. Worth, Wheaton and Beyond* (Nashville: Broadman and Holman Publishers), 112-113.
10. John Kilpatrick, *Feast of Fire—The Father's Day Outpouring* (Pensacola: John Kilpatrick Publishers), 10-11.
11. Charisma Magazine, *"The Holy Spirit Around the World,"* (January, 1996), n.a.

Chapter 3

DISCOVERING DIVINE STRATEGY

*T*he church is expected to encounter increasing decay and hostility in the surrounding culture of the last days. Spiritual decline has been an ever-present threat for the people of God, both now and in past history.

The inter-relationship between reformation of doctrine (and structure) and spiritual revitalization in the church is important and complex. These two factors are linked together for spiritual advancement and spiritual renewal. Reformation grows out of an awakened spiritual interest, which obviously could come through revival-type atmosphere. Whenever the Holy Spirit moves upon the church, there is a reformation, that is, a resurfacing of strong teaching and doctrine, along with certain structural changes to accommodate the new moving of the Spirit.

There are cycles of decline and renewal in the church, as we can see in the church's past and present and in biblical times. God acts to turn the cycle of decline toward heaven. In the cycles of decline and renewal, we usually see the appearance of a new generation and then popular apostasy in that generation. Next, there is a recognizable degeneration that takes place, and after that an extensive repentance that includes agonized prayer. This usually results in the raising up of a new leadership that speaks to that generation to prepare them for the moving of the Holy Spirit. There is no doubt that in our nations today, we have experienced a cycle of decline. We are praying that we would enter into the cycle of renewal.

GOD'S PURPOSES FOR REVIVAL

Ezra 9:8-9 gives us God's five stated purposes for revival being released in the midst of His people. Ezra prays for these purposes to be fulfilled in his people, as we should also pray today: "And now for a little while grace has been shown from the Lord our God, to leave us a remnant to escape, and to give us a peg in His holy place, that our God may enlighten our eyes and give us a measure of revival in our bondage. For we were slaves. Yet our God did not forsake us in our bondage; but He extended mercy to us in the sight of the kings of Persia, to revive us, to repair the house of our God, to rebuild its ruins, and to give us a wall in Judah and Jerusalem."

> "God desires to leave Himself a remnant. I am not referring here to quantity—as in a small group of people—but to quality."

"To leave us a remnant . . ." The word remnant means that which is left after the separation and purification of the people. It refers to what is set apart for a special purpose. It speaks of those who have escaped from something and are entering into something else.

God desires to leave Himself a remnant. I am not referring here to quantity—as in a small group of people—but to quality. God wants a separated people who have escaped the destruction of this world and the vain philosophies of this day to be separated unto the gospel of the kingdom of God (also see Zephaniah 2:7, 3:12-13; Romans 9:27; Revelation 11:13, 12:17, 19:21; Psalm 124:7; 2 Peter 1:4).

"To give us a peg in His holy place . . ." A nail driven into the wall or a tent peg into the ground symbolically spoke of stability of position. It also spoke of a place of blessing and leadership. The "peg in His holy place" gives us an established place and a firm hold on God's holy purposes for this generation. A footing in God's sacred place means that we have a secure place in His presence. His power and holy anointing are the secure place from which we move out to minister to a sick and dying world. We are a nail in a holy place. We are a peg that God has hammered down securely unto His purposes.

God desires to call the church to a stable place where He can bless His people, release leadership, and reach the world. We need to be fixed in our pursuit of God through our praying and teaching. We need to be fixed in our convictions and not swayed by the spirit of our day. We need to be fixed by our visible values—our kingdom beliefs—and not be swayed by the decaying philosophies of our culture. We need to have fixed in our spirits, the passion for worship, not allowing the world to pollute our sacred sacrifices to God.

> "God desires to call the church to a stable place where He can bless His people, release leadership, and reach the world."

"That our God may enlighten our eyes . . ." This means to increase the light of the Holy Spirit in our lives and in our perspectives for what God desires to do through us. God wants us to have open eyes to see His kingdom and His power. God wants us to have a perspective that would be reflected in the way we live, in what we believe, and in how we understand the teachings of the holy Word of God (also see Ephesians 1:17-18).

"To repair the house of our God . . ." God desires to repair His house. This speaks of the restoration and revitalization of the church of the Lord Jesus Christ today. God wants to take the ruined, wasted, destitute places and restore them back to where they should be (also see Isaiah 2:1-4; Haggai 2:6-7, 2 Chronicles 29:32, 9:3-7).

"To revive us . . ." God desires to revive our spiritual vitality. That is, He wants to revive the dead areas of our lives. This word is used eight times in the Old Testament to mean to bring relief or to bring new life.

When there is life in our spirits and we respond to the living God because of that life, we have a deep sense of being in God's sight and presence. God's truth is overwhelmingly powerful to us personally, and the conviction of sin becomes intolerable. Repentance comes easily and goes deeply within us. Then, faith springs up and grasps the things of God.

We are spiritually revitalized when we are filled with the Holy Spirit. We are Christ-centered and our emotions find expressions in holy and right things. Our prayer lives increase and we find ourselves becoming very liberal in our giving (see Ephesians 3:16-19; Philippians 3:13-14; Matthew 4:23-25, 9:35).

THE DANGERS OF RESISTING REVIVAL

In many quarters of the church, people can be so spiritually traditionalized that many kinds of spiritual activity and responses to the presence of God would probably seem out of order to them. Some people reject or resist revival out of ignorance. Others may resist revival because of doctrinal stances or learned responses to church culture. They may resist things they are not familiar or uncomfortable with. It is usually human nature to be uncomfortable with or even espouse an attitude of prejudice against things that we have not experienced ourselves.

Some object to revival because they associate it with the excesses and other undesirable features that usually accompany renewal. Historically, we see that these things are features of revival, but we should not allow the fear of these things to stop us from welcoming an outbreak of God upon the human soul.

In 1947, at the opening of the First World Pentecostal Conference in Zurich, Switzerland, General Secretary David Duplesis preached an address that ended with the following words: "There is nothing that can ever take the place of the Holy Spirit in the church. Let us pray for a greater outpouring than ever and remember when the floods come, it will not keep to our well-prepared channels, but it will overflow and most probably cause chaos in our regular programs."

Some desire revival until it comes, then bitterly oppose it because it does not come in the way they had anticipated it. The instruments that God uses or the channels through which the blessing flows are not what they had expected. The manner in which the Spirit works or the manifestations through which God chose to exhibit His power may be contrary to their expectations or foreign to their experience.

The history of revivals shows very clearly that people often behave in a most unusual manner as they respond to God's presence. I am not espousing chaos or emotional outbursts without any spiritual substance, but we have to understand that both in Scripture and out, people have done what we might consider some pretty bizarre things as they responded to the Holy Spirit.

We must be sure never to resist revival because we are not familiar with or used to the means by which the Holy Spirit chooses to move in and through His people.

HOLY SPIRIT TIMING

Evan Roberts, the leader of the Welsh Revival in the last century, continually preached the message of "Honor the Holy Spirit." Roberts said that the Welsh Revival came as a definite outpouring of the Holy Spirit that could be logged according to the time that it came: "The outpouring of the Spirit came dramatically with precision in the second week of November 1904, on the same day both in the north and in the south."

Henry Theissen, a respected theologian, stated: "There are occasions in which God, as it were, comes forth from His hiding place and shows to men that He is a living God and that He is still on the throne of the universe and that He is sufficient for all men's problems."

There are times when the Holy Spirit just seems to open the heavens and pour forth upon hungry hearts, sometimes simultaneously in different countries. These are times of what we would call a "measure of revival." Ezra 9:8 refers to this measure or space of revival that we see happen as windows in history where God appears in dramatic ways.

Martin Luther once said that thirty years constitutes the outer limit of an awakening. The sun will set on all revivals, yet there is a set time, a limited space set by the divine boundaries of God upon every revival. Revival comes suddenly, often breaking out of obscure places through the ministries of obscure people. Exodus 33:5: "For the Lord had said to Moses, 'Say to the children of Israel, "You are a stiff-necked people. I could come up into your midst in one moment and consume you. Now therefore, take off your ornaments, that I may know what to do to you.' "

Revival can be classified as a one-moment experience in the life of a generation. God comes in quickly during revival seasons and then it subsides. It is the one moment of sovereignty, the moment of revival.

"In that day sing to her, 'A vineyard of red wine! I, the LORD, keep it, I water it every moment; lest any hurt it, I keep it night and day' " (Isaiah 27:2-3).

"There are times when the Holy Spirit just seems to open the heavens and pour forth upon hungry hearts, sometimes simultaneously in different countries."

"And He said to them, 'It is not for you to know times or seasons which the Father has put in His own authority' " (Acts 1:7).

These Scriptures refer to God's choosing the divine moments, the divine turning points, the fixed seasons, where He moves by His own hand, with His own authority to establish truth in Spirit in the life of a generation (also see Ezekiel 34:26; Isaiah 35:1-7; Deuteronomy 11:11-14; Zechariah 10:1; Job 12:15).

GOD MOVES US OUT OF OUR COMFORT ZONES

God is omnipresent, meaning He is everywhere all the time. You cannot escape the sovereign presence of the living God, but there are different levels to His revealing of Himself. During times of revival or renewal, we have a new awareness of God's manifested presence.

It seems we are once again experiencing a fresh new touch of the Holy Spirit upon His church today. Whenever this happens, it always provokes different responses in different people—some positive, some negative, some bewildered, and some confused.

Comfort level is an important factor in business today. Banks, restaurants, and other businesses all endeavor to make people feel comfortable so they will stay and do business. The same is true with God and His church. How can we feel comfortable with God and comfortable in His presence, especially His revival presence?

There are times when the Lord will push us out of our comfort zones as He comes in His power and presence. There are also times when we ourselves might do things we are uncomfortable with. When God comes down, people's emotions are stirred, their minds are opened, and their spirits are renewed.

Jonathan Edward's wife, Sarah, was powerfully touched by revival. She recorded, at her husband's request, a record of seventeen days of her experience. This is not to imply that her experience ended after seventeen days, only that she recorded a seventeen-day period of her experience.

Her narrative begins Tuesday night, January 19, 1742. While seeking God, her thoughts turned to the subject of the fatherhood of God and she writes, "I cannot find language to express how certain this appeared. My safety, my happiness and eternal enjoyment of God's immutable love seemed as durable and unchangeable as God Himself. Melted and overcome by the sweetness of this assurance, I fell into a great flow of tears and could not forbear weeping aloud. It seemed certain to me that God was my Father, Christ my Lord and Savior. That He was mine and I was His. Under a delightful sense of the immediate presence and love of God, these words seem to come over and over in my mind: 'My God, my all. My God, my all.' The presence was so near, so real that I seemed scarcely conscious of anything else. This continued for four days, day and night, without letup."

When God comes down for a season of revival He often pushes us out of our comfort zones and we do things we normally would not do. There are times when the Holy Spirit's presence so rests on us that our emotions seem like putty in God's hands and we just fall apart. The tears flow easily and we find ourselves sobbing in His presence. We might find ourselves groaning under the heavy hand of God, under intercessory prayer, or under God dealing with our own sin.

GOD INITIATES REVIVAL AND WE RESPOND

God produces, promotes, and sustains revival according to His sovereign Holy Spirit. God is the initiator of revival and we are the responders.

In order for us to understand God's strategies for revival, we must understand who God is. We must understand what His attributes are. We must understand what makes God, God.

God is alive. In the Scriptures, He is called the living God (see Deuteronomy 5:26; Joshua 3:10; 1 Samuel 7:26).

"Living" implies feeling, power, and activity. God is not just a name, but a living person.

God has become very personal with His people, and that is the redemptive message that we preach. God can be seen and felt. Even though God is spirit and invisible, we can feel and receive His Spirit into our emotions, affections, minds, and hearts. We can reflect what we feel in God. He can speak to us and hear us, and we can speak to Him and hear Him as He speaks. We can touch His throne with our prayers and He can touch us by His Spirit. We can experience His grace and love, and we can worship Him as we would a living person, for He is the living God.

> " 'Living' implies feeling, power, and activity. God is not just a name, but a living person."

God is not a lifeless idol. He is not a dogma, a belief, or something we read about in a book. God is alive now, and He is alive in us. And we can respond to the living God when He appears to us in more power and more presence.

We want to be people who understand God and grasp the day of God's visitation. The words visit or visitation in Scripture could have three different meanings that break down into three different concepts of revival:

The word visitation could mean to heal because God comes as the doctor.
(See Psalm 41:4; Jeremiah 3:22, 37:2; Luke 9:11; Acts 10:38; 1 Corinthians 12:9; Revelation 22:2.)

The word visitation could mean to adjust because God comes as the chiropractor.
(See Jeremiah 30:11; Hebrews 12:9-15; Proverbs 3:12.)

The word visitation could mean to make a deposit because God comes as the wise investor.
(See Matthew 25:1-10; 1 Corinthians 12; Ephesians 4:12-16.)

THE GRACE OF GOD

God breaks in upon a generation in a moment of time. It says in Ezra 9:8 that they prayed for grace to be shown from God. In Zechariah 12:10, it says, "I will pour . . . the Spirit of grace and supplication."

The word grace, both in the Old and New Testaments, is a rich word that has numerous meanings. It contains the idea of unmerited favor, supreme graciousness, and condescension of a superior. Grace is that which is undeserved and not secured by our own works. To the church, revival means humility, a bitter knowledge of unworthiness, and an open, humbling confession of sin on the part of the leaders and sheep.

Grace also means to create an intense desire toward something. It means to bend or stoop or to stir expectations. God desires to bend or stoop down and visit hearts that are filled with expectation and bring unmerited favor and supreme graciousness into their lives. God also wants to create an intense desire in the hearts of the people for prayer, worship, and communion with Him. This intense desire is not worked up by the people themselves, but is a desire that is divinely sent. It is actually the work of grace in the hearts of the people to prepare them to enter into what God would do in their day.

God not only prepares His people, but He leads His people through chosen leaders who will speak the words of God that stir their hearts and motivate them to run hard after the Lord. He also sends His sovereign Spirit to visit these hungry hearts.

God is truly the initiator and governor of all revival. Ezra prayed that God would send a little space of grace and a measure of revival. This measure of revival comes to us in mercy drops, tiny trickles of grace that flow down from above. Each little space of revival could be called a divine mercy drop, a divine measure of revival moving upon a generation.

MERCY DROPS OF REVIVAL

On Bernera, a small island off the coast of Lewis, Duncan Campbell assisted at a communion service. Halfway through his address, he stopped, leaned over the pulpit, and said to a boy in front of him who was visibly moved, "Donald, would you lead us in prayer?" The boy prayed, "Oh God, I seem to be gazing through an open door. I see the Lamb in the midst of the throne with the keys of death and of hell at his girdle." According to Andrew Woosley, the boy began to sob, then lifting his eyes toward heaven, he cried, "Oh God, there is power there. Let it loose!" With the force of a hurricane, the Spirit of God swept into the building and the flood gates of heaven opened. The church looked like a battlefield. On one side, many were prostrated over the seats, weeping and sighing; on the other side, some had thrown their arms in the air in rigid posture. God had come down.

> "God is truly the initiator and governor of all revival."

These mercy drops we are speaking about, these times of measured revival, these times of grace releases, are what God desires to do in our day and age. A work of God's Spirit among His own people—what we call revival—is simply a return to Scripture, a return to Bible morality. The saints getting together to experience this means that heaven can be opened. The throne of God is filled with God's power, and He wishes to release that power into the midst of His people.

We can pray a prayer as in Habakkuk 3:2: "O Lord, I have heard your speech and was afraid; O Lord, revive Your work in the midst of the years! In the midst of the years make it known; in wrath remember mercy."

REVIVAL—A SPECIAL TIME OF DELIVERY

God is interested in flowing into this generation with the redemptive message of Jesus Christ. He is also interested in moving within the church today to revive its spirit and its vision to take the gospel to the ends of the world. God desires that we all have a burden for Him to move in our generation, as He wishes to do in every generation (see Psalm 119:90, 89:4, 71:18; Judges 2:10; Acts 3:19).

God has a divine strategy for times of visitation. These spaces or measures of time where God seeks to pour out His Spirit upon a generation are indeed special times.

During the times of the Old Testament kings of Judah, there were seasons of spiritual renewal, and there were always common characteristics and results of the revival atmospheres. Each revival occurred during the darkest hour of deep moral decay, national depression, and spiritual hardness of heart. These revivals began with a consecrated servant who was not afraid to speak truth with a prophetic voice to that particular generation. In spite of the opposition and the threats that would come against that person's life, the servant would still give a clear word to the kings— sometimes to the backslidden priests—of the land in that day. The resulting revivals brought radical repentance that was evidenced by drastic reform and turning back to God. It was a time of change and of removing all things that were not of God. These seasons of revival produced men like Elijah, who would confront the Ahabs, and Gideon, who would tear down the works of the enemy and motivate 300 men to go against all odds.

Revival times cause a rebuilding of the altar of prayer and a new commitment to seeking God. And, many times, the restoration of worship, under the Davidic worship order, would bring in a new presence and a new sense of awe toward God.

> "Each revival occurred during the darkest hour of deep moral decay, national depression, and spiritual hardness of heart."

These revival times restored the power of the written Word with new respect, and the emphasis on purity and holiness became part of the revival message.

I believe that the church is in desperate need of a mighty move of the Holy Spirit that we in the body of Christ have prayed for earnestly. Let us pray with all sincerity of heart that we would enter into the measure of time of revival that God desires to send upon this generation. As we seek God's strategy for revival, we need to pray for deliverance from the attitudes and mind sets that stifle that renewal.

The Need to be Delivered from Elitism

We should pray with all diligence that God would deliver us from elitism, which is thinking that our particular group, denomination, or movement is superior to the rest. Elitism causes judgmental attitudes toward anyone or anything that is different. These feelings of superiority will cause us to cultivate a pharisaic attitude, which will cause us to miss the moving of the Spirit of God. We need to pray that God will remove from us sectarianism, which in this context means limiting ourselves to only that which we can accept and that which we can believe. This includes reading only the books we agree with and listening only to speakers who say what we like to hear.

The Need to be Delivered from Emotionalism

We need to ask God to deliver us from emotionalism. There is a fine line between healthy emotions and unhealthy ones and a fine line between learned behavior and natural, spontaneous responses to the supernatural presence of the living God.

Of course, there will be emotional times when people will weep, fall, laugh, shout, or cry out. This has happened in every revival, including the ones in the Scripture. But emotions must be governed by the Word of God. We should not give in to emotionalism, but neither should we react negatively to emotions caused by the presence of God simply because they make us uncomfortable.

> "Revival times cause a rebuilding of the alter of prayer and a new commitment to seeking God."

The Need to be Delivered from Anti-intellectualism

We should also pray that God would deliver us from anti-intellectualism, the attitude that makes us so subjective that the moving of the Holy Spirit begins to shroud and shrink the preaching of the written Word of God.

The Word of God is the foundation and the river banks to every revival. We want to have intensity with stability. We want to have insight with intelligence. We want to have the Word of God with the moving of the Holy Spirit.

REVIVAL IN OUR GENERATION

"When all that generation had been gathered to their fathers, another generation arose after them who did not know the Lord or the work which He had done for Israel" (Judges 2:10).

We are living in another generation that does not know the Lord or His supernatural and sovereign ways. But God has granted His people a little grace in this time. A small remnant of His people has found its weary way back home and driven a single peg into its soil.

A heart-cry for revival ascends from every quarter. There is much interest, not only in the teaching and knowledge of revival right now, but in experiencing revival in our generation. Not for decades has there been such interest, even burden, for spiritual refreshing and awakening as there seems to be as the twenty-first century approaches.

> **"God desires to send revival, and He has a plan, a strategy to bring a new outpouring of His Holy Spirit into the hearts and lives of His people today."**

God desires to send revival, and He has a plan, a strategy to bring a new outpouring of His Holy Spirit into the hearts and lives of His people today. We are praying for a measure of revival. We are praying that God will give us a little space, a little time to respond to the window of His sovereign moving of the Holy Spirit in our generation.

Chapter 4

THE LAW OF EXPECTATION

*T*here are certain characteristics that distinguish this divine activity we call revival from the more "day-to-day" operations of the Holy Spirit. Revival is a time when God gives us an awakening, an opening of ourselves to receiving a greater outpouring of the Holy Spirit. We must pray that God will give us a spirit of expectation for what He wants to do in and through us as His Spirit moves on us in a season of revival.

There is an urgent need for revival today, for a move of God to renew His church, for a visitation from the Holy Spirit that has lasting effects. That is God's promise and our hope—our expectation.

WAITING WITH EXPECTATION

One of the keys to seeing the hand of the Lord move in a mighty way is faith, and faith can otherwise be defined as expectation. Expectation is the ability to see in the Spirit and by the Spirit things God wishes to bring into our lives. It is the art of seeing with the hidden eyes of the hidden spiritual man.

The word expectation means to wait for something in suspense, to wait in hope. It means to continually remain in one place—maybe permanently—to receive something, you have faith that it will come to pass. This is expectation that is kindled by a promise.

Early in the book of Acts, we have a verse that gives us an example of what it means to wait with expectation:

"And being assembled together with them, He command-ed them not to depart from Jerusalem, but to wait for the Promise of the Father, 'which,' He said, 'you have heard from Me' " (Acts 1:4).

"Wait" does not mean to idly stick around in one place for something you think might happen, but to wait, know-ing that God will fulfill His promises. There are five Greek words used in the New Testament to define the English word wait in the context of expectation:

"Anameno"—to wait patiently and anticipate in advance. "And to wait for His Son from heaven, whom He raised from the dead, even Jesus who delivers us from the wrath to come" (1 Thessalonians 1:10).

"Apodechomai"—to intensely and eagerly wait. "Not only that, but we also who have the firstfruits of the Spirit, even we ourselves groan within ourselves, eagerly waiting for the adoption, the redemption of our body. For we were saved in this hope, but hope that is seen is not hope; for why does one still hope for what he sees? But if we hope for what we do not see, we eagerly wait for it with persever-ance" (Romans 8:23-25).

"Ekdechomai"—to look forward to something with open anticipation as you would welcome someone into your presence. "For he waited for the city which has foun-dations, whose builder and maker is God" (Hebrews 11:10).

"Prosdechomai"—to receive or welcome, to accept something openly. "But do not yield to them, for more than forty of them lie in wait for him, men who have bound themselves by an oath that they will neither eat nor drink till they have killed him; and now they are ready, waiting for the promise from you" (Acts 23:21).

"Prosdokao"—to wait for, look for, anticipate with great expectation. "Now as the people were in expectation, and all reasoned in their hearts about John, whether he was the Christ or not" (Luke 3:15).

WAITING AND KNOWING

We have an example of this kind of faith in Luke 2:25, where we see Simeon the priest practicing the law of expectation as he waited for the Messiah: "And behold, there was a man in Jerusalem whose name was Simeon; and this man was righteous and devout, looking for the consolation of Israel; and the Holy Spirit was upon him."

Luke 2:36-38 tells us about Anna, a prophetess who was waiting with expectation for the coming of the promised deliverer: "Now there was one, Anna, a prophetess, the daughter of Phanuel, of the tribe of Asher. She was of a great age, and had lived with a husband seven years from her virginity; and this woman was a widow of about eighty-four years, who did not depart from the temple, but served God with fastings and prayers night and day. And coming in that instant she gave thanks to the Lord, and spoke of Him to all those who looked for redemption in Jerusalem."

Anna practiced the law of expectation with fasting and prayers night and day, as she anticipated the moment when the deliverer would come to Jerusalem. She was looking and believing for this redemption. The law of expectation worked so deeply within this woman that she became an intercessor. The law of expectation is foundational to the spirit of intercessory prayer and the dedication to fasting that Anna practiced.

Simeon and Anna had that spirit of expectation that we need to produce revival. Revivals will always produce in us a spirit of expectation and, expectation produces revival. The two work together.

STIRRING WATERS OF REVIVAL

> "Revivals will always produce in us a spirit of expectation and, expectation produces revival. The two work together."

John 5:3 gives an account of a multitude of people at Bethesda waiting for the moving of the water. There were sick, blind, lame, and withered people who were eagerly anticipating a moving of the Holy Spirit. Bethesda was the house of mercy, the house of the olive tree, or the house of oil. This was a place of healing by the supernatural moving of God upon the human body. There were certain seasons when the angel of the Lord would come down and stir the water, and whoever stepped into it first after the stirring was healed from whatever disease afflicted them. This great multitude of sick people had an expectation that their pitiful states could be changed by the moving of the Holy Spirit.

The divine law of expectation is that we believe there are seasons when God stirs the water and touches people's hearts, where those who are spiritually dry can be watered and those who are lame can be healed. The water must be stirred before we can step into it. We must expect that stirring, and we must step into the water with high expectation, knowing that there is enough for everyone and everything. This is the kind of faith that God responds to.

God once again is stirring the waters of revival and we, in faith, must anticipate that He will move with supernatural miracles and healings upon those who are sick and upon those who need to be miraculously raised up. We must anticipate that He will also move upon the spiritually dry— those who have been at one time born again, who have walked with the Lord, but maybe are not now walking closely with Him. These are the people who are dried up and withered away spiritually, the people who have no anticipation in their hearts for anything to do with God or His promises. We must believe God that he will stir in them that spirit of expectation.

NURTURING A SPIRIT OF EXPECTATION

We have an example of the divine law of expectation as practiced in the early church in Acts 10:24, where Cornelius, a man of faith and prayer, expected a move of the Holy Spirit upon whoever might enter his house: "And on the following day he entered Caesarea. Now Cornelius was waiting for them and had called together his relatives and close friends."

Cornelius so believed that God would minister through his home that he called together all of his relatives and close friends. The Bible says that when Peter entered the house, Cornelius fell at his feet and worshiped, but Peter told him to stop because he, too, was just a man. This shows us that Cornelius was a man of anticipation, a man who knew he would receive something from Peter.

We need to somehow nurture in our hearts an expectation to receive not only from the Holy Spirit, but also from the ministries that God has raised up in order for us to receive from them. As we have an expectation for receiving, we will want to gather into the house all our friends, relatives, and everyone else who could be touched by the Holy Spirit.

ASKING WITH EXPECTATION

Sadly, there are people who, though they stand in seasons of revival, ask to receive nothing, even to be prayed with. And nothing is just what they will receive. Why? Because they have no expectation, no hunger. They have no anticipation to receive anything from God.

Then there are others—even though they are sick, lame and dry—who have great faith to receive. They are the people who will ask for prayer or for help, and ask God to give them what they need. Faith to receive is vital in a time of revival. We can see a wonderful example of this kind of faith in Acts 3:1-6, the account of the lame man at the Gate Beautiful who was healed through a prayer of faith:

"Now Peter and John went up together to the temple at the hour of prayer, the ninth hour. And a certain man lame from his mother's womb was carried, whom they laid daily at the gate of the temple which is called Beautiful, to ask alms of those who entered the temple; who, seeing Peter and John about to go into the temple asked for alms. And fixing his eyes on him, with John, Peter said, 'Look at us.' So he gave them his attention, expecting to receive something from them."

The man at the gate had an attitude of expectation and faith. Verse 3 tells us he asked to receive something from Peter and John. Verse 5 than tells us that he expected to receive something, from these men.

This should always be the condition of a hungry heart in the midst of revival. Like the lame man who was asking for money because he was hungry and thirsty, our hunger and thirst for a move of the Holy Spirit should move us to ask and expect Him to move upon us.

The lame man's asking and expecting paid off, too, as Peter looked at him and said, "I do not possess silver and gold, but what I do have I give to you. In the name of Jesus Christ, rise up and walk."

The Bible does not tell us of any other miracles worked at this gate. The lame man in this passage probably was not there that day looking for a miracle. He did not come expecting the healing that he had only dreamed of. The Gate Beautiful was simply a place for him to receive money. But when Peter and John looked at him, something happened in his heart. He knew they had something to give and that he should receive it. This man had a spirit of expectation that was stirred in him during the few minutes that he had with Peter and John.

Receiving is an active form of faith where we take hold of something, where we seize it, grasp it, and get it. We need to receive with open hands, to open up so as not to miss anything that God might want to do in our lives. The law of expectation will push us into a new realm of believing for our own personal lives, a realm of believing for what God wants to pour into us now.

IMPARTING EXPECTATION

In Acts 3:6, we see the power of the spiritual impartation that resided in Peter's life. He did not have silver or gold, nor did he want to just give the temporal. But what Peter had he gave to this man. It was a supernatural faith, a moving of the Holy Spirit. Peter himself had been nurtured in this spirit of faith, as he had seen many miracles worked through the ministry of the Lord Jesus Christ. Therefore, Peter had a faith to impart. Peter had a knowledge of the supernatural to give away. What he gave to this man was an impartation of that supernatural faith, a vision to receive from God whatever he needed.

> **"Receiving is an active form of faith where we take hold of something, where we seize it, grasp it, and get it."**

Just as Peter did at the Gate Beautiful, we need to impart to others what we have received from the Lord. In revival, there are times of impartation when we receive from the Holy Spirit the presence of God and the ministry of the Word, and we get filled up. We get filled to the point that we need to give out, to impart to others what God has imparted to us. It happens through the ministry of laying on of hands, as we pray for the sick, or as we pray for someone to be encouraged, or as we teach the Word of God and serve.

But one of the greatest things we can impart to others is expectation. When Peter said to the man, "look on us," he wanted to arouse his expectation to receive.

LOOKING WITH EXPECTATION

Expectation is the ability to see in the Spirit and by the Spirit things that God wishes to bring into our lives. It is the art of seeing with the hidden eyes of the hidden spiritual man. "After that He put His hands again upon his eyes and made him look up and he was restored and saw every man clearly. Once more Jesus put His hands on the man's eyes and his eyes were opened, his sight was restored and he saw everything clearly" (Mark 8:25).

We need to allow the Holy Spirit to anoint our eyes so that we might see clearly the provision that God has for us and the wonderful outpouring of the Holy Spirit available to us.

"And the Lord said unto Abraham after that Lot was separated from him, 'Lift up, thou, thine eyes and look from the place where thou art northward, and southward, and eastward, and westward' " (Genesis 13:14).

> "We get filled to the point that we need to give out, to impart to others what God has imparted to us."

We need to look with expectation from our present positions to our future potential. We need to look to the Word of God as we, in faith, seek out what God has for us.

LOOKING FROM A SPIRITUAL AND EMOTIONAL PERSPECTIVE

We can become discouraged or disillusioned about our spiritual growth and our future, about our failed relationships or broken dreams. But we can look beyond those things and lift up our eyes in faith to see what the Lord has for us: things that are broader and deeper and more exciting than what we might expect.

We need to lift up our eyes and trust God. Then, in the days of revival and restoration, God will bring into our lives, our families, and our circumstances an outpouring of the Holy Spirit. God will do better for us, when we trust Him, than we can ever do for ourselves. There is nothing lost and everything to be gained by meekness and yielding.

In Genesis 13, we read about Abraham and Lot separating. Their relationship had been damaged, and now Abraham is left alone. This is the time the Lord chose to speak afresh to him about his future.

God's voice is more distinctly heard in our solitude. We require a renewed sense of the divine approval of God after testings and disillusionments. The divine promises are more clearly comprehended when God speaks a word of faith to us and we lift up our eyes and look from where we are and into the future. We are more free to survey the greatness of our inheritance when we respond to a spirit of faith. We have an enhanced idea of the divine resources.

Lift up your eyes of the inner man and see all that the Lord has given. Lift up your eyes and see, by the Spirit, the good and mighty things the Lord has planned for you and your future. Put the past in perspective by releasing it and putting it under the mighty hand of God. The past can never be relived, so do not keep reliving it in your mind. The past is not a prophecy of the future. Isaiah 43:18-19 says, "Remember not the former things for behold I will do a new thing." Revival is a time of faith and expectation, not a time of sorrow and looking to the past.

LOOK FOR REFRESHING IN TIMES OF REFINING

"And she went and sat her down over against him a good way off, as it were a bowshot, for she said, 'Let me not see the death of the child.' And she sat over against him and lifted up her voice and wept. And God heard the voice of the lad, and the angel of God called to Hagar out of heaven and said, 'What aileth thee, Hagar? Fear not for God hath heard the voice of the lad where he is. Arise, lift up the lad and hold him in thine hand for I will make him a great nation.' And God opened her eyes and she saw a well of water and she went and filled the bottle with water and gave the lad drink. And God was with the lad and he grew and dwelt in the wilderness and became an archer" (Genesis 21:16-20).

Hagar was in desperate need, and God provided for her. How did the well come to be there just when Hagar needed it? The Arab shepherds did not dig the well for the wandering traveler, but for their own flocks. Yet God guided Hagar's steps.

> **"Life is full of hidden wells and stored up blessings, which are ready at the right time and the right moment to supply those who are in the wilderness."**

Life is full of hidden wells, and stored up blessings, which are ready at the right time and the right moment to supply those who are in the wilderness. God has plenty of hidden water wells during seasons and times of revival. The Holy Spirit must open our eyes so that we might receive from these hidden wells.

ASKING AND RECEIVING

What are you asking for? What are we believing for this day? What might the church have if we would move in the law of expectation?

Revival spirit is available to us if we would move into it, if we would just receive it. Maybe revival spirit is always available to the church, every year, every decade, every age, but we do not pay the price to move into it. Yet when God initiates revival, how much more should we move into it and pray and receive what we expect.

When God comes down things begin to happen. Our expectation and desire for more will prepare us to embrace God's coming in power.

Chapter 5

THE RECEIVING MORE FACTOR

*I*n seasons of revival, we need to understand who the Holy Spirit is, what we can expect when He takes up residence in our hearts and minds, and what we can do to open the river bed of our personalities for His flow.

The law of receiving more, which is built upon the foundation of the law of expectation, tells us what we must do to allow the Holy Spirit to move in our lives as we enter into a time of revival.

The law of receiving more moves us from salvation to water baptism, from water baptism to baptism in the Holy Spirit, from baptism in the Holy Spirit to fillings of the Holy Spirit, from fillings of the Holy Spirit to more power of the Holy Spirit, and from more power in the Holy Spirit to the release of more gifts of the Holy Spirit.

"For John truly baptized with water, but you shall be baptized with the Holy Spirit not many days from now" (Acts 1:5).

"If you then being evil know how to give good gifts to your children, how much more will your heavenly Father give the Holy Spirit to those who ask" (Luke 11:13).

To receive more, we must move from the old to something new. In John 7:37-39, Jesus demonstrated this idea when He promised the Jews rivers of living water, not just trickles. He was telling them that they had to move from the law to grace, from the old to the new. They had to move from what used to be to what could now be under the new dispensation of grace. Jesus was telling them that under grace, there would be rivers of the Holy Spirit, not just a presence that would come and go. It would be a presence that would abide permanently.

MOVING FROM THE OLD TO THE NEW

Jesus' promise of the coming of the Holy Spirit upon His people necessitated a change in how believers approached baptism. The physical act of being baptized in water is still important, but there came a new baptism, a spiritual baptism.

To move from John's baptism to a new baptism was difficult because it meant moving from the old to new. Sometimes, when we try to move from the old to the new, we compare and say that the old is better than the new. But the old is not really better than the new. We just have not had enough of the new in order to properly judge the old.

"We must receive more of the new—more of the rivers of living water that Jesus promised—in order to put the old in perspective."

Jesus said in Luke 5:37-39: "No one having drunk the old immediately desires new, for he says the old is better."

We must receive more of the new—more of the rivers of living water that Jesus promised—in order to put the old in perspective. The old baptism was with water; it was tangible, something that could be felt and seen. But the new baptism in the Holy Spirit is with the invisible Spirit of God. When we move from the old to the new, we move from the visible and tangible to the invisible and non-tangible.

In water baptism, you submit as another person immerses you. You have a certain confidence in the event. It is easily understood because it is still in elements of nature that you can understand. You know that another person holds you, immerses you in water, and you come up wet. You can see, feel, and somewhat be in control of what is happening.

But the Holy Spirit is something new, something different. The Holy Spirit is invisible. No human hands can immerse you into the river of the Spirit. You receive more of the Holy Spirit as you immerse yourself through a spirit of faith.

"If you then, being evil, know how to give good gifts to your children, **how much more** will your heavenly Father give the Holy Spirit to those who ask Him!" (Luke 11:13).

"The thief does not come except to steal, and to kill, and to destroy. I have come that they may have life, and that they may have it **more abundantly**" (John 10:10).

The meaning of the word "more" means we go beyond what we had. It is more in quality, not just in quantity. We are praying for more of Jesus, more of the Holy Spirit, more of the love of God, more brokenness, more victory, more bondage broken, more power to minister, more intensity in prayer and worship, more reaching out to the nations in prayer and missionary work (Psalm 10:18, 115:14, 119:99; Matthew 13:12).

The law of receiving more means that we cannot approach God as spectators. We must come to Him as participators. We can not approach God with preconceived ideas of what might happen. We must come with abandonment, with a yielding and a cooperation with the Holy

Spirit. We must come with an open hand and an open heart. We must come with a spirit that is reaching out so that we might receive the power and the dimension of the Holy Spirit that God wants to place into our lives. "And whatever we ask we receive from Him" (1 John 3:22).

MOVING BEYOND WATER BAPTISM

All believers should experience the baptism of water unto repentance. In Acts 19:1-6 the two baptisms—in water and in the Holy Spirit—are side by side, but there are important differences between the two:

"And it happened, while Apollos was at Corinth, that Paul, having passed through the upper regions, came to Ephesus. And finding some disciples he said to them, 'Did you receive the Holy Spirit when you believed?' So they said to him, 'We have not so much as heard whether there is a Holy Spirit.' And he said to them, 'Into what then were you baptized?' So they said, 'Into John's baptism.' Then Paul said, 'John indeed baptized with a baptism of repentance, saying to the people that they should believe on Him who would come after him, that is, on Christ Jesus.' When they heard this, they were baptized in the name of the Lord Jesus. And when Paul had laid hands on them, the Holy Spirit came upon them, and they spoke with tongues and prophesied."

JOHN'S BAPTISM

In Mark 1:3-5, we have a summary of John's message on his baptism: "The voice of one crying in the wilderness: 'Prepare the way of the Lord; make His paths straight.' John came baptizing in the wilderness and preaching a baptism of repentance for the remission of sins. And all the land of Judea, and those from Jerusalem, went out to him and were all baptized by him in the Jordan River, confessing their sins."

John's baptism was to prepare people's hearts for the event in revelation of the long-awaited Messiah. It was a baptism of repentance and public confession of sins with commitment to live a true life of righteousness.

"But when he saw many of the Pharisees and Sadducees coming to his baptism, he said to them, 'Brood of vipers! Who warned you to flee from the wrath to come? Therefore bear fruits worthy of repentance.' " (Matthew 3:7-8).

John's baptism was an outward seal demonstrating an inward transformation that had already taken place. It was an assurance that those who were being baptized had already passed through the experience of repentance and forgiveness.

There must always first be repentance and faith before there can be the immersing into water in Christian baptism. "Now when they had heard this, they were cut to the heart, and said to Peter and the rest of the apostles, 'Men and brethren, what shall we do?' Then Peter said to them, 'Repent, and let every one of you be baptized in the name of Jesus Christ for the remission of sins; and you shall receive the gift of the Holy Spirit' " (Acts 2:37-38).

The first step toward water baptism is repentance—a turning around, a change of mind, and change of heart through asking God to forgive our sins. In Acts 8:36-38, the eunuch was baptized in water after he understood the meaning of baptism. The baptism of repentance is a prerequisite to the baptism in the Holy Spirit.

THE BAPTISM OF THE HOLY SPIRIT

All who believe in Christ and accept the doctrine of the Holy Spirit as truth have been filled with the Holy Spirit. But the baptism of the Holy Spirit is distinct from and subsequent to regeneration. This baptism empowers believers for Christian service. The Holy Spirit baptism was not exclusively for the apostles or for their age, but for all who are far off even as many as the Lord our God shall call (Acts 2:39). It is for every believer of the church age.

To move in the true power of the anointing of God, we need to be filled with the Holy Spirit just as Christ was filled. Believers need to cry out to God for the baptism of the Holy Spirit. We need the Holy Spirit not only to come upon us, but to fill, permeate, and saturate us.

In *Renewal Theology*, there is the following definition of the baptism of the Holy Spirit: "By extension, since we have noted the use of such terms as outpouring, falling on, coming on, associated with the baptism of the Holy Spirit. Baptism depicts vividly the idea of being enveloped in the reality of the Holy Spirit. To be baptized means to be immersed in, plunged under, drenched or soaked with the Spirit, the entire person being saturated. A gateway into a new dimension of the Holy Spirit's presence and power."[1]

The baptism of the Holy Spirit has also been defined in the following ways:

Jack Hayford: "To be spirit filled is an expansion of our capacity for worshiping. An extension of our dynamic for witnessing, and an expulsion of our adversary to our spiritual warfare."[2]

R.A. Torrey: "Baptism of the Holy Spirit is a definite experience which one may know whether he has received or not. It works separate and distinct from salvation or regeneration imparting power and clothing the believer with the new power."[3]

Derek Prince: "Baptism with the Holy Spirit is to drink of the Holy Spirit or be filled with the Holy Spirit. To receive the Holy Spirit is a definite new experience in which the believer receives the fullness of the Holy Spirit inwardly within himself. His whole personality immersed, surrounded and enveloped in the presence and power of the Holy Spirit coming down over him from above and from without."[4]

Samuel Chadwick: "Baptism in the Spirit is to be overflowed by the Holy Spirit. Your heart filled with God's love, your mind filled with God's truth, your soul filled with God's life, your body overflowing with God's goodness."[5]

Charles Ryrie: "To come under the control of the Holy Spirit is to act in ways unnatural to him as a drunk person is controlled by the influence of liquor."[6]

In Holy Spirit baptism, the invisible, but absolutely real, presence and power of the Holy Spirit comes upon the believer from above, completely surrounding, enveloping, and immersing the believer. Holy Spirit baptism takes place inwardly with an internal force. The believer receives the presence and power of the Holy Spirit within himself or herself until there comes a point in which the Holy Spirit wells up within the believer and flows forth like a mighty river from within, from the innermost depths of the spirit man.

To be filled with the Holy Spirit is to experience Christ as He unselfishly shares with us the same power for living and serving that He Himself experienced. To be Spirit-filled is to have the Holy Spirit, the oil of heaven, poured from God's throne into our own being.

TO BE FILLED WITH THE HOLY SPIRIT HAS SEVERAL POSITIVE RESULTS:

1. Our worship and praise are intensified because as the Holy Spirit fills our heart more, there is intensified sensitivity and gratefulness toward God and His presence.

2. The inner devotional life of prayer is intensified and enlarged. Our prayer capacity is enlarged because the Holy Spirit has filled our hearts, and we learn to pray more intensely and more directly. Our inner devotional lives are changed because we want to drink of the Spirit and eat of the Word. A thankful heart is always a result of a person who is filled with the Holy Spirit.

3. Humility and submission in serving one another is always the result of a person who is soft hearted and filled with Christ. Service becomes easy as pride, ego, and selfishness are set aside. A serving heart is developed. We must drink deeply of the Holy Spirit, expecting God to fill us and give us more.

The baptism of the Holy Spirit is referred to directly in seven passages in the New Testament where baptism is used in connection with the Holy Spirit.

"I indeed baptize you with water unto repentance, but He who is coming after me is mightier than I, whose sandals I am not worthy to carry. He will **baptize** you with the **Holy Spirit** and fire" (Matthew 3:11).

"I indeed baptized you with water, but He will **baptize** you with the **Holy Spirit**" (Mark 1:8).

"John answered, saying to all, 'I indeed baptize you with water; but One mightier than I is coming, whose sandal strap I am not worthy to loose. He will **baptize** you with the **Holy Spirit** and fire' " (Luke 3:16).

"I did not know Him, but He who sent me to baptize with water said to me, 'Upon whom you see the Spirit descending, and remaining on Him, this is He who **baptizes** with the **Holy Spirit**' " (John 1:33).

 "For John truly baptized with water, but you shall be **baptized** with the **Holy Spirit** not many days from now" (Acts 1:5).

"Then I remembered the word of the Lord, how He said, 'John indeed baptized with water, but you shall be **baptized** with the **Holy Spirit**' " (Acts 11:16).

"For by one Spirit we were all **baptized** into one body—whether Jews or Greeks, whether slaves or free—and have all been made to drink into one **Spirit**" (1 Corinthians 12:13).

The word baptism illustrates the experience. The word *baptizo* in the Greek means to dip something into a fluid and then take it out again, plunged into so as to cover wholly. Baptism is total in the sense it involves the whole person and the whole personality of the one baptized. Baptism is transitional for the person being baptized and marks a transition of passing out of one stage or realm of experience into another that was never previously entered into. Baptism occurs outwardly with external force.

RECEIVING THE BAPTISM OF THE HOLY SPIRIT

To receive the baptism of the Holy Spirit, we must move into the law of expectation and a spirit of faith. We must believe that it is biblical and that it is something that we can receive now. There must be a spirit of faith and anticipation to open the heart and mind so that this truth will become an experienced truth, not just a dogma.

When a person receives the scriptural baptism of the Holy Spirit, there can also be with that a new spiritual language. This new spiritual language can be embraced by all who receive the baptism of the Spirit (see Mark 16:17; Acts 2:4, 4:31, 8:14-17, 8:38-39, 9:17, 10:44-46, 19:1-6; 1 Corinthians 12:10, 12:28, 13:1).

THE "MORE" FACTOR

After we receive Christ as Lord in a salvation experience, are water baptized, then receive the baptism of the Holy Spirit, there is still another step in moving into more of what God has for us. We still must believe God for the more factor. We must believe that there is still more of God yet to come into our lives, more of the Holy Spirit yet to overflow in us.

Even after salvation, water baptism, and Holy Spirit baptism, there are still more infillings of the Holy Spirit. In 1 Corinthians 12:13, it says: "For by one Spirit we were all baptized into one body—whether Jews or Greeks, whether slaves or free—and have all been made to drink into one Spirit."

REFILLING: A CONTINUOUS EXPERIENCE

Being filled with the Holy Spirit is a continual act of the believer. It is something we need to do repeatedly and frequently. To be filled, in the Greek, is a present tense of the imperative, which indicates a continuous action.

The Bible repeatedly uses the word drink when referring to this refilling. Just as drinking water once does not mean that your physical body will never again thirst, being filled with the Holy Spirit does not mean you can drink once then never thirst for Him again. Drinking is a daily experience (see John 4:7-10, 6:53-55; 1 Corinthians 10:4, 12:13).

> "We must believe that there is still more of God yet to come into our lives, more of the Holy Spirit yet to overflow us."

Refillings are fresh visitations of the Holy Spirit available to each of us. And they are necessary to continue an increase of power. Refillings or infillings of the Holy Spirit are biblical.

"On the last day, that great day of the feast, Jesus stood and cried out, saying, 'If anyone thirsts, let him come to Me and **drink**' " (John 7:37).

" 'He who believes in Me, as the Scripture has said, out of his heart will **flow rivers** of living water.' But this He spoke concerning the Spirit, whom those believing in Him would receive; for the Holy Spirit was not yet given, because Jesus was not yet glorified" (John 7:38-39).

"But the land which you cross over to possess is a land of hills and valleys, which **drinks water** from the rain of heaven" (Deuteronomy 11:11).

"And do not be drunk with wine, in which is dissipation; but be **filled** with the Spirit" (Ephesians 5:18).

"Jesus answered and said to her, 'Whoever **drinks** of this water will thirst again, but whoever **drinks** of the water that I shall give him will never thirst. But the water that I shall give him will become in him a fountain of water springing up into everlasting life' " (John 4:13-14).

"Then Peter, filled with the Holy Spirit, said to them, 'Rulers of the people and elders of Israel' " (Acts 4:8).

"And when they had prayed, the place where they were assembled together was shaken; and they were all **filled** with the Holy Spirit, and they spoke the word of God with boldness" (Acts 4:31).

To be filled means we begin to minister out of our over-flow. We are not satisfied with meeting our own needs, but we overflow into spiritual service to others.

We must avoid quenching the Holy Spirit and begin to encourage drinking of the Holy Spirit. "And do not be drunk with wine, in which is dissipation; but be filled with the Spirit, speaking to one another in psalms and hymns and spiritual songs, singing and making melody in your heart to the Lord, giving thanks always for all things to God the Father in the name of our Lord Jesus Christ" (Ephesians 5:18-20).

God has given us everything we need to live in Him and for Him. But the key is that we need to seek more. We need to hunger for and seek more of God's Holy Spirit as we move into times of revival. He is here for us if we will but ask in faith.

NOTES

1. Renewal Theology, (Grand Rapids: Zondervan Publishing House), n.a.

2. Jack Hayford, *Spirit-Filled—The Overflowing Power of the Holy Spirit* (Wheaton: Tyndale House Publishers), 8-9.

3. R.A. Torrey.

4. Derek Prince, *Foundation Series—From Jordan to Pentecost* (Ft. Lauderdale: Derek Prince Publications), 56.

5. Samuel Chadwick.

6. Charles Ryrie.

PART 2

RIDING THE WAVE OF REVIVAL

Chapter 6

REVIVAL - A MIXED BLESSING

*W*hen the Holy Spirit begins to move on His people, there is an empowerment in evangelism, a renewed reaping of the harvest for Jesus Christ. There is a rejuvenated spiritual life in the church that becomes more effective in confronting a culture that is falling further and further away from God. When revival comes, miracles happen. People's bodies and minds are healed, and many begin to move supernaturally in the gifts of the Spirit.

But there can be a downside to revival. Revival can be dangerous because of weak foundations and flaws that are present within individual people and in church bodies. The danger is not in the moving of the Holy Spirit Himself, but in the actions and reactions of the people He moves through.

Most Christians have attended or participated in revival meetings at some time in their lives. I have seen what has taken place in some of these meetings firsthand, and I have also viewed many of these meetings on videotape and television. I have read hundreds of articles and just about any book even remotely related to the subject of revival.

I must be honest and say that I do not endorse everything that goes on in some of these meetings. I do not claim to be the final authority on revivals or on the activities that take place at revival meetings. But I can speak as a pastor and leader who has taken part in two or three historical revival movements and Holy Spirit activities in our nation. I have seen some wonderful outcomes of these revivals, but

I have also seen the extremes and excesses that often accompany these outpourings.

My hope in writing this book is that we in the body of Christ can keep the excesses to a minimum, while at the same time avoid doing anything that would quench what the Holy Spirit may be doing in our midst.

INTERPRETING CURRENT RENEWAL ACTIVITY

In a recent book entitled, *Holy Laughter and the Toronto Blessing: An Investigative Report*, the author gives five interpretations of current renewal activity. Most of what he has to say is focused on what is called the "Toronto Blessing," yet it could be applied to any revival activity around the nation right now. Here are his five interpretations of the current renewal activity:

> 1. The most optimistic interpretation is the view that the Toronto Blessing represents a renewal that is prophetic and significant. This renewal is part of God's will in bringing the church to its final preparation for the return of Jesus Christ.

> 2. It is true that the Toronto Blessing is a great renewal, but it should not be interpreted as having eschatalogical significance in any other way than any church or part of the body of Christ has eschatalogical significance in being part of the kingdom of God. According to this view, the Toronto Blessing is acknowledged primarily as a supernatural and miraculous outpouring of the Holy Spirit.

3. A third interpretation uses the phrase "mixed blessings" to describe the Toronto Blessing. Simply put, the renewal connected with Rodney Howard-Browne and the Vineyard offers a mixture of good and bad, of positive and negative.

4. In a more critical position, many believe that the Toronto Blessing is fundamentally a negative reality. This renewal is not in keeping with the authentic revivals of church history, and its weaknesses are so great that Christians worldwide must be warned against it.

5. The final interpretation is the most negative. It is rooted, like the first one, in a prophetic or eschatalogical understanding. According to those who take this view, the Toronto Blessing is part of the work of the Antichrist to bring about world apostasy and the creation of a one-world church under satanic delusion.[1]

REVIVAL: A MIXED BLESSING

Of these five responses to the Toronto Blessing—and possibly to many of the Holy Spirit activities in our nation today—I would say that number three most closely describes most every revival: They are always a mixed blessing. No revival—the renewal with Rodney Howard-Browne, the Vineyard churches, Toronto Revival, Melbourne Revival, or the campus revivals—will offer a completely pure river where everything that is happening, everything that is preached or taught, everything that goes on in the church service, is a pure product of the Holy Spirit.

There are positives and negatives to every revival. Why? Because humans are involved, and whenever humans are involved there is a mixture of flesh, the human mind, and Holy Spirit activity. Revivals are messy by nature because the Holy Spirit is moving within a human environment that has been molded by sin, encumbering religious traditions, and demonic presences. Revival manifestations of the Holy Spirit are contaminated by the human element, which often leaves room for emotionalism, incorrect direction, and inaccurate interpretation of God's leading.

Put these things together and you will have a mixed blessing. It does not necessarily mean that the manifestations we see have a spirit of antichrist, and it does not necessarily mean that they will lead anybody into delusion or harmful doctrine as they try to respond to the Holy Spirit. But as we move into a season of revival, we need to keep in mind that certain fleshly human responses can quench the moving of the Holy Spirit or cause excesses.

> "There are positives and negatives to every revival. Why? Because humans are involved."

As we respond to the moving of the Holy Spirit, I believe we can obey Scripture's admonition to "Quench not the Holy Spirit and test everything." Our responsibility is to test everything, while making sure that we do not quench what God might be trying to accomplish.

John Wesley articulated clearly what our perspective ought to be in times of revival: "Lord, send us revival without its defects, but if this is not possible, send revival, defects and all." This is the perspective of a man who had experienced revival with all of its confusion, excitement—

and fruit. May we be so wise as to tolerate some excesses and defects without rejecting revival itself.

HUMAN RESPONSE TO REVIVAL

The revivalist Jonathan Edwards offered this jewel of wisdom on our judgment or evaluation of revival: "A work of God without stumbling blocks is never to be expected." Arthur Wallis, in his book, *In The Day of Thy Power*, entitles a chapter "A Sign Spoken Against." In this chapter, he suggests that, "If we find a revival that is not spoken against we had better look again to ensure that it is a revival."[2]

We should eagerly seek to allow the Holy Spirit to move in a more powerful and impacting way in our lives and in our churches, keeping in mind that any time He moves in a revival fashion that there will be human reactions and responses.

When revival comes, there can be two extremes in human response. The first is to be reactionary, maybe to the point of resisting the season of revival. The other extreme is to over-respond, ultimately in an unreasonable, gullible manner.

We do not want to go to either of these extremes. We do not want to react by resisting the Holy Spirit as He moves upon us, and we don't want to be so trusting that we have no boundary lines or doctrinal grid by which to understand what God is doing.

Revival activities, beliefs, and behaviors must be spiritually discerned. We must not attempt to understand the moving of the Holy Spirit by using our emotions, opinions, religious background, or personal likes or dislikes. We must cling to biblical principles as we move in times of revival.

If we can balance our response to God's presence and to the subjective movings of the Holy Spirit by grasping the objective written Word of God, we will walk a balanced walk during seasons of revival.

HOLDING ON TO THAT WHICH IS GOOD

My desire is to embrace all that is positive about renewal and revival while correcting that which is excessive, hurtful in the long term, or contrary to biblical mandates. As we walk during these seasons of revival, there are principles of wisdom that we can apply to our situation so as to build a bank for the river, so to speak.

"My desire is to embrace all that is positive about renewal and revival while correcting that which is excessive, hurtful in the long term, or contrary to biblical mandates."

Revivals are God's design to "dig the wells of refreshing" for His people. God desires to unblock these wells by removing all the rocks of wrong traditions, wrong theology, and wrong ideas that have kept God's people from the pure water in the well. "Then Isaac departed from there and pitched his tent in the Valley of Gerar, and dwelt there. And Isaac dug again the wells of water which they had dug in the days of Abraham his father, for the Philistines had stopped them up after the death of Abraham. He called them by the names which his father had called them" (Genesis 26:17-18).

Let us not react to the excesses or ideas of men during times of revival by rejecting the revival itself. We must hold to that which God is doing in our midst. We must test the water of revival activities, knowing that God may want to touch us in a supernatural way. Leaders from many different denominations, belief systems, geographical locations, and spiritual passions are speaking about the need for more of God. Let us be careful not to allow any human imperfections or religious mind sets to overwhelm our passion for authentic revival.

DEFINING REVIVAL

We can define revival or renewal as a move of the Holy Spirit that refreshes and enables us, that gives us a season of new beginnings.

Dr. Martyn Lloyd Jones, who served as minister of Westminster Chapel in London for twenty-five years and is recognized as one of this century's most gifted preachers and writers, defines the moving of the Spirit as, "People becoming aware of the presence and power of God in a manner they have never known before. The Holy Spirit literally is presiding over the meeting, directing the meeting, taking charge of it, guiding them, and leading them."

Jones, who preached extensively throughout the United States and Europe, wrote, "We have seen some of the general characteristics of revival—a sense of the majesty of God, of personal sinfulness, of the wonder of salvation through Jesus Christ and a desire that others might know it. And we have seen, too, that in a time of revival, people are aware of the presidency of the Holy Spirit over everything and the life of the whole community."[3]

In defining revival so far, I have quoted three words: "God comes down." But in order for us to properly evaluate our responses to revival, we need a more detailed examination of what revival really is.

Webster's Dictionary defines the word revival this way: Return, recall or recovery to life from death or apparent death, revival brings something back to life that is either now dead or seemingly dead. Renew the mind or memory, to recover from a state of neglect or depression, to awaken, reinvestigate.

Hayah-chayah, the Hebrew word for revival, literally means to recover, to repair, to give new life, to refresh, to reestablish, to restore, to make alive again.

SCRIPTURAL DEFINITIONS OF REVIVAL

When we use the words renewal or revival, we simply mean an intensified activity of the Holy Spirit on hungering and thirsting believers. Here are a few Scriptures that refer to this concept:

"On the last day, that great day of the feast, Jesus stood and cried out, saying, 'If anyone **thirsts**, let him come to Me and **drink**. He who believes in Me, as the Scripture has said, out of his heart will **flow rivers** of living water.' But this He spoke concerning the Spirit, whom those believing in Him would receive; for the Holy Spirit was not yet given, because Jesus was not yet glorified" (John 7:37-39).

"And the Spirit and the bride say, 'Come!' And let him who hears say, 'Come!' And let him who **thirsts** come. Whoever desires, let him take the water of life freely" (Revelation 22:17).

"Will You not **revive** us again, that Your people may rejoice in You?" (Psalm 85:6).

"Not by works of righteousness which we have done, but according to His mercy He saved us, through the washing of regeneration and **renewing** of the Holy Spirit, whom He poured out on us abundantly through Jesus Christ our Savior" (Titus 3:5-6).

The words revival or renewal appear throughout the Scriptures. Here are just a few of many, many examples:

"And he spoke before his brethren and the army of Samaria, and said, 'What are these feeble Jews doing? Will they fortify themselves? Will they offer sacrifices? Will they complete it in a day? Will they **revive** the stones from the heaps of rubbish—stones that are burned?' " (Nehemiah 4:2).

"For thus says the High and Lofty One Who inhabits eternity, whose name is Holy: 'I dwell in the high and holy place, with him who has a contrite and humble spirit, to **revive** the spirit of the humble, and to **revive** the heart of the contrite ones' " (Isaiah 57:15).

In the context of Scripture, the words renewal, revival, and reformation are all words that speak about dynamic changes taking place in the church and in people's lives.

The words used to describe spiritual awakenings are usually revival, reformation, or renewal.

Revival is traced back to biblical metaphors for the infusion by the Holy Spirit of spiritual life into Christian experience so that He can work in renewing spiritual vitality in the church, which fosters kingdom expansion.

Renewal is sometimes used to encompass revival and reformation, and also to denote the updating of the church, which leads to new engagements with the surrounding world.

Reformation refers to the purifying of doctrine and structure in the church, but implies a component of spiritual revitalization.

Usually, revival and renewal are a sovereign work, while reformation can be led by insightful leaders who seek to bring a refreshing to the church through restructuring and reteaching.

Many spiritual leaders of the past and present have had a lot to say about revival. The late Arthur Wallis, an English writer and Christian statesman whose influence was felt in England for over four decades, once defined revival this way: "Revival is divine intervention in the normal course of spiritual things. It is God revealing Himself to man in awesome holiness and irresistible power. It is such a manifest working of God that human personalities are overshadowed and human programs are abandoned. It is man retiring to the background because God has taken the field. It is the Lord working in extraordinary power on saint and sinner. Revival accomplishes what our best spiritual efforts cannot."

Other godly leaders have given these insights to the understanding of true revival:

J. Edwin Orr: "Spiritual awakening is a moment of the Holy Spirit bringing about a revival of New Testament Christianity in the church of Christ and its related community. The best definition for revival is simply times of refreshing from the presence of God."[4]

R.A. Torrey: "A revival is a time when God visits His people, and by the power of the Holy Spirit imparts new life to them, and through them imparts life to sinners. Revivals are not religious excitements stirred up by cunning methods and the hypnotic influence of the mere professional evangelist."[5]

Ralph Mahoney: "What is revival could be answered in these two words: GOD CAME. That is the summation of what we mean by revival—God coming."[6]

Stephen Olford: "Revival is the sovereign act of God in which He restores His own backsliding people to repentance, faith and obedience."[7]

Charles Finney: "Revival presupposes that the church is sunk down in a backslidden state and revival consists in the return of the church from her backslidings and reaping the harvest of souls."[8]

D.M. Panton: "The inrush of the Spirit into the body that threatens to become a corpse."[9]

Arthur Wallis: "Revival can never be explained in terms of activity, organization, meetings, personalities, preachings. These may or may not be involved in the work, but they do not and cannot account for the effects produced. Revival is essentially a manifestation of God, it has the stamp of deity upon it, which even the undegenerate and uninitiated are quick to recognize. Revival must of necessity make an impact on the community, and this is one means by which we may distinguish it from the more usual operations of the Holy Spirit."[10]

Andrew Murray: "The true meaning of the word is far deeper. The word means making alive again. Those who have been alive but have fallen into what is called a cold, or dead state. They are Christians and have life, but they need reviving to bring them back to their first love again. The healthy growth of the spiritual life to which conversion was mean to be the entrance."[11]

Walter C. Kaiser: "Accordingly, revival presupposes a serious decline in the church's appetite for spiritual things and in her championing the cause of morality and justice in human affairs."[12]

COMPONENTS OF SUCCESSFUL REVIVAL

If we are to hold on to that which is good during times of revival, we will need to understand what our attitudes and actions should be as we seek a visitation of God's Spirit. In Dan Crawford's book, *The Emerging Movement*, he gives nine components of any successful revival, and it bears quoting here. The nine components for successful revival he gives are:

Components of 9 SUCCESSFUL REVIVAL

1. Humility
2. Prayer
3. Discernment
4. Genuineness
5. Moderation
6. Propriety
7. Empathy
8. Bible Focus
9. Maturity

1. **Humility** - Revival is to serve God's purpose, not feed mortal egos.

2. **Prayer** - Pray before revival, during, and especially after, when excitement wanes and the novelty is gone, prayer is still the key instrument.

3. **Discernment** - Listen carefully to God's call in order to generate a spiritual response, not merely an emotional one.

4. **Genuineness** - Firmly reject anything counterfeit.

5. **Moderation** - Extremists, even well-meaning ones, will seriously jeopardize the credibility of your efforts.

6. **Propriety** - Sins committed publicly must be confessed publicly. Private sins, especially of a sexual nature, must be confessed privately.

7. **Empathy** - Reach out to those in the congregation who are suspicious of or resistant to revival.

8. **Bible Focus** - Revival must be Bible-centered, not experience-centered. Experience and testimony are important, but must never overshadow the Word.

9. **Maturity** - Rely on spiritually mature people for testimony. Most newly planted Christians should not be tempted to pridefulness by sharing their testimony before they are ready.

If we can apply these components to our own lives and to our church bodies, we will find it much easier to root out the excesses and extremes of revival, while at the same time avoid quenching a move of God's Spirit.

Revival is a time when God makes known His inescapable presence as the only true God, as the One who is mighty and majestic. God's presence confronts His people, both to humble them and to exalt them at the same time. God's presence forces people to realize His awesome power and to assimilate into their lives His unchangeable principles.

NOTES

1. *Holy Laughter and the Toronto Blessings—An Investigative Report*, (Grand Rapids, Zondervan Publishing House), 22-25.
2. Arthur Wallis, *In The Day of Thy Power: A Picture of Revival from Scripture and History*, (Columbia: Cityhill Publishing), 26.
3. Dr. Martyn Lloyd Jones, *Revival*, (Wheaton: Crossway Books), 105.
4. J. Edwin Orr.
5. R.A. Torrey.
6. Ralph Mahoney, from author's personal notes taken at Mahoney's lectures.
7. Steve Olford, *Heart Cry for Revival: Expository Sermons on Revival*, (Westwood: Revell Publishing), 33.
8. Charles Finney, *Revivals of Religion*, (Westwood: Revell Publishing), 7.
9. D.M. Panton.
10. Arthur Wallis, *In the Day of His Power*, (Columbia: Cityhill Publishing), 22-23.
11. Andrew Murray, *Revival*, (Minneapolis: Bethany House Publishers, 1990), 17.
12. Walter C. Kaiser, Jr., *Quest for Renewal*, (Moody Press),n.a.
13. Dan Grawford, *The Emerging Movement*.

Chapter 7

DISCERNMENT IN REVIVAL TIMES

*W*ithout a doubt, we are living in some of the most exciting days of our lives. As the people of God, we have heard a particular call of the Spirit, an urging to get involved and build with the Holy Spirit the eternal purposes of God. What a terrific call! What a way to live!

Yet along with the excitement, there is potential danger in living on the edge of what God is doing and is challenging us to do. These are exciting times if we will live within God's guidelines and eternal principles. Seasons of revival necessitate a certain level of maturity in responding wisely to God's Spirit without reacting negatively to the revival atmosphere.

Revival seasons emphasize the working of the Holy Spirit. Prayer, worship, gifts of the Spirit, healing, and power manifestations are all elements of revival, and during times of revival, it is vitally important that we secure our hearts with discernment. Believers are biblically exhorted to use "discernment" and "good judgment." Discernment is the ability to live life successfully in all seasons, applying biblical truth without becoming weird, out of touch with reality, or a hindrance to true kingdom expansion.

The spirit of discernment can be defined as sound judgment and following God's divine principles. We need this because our modern times have introduced the age of imitation. Imitation of anything is possible today, from clothes to perfumes to golf clubs. And imitated goods are much cheaper because they are not the real thing.

HOLDING ON TO WHAT IS REAL

Scripture exhorts believers to live soberly, wisely, and discerningly, lest we be swayed and captured by the untrue, unreal, and unbiblical. In today's world of religion and religious experiences, there are many imitations: imitations in philosophies, in ministries, in churches and in experiences. As believers, we must develop eyes for the authentic so we are not taken in by the imitations. Discernment is not just a word that denotes spiritual capacity, but spiritual survival.

> "A lack of spiritual discernment or 'kingdom common sense' will result in spiritual immaturity."

A lack of spiritual discernment or "kingdom common sense" will result in spiritual immaturity. In Philippians 1:9, Paul exhorts the church this way: "That I pray, that your love may abound still more in real knowledge and all discernment." Discernment here is a broad range of perception and practical wisdom. In Hebrews 5:11-14, the writer exhorts believers to maturity, that is, to have their spiritual senses trained to discern good and evil.

In the Old Testament, there are several Hebrew words in the discernment family:

"Nakar"— To be able to distinguish, inspect, or look over something with the intention of recognizing it, and discerning its true identity (see Ezra 3:13; Job 4:16).

"Shama"— To hear or listen. This word implies perceiving a message and giving special attention. Effective hearing involves perception, understanding, and discernment.

"Yada"– A knowledge gained by the senses so as to be able to discern. To recognize what is beneficial or what is harmful. Ordinarily gained by experience, knowledge is contemplative perception possessed by a wise man (see Proverbs 1:4, 2:6, 5:2).

"Raal"– To see, look at, respect, perceive, understand, learn and, enjoy. It denotes the use of understanding that comes by accepting the word of God as delivered by His accredited messengers.

"Tebuna"– Understanding or insight. Discernment leads to understanding. To be perceptive and use good judgment (see 1 Kings 3:9; Proverbs 29:19; Job 6:30).

We must lift up our voices for godly spiritual understanding. While discernment is available for all believers, it is not a gift. It does not come automatically. It is more than I.Q. It connotes character. The possession of discernment requires a disciplined diligence in adding judgment capacity to a life. One is at fault if he or she does not possess it, and, in fact, not to pursue it will lead to spiritual damage.

A summarized conceptual definition of discernment is: Spiritual perception through the combination of God's Spirit bearing witness with our spirits in harmony with Scripture, godly principles, and wisdom, resulting in spiritual insight into what is false or true, whether in concepts, motives, ministries, philosophies, thoughts, or experiences.

The Word of God has several references relating to discernment. The following is an example: "The LORD is exalted, for He dwells on high; he has filled Zion with justice and righteousness. Wisdom and knowledge will be the stability of your times, and the strength of salvation; the fear of the LORD is His treasure" (Isaiah 53:5-6).

DISCERNMENT IN THE PROVERBS

The Book of Proverbs deals with those who are in need of discernment. It describes people who will vanish because of their lack of discernment. Each one of these characters in the Proverbs can apply to those in revival seasons who must grasp the art of discernment so that they do not vanish with their lack of judgment.

The Simple Person

The word simple is used twenty-seven times in Proverbs. It is translated from the word *pata*, which means to be open, spacious, wide, gullible, silly, or empty-headed. It also means to be aimless and drifting. This word speaks of a person who is immature and simple, one who is open to all kinds of enticements and does not have sound judgment as to what is right and wrong.

Enticement is what happens when a man refuses to follow God's directions. He is enticed to do wrong, and this will ultimately lead to discipline or judgment for rejecting the Lord's wisdom. This is the naive one of Proverbs. He is not deranged or possessing a mental handicap. This is a spiritual state, not a mental state. This is a person whose instability could be rectified, but who refuses to accept discipline in the school of wisdom. This person refuses to hear and obey, so he inherits folly, is morally confused, and has twisted spiritual values.

"To give prudence to the simple, to the young man knowledge and discretion" (Proverbs 1:4).

"How long, you simple ones, will you love simplicity. For scorners delight in their scorning and fools hate knowledge" (Proverbs 1:22). (Also see Proverbs 7:7, 8:5, 9:4, 9:13, 9:16, 14:15, 19:25, 22:3.)

The Foolish Person

The second person without discernment in Proverbs is the foolish person. The Hebrew words *hesil, ewil,* and *nabal* are the words used to refer to the person translated in our English Bible as "fool." The Hebrew words simply refer to one who has a twisted sense of values and to a person with a dull and obstinate mental outlook. It does not refer to mental deficiency, but to a propensity to make wrong choices because of a stubborn attitude. This word refers to a person who has shallow insights, to a person whose lifestyle will lead to deception and destruction.

> "The fool's eyes are unable to see principles of wisdom and discernment."

The fool's eyes are unable to see principles of wisdom and discernment. He may roam the earth seeking it, but he will miss it completely because of his attitude. His mind fluctuates at the mercy of the winds of opinion in the world around him, and he desperately needs some set of principles to fix his purposes, his choices in life, and his conduct.

"He who troubles his own house will inherit the wind and the fool will be a servant to the wise of heart" (Proverbs 11:29).

"The way of a fool is right in his own eyes but he who heeds counsel is wise" (Proverbs 12:15). (Also see Proverbs 7:22, 10:10, 15:5, 17:7, 17:24, 18:2, 19:1, 20:3.)

The Scorner

The third person who is in dire need of discernment and proper judgment is the scorner or the proud person. In the Hebrew, the word for scorner is *lason*, which means to be resistant of reproof, to hate rebuke, to mock sin or sound judgment, or to be proud and haughty. A scornful person is contrasted with the wise and coupled with the foolish. He has been put into the fool's gallery, and his presence there makes it clear that attitude, not mental capacity, classifies the person. He shares with his fellows a strong dislike for correction, and it is this, not any lack of intelligence, that blocks any move he makes toward wisdom. He has no grasp on spiritual principles, so he scorns what is sound judgment. James 4:6 says that, "God resists the proud but He gives grace to the humble."

"How long, you simple ones, will you love simplicity? For scorners delight in their scorning, and fools hate knowledge" (Proverbs 1:22).

"The scoffer seeks wisdom and does not find it, but knowledge is easy to him who understands" (Proverbs 14:6). (Also see Proverbs 19:29, 15:12, 21:11, 22:10; Psalm 1:1.)

The Lazy Person

The fourth type of person in Proverbs who has an attitude that must be changed to receive spiritual discernment is the lazy person. The lazy person of Proverbs refers to more than physical laziness. This person will not begin things and will not end things. He has an attitude that will not allow him to be a disciplined person who takes care of details.

To ask the questions "how long?" or "when?" is being too precise for this type of person. All he knows is his delicious drowsiness. He does not commit himself to refusal, but deceives himself by the smallness of his surrenders. By inches and by minutes, his opportunities slip away. He will not finish things. The rare effort of beginning has been too much. He will not face things. He comes to believe his own excuses to rationalize his laziness. He is wiser in his own conceit than seven men who can render a reason. He avoids trouble and responsibility.

"How long will you slumber, O sluggard? When will you arise from your sleep? A little sleep, a little slumber, a little folding of the hands and in comes poverty" (Proverbs 6:9-10).

The Deceived Person

The fifth type of person is the most important profile in the Proverbs. This is the deceived person. The word deceived in the Book of Proverbs, and in the rest of the Old Testament, means to be restless, to be led astray, to stagger, or to be confused. It is used to describe those who are carried off into a trackless wilderness. It describes horses that wander off the race course, or wild bees and wasps that have neither leader nor goal. It is also used on wandering stars that have no fixed orbit, plan, or rule. This word describes those who have been seduced off their course by right-sounding words but wrong principles that lead to digression. Deception is always brought about by a failure in judgment or discernment. To lack discernment is to vacillate in judgment without the ability to fix convictions or goals according to one's principles.

The world's wise man is stayed from his error by turning aside from the world of the senses to the world of ideas. Here, too, is a detour to the goal of true knowledge. It is a different kind of deception, but is nevertheless a deception.

To look to materialism as the source of security is to believe in the external things and to be overtaken by that which is temporary. On the other hand, to believe in idealism as the answer to one's problems is using one's imagination, which results in vain conceptions. Neither materialism nor idealism can be a foundation for true spiritual discernment or sound judgment. A society that runs hard after fantasy, eastern religion, and human philosophy will nurture an internal deception that will end in disaster.

A SATANIC STRATEGY

To take advantage of our lack of discernment is one of the strategies of the enemy. During revival seasons, subjectivity and misuse of Scriptures, dreams, visions, and gifts of the Spirit can be a great source of error and deception.

Revival seasons necessitate strong discernment, sound judgment, and an anchor in the Word of God. Man does not err simply because he is weak or open to deception. He is deceived when he does not listen to or obey God's Word. We are all responsible to read and study God's Word for ourselves. If we are deceived, we cannot blame the deceiver. It is our own allowed weakness that eventually leads us astray (see Proverbs 11:18, 12:5, 12:20, 14:8, 14:25, 23:3, 27:6, 31:30).

DEVELOPING DISCERNMENT

The spirit of discernment can and must be cultivated during revival seasons. There are five basic steps to developing spiritual discernment. The following chart gives the believer a simple, practical strategy to develop the important quality of spiritual discernment.

DISCERNMENT

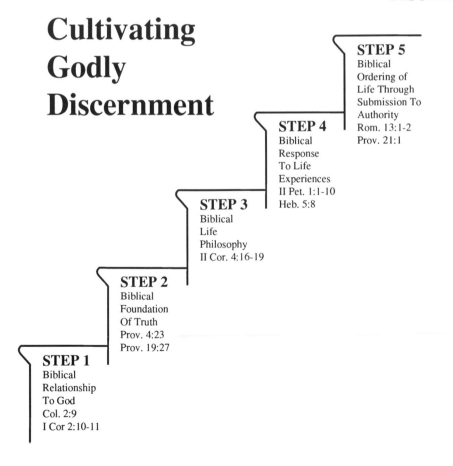

Cultivating Godly Discernment

STEP 5
Biblical
Ordering of
Life Through
Submission To
Authority
Rom. 13:1-2
Prov. 21:1

STEP 4
Biblical
Response
To Life
Experiences
II Pet. 1:1-10
Heb. 5:8

STEP 3
Biblical
Life
Philosophy
II Cor. 4:16-19

STEP 2
Biblical
Foundation
Of Truth
Prov. 4:23
Prov. 19:27

STEP 1
Biblical
Relationship
To God
Col. 2:9
I Cor 2:10-11

Discerning the Multitudes of Voices

There are multiple voices that surface during seasons of revival. This is why it is time to be careful.

In 1 Corinthians 14:7-8, it says: "Even things without life, whether flute or harp, when they make a sound, unless they make a distinction in the sounds, how will it be known what is piped or played? For if the trumpet makes an uncertain sound, who will prepare himself for battle?"

There are many sounds released during seasons of revival. These sounds come from different teachers, preachers, truths and trends, ideas, concepts, and perspectives. We must make sure that there is a distinction in the sounds, and that distinction should be through clear biblical elements that we can see and hear in the teachings that surface during revival.

> **"We need to inspect fruit and examine doctrine, but not with an attitude of judgement or criticism."**

Every voice has behind it a philosophical and doctrinal stance, and we must discern what is behind every voice that speaks. Every voice is nurtured with its own personality and its own passions. Every voice has certain theological frameworks to work from and an eschatalogical bias that influences all decisions.

Discerning the Motives of Our Responses

We must not nurture reactionary attitudes. This is what we need to avoid during times of the moving of the Holy Spirit. An attitude of defensiveness usually is from the root of insecurity, and causes a person to become dogmatic without need. The attitude of, "That's not the way we do it here, so it is wrong" is certainly a wrong attitude. The attitude of spiritual superiority and separation is an attitude that will breed rejection and isolation.

We need to inspect fruit and examine doctrine, but not with an attitude of judgment or criticism. We must ask ourselves questions continually as we respond during seasons of revival. Revival is a time to be careful and a time to be mature.

As we discern the motivation behind our own responses, we need to ask ourselves the following questions:

Discerning our motivations CHECKLIST

✓ Are we responding to truth or trend?
✓ Are we responding to personality or personal conviction?
✓ Are we responding for spiritual reasons or selfish reasons?
✓ Are we using truth to profit our own ministries and our own pocketbooks?
✓ Are we using people to reach our own goals and visions?
✓ Are we building people to reach their goals and destiny?
✓ How do we perceive what we are doing in light of the moving of the Holy Spirit in days of revival?
✓ Are we responding cautiously or hastily?

(See Psalm 85:11, 86:11, 117:2; Proverbs 23:23, 25:8, 14:29, 29:20.)

Discerning the Proper Foundation

Revival seasons are times for the people of God to develop sound judgment. A spirit of discernment is of great necessity when there is a great deal of subjectivity involved (see 1 Kings 34:9-11, Matthew 16:3-5). Subjectivity is dangerous because its roots are in ourselves, our experiences, our moods, our giftings, and our biases. Subjectivity can be confused with prophetic feelings or the inner voices of the spiritual man, when in reality it is simply a strong opinion, a strong view, or a strong desire.

"The clear statements of the Word must always judge the obscure feelings of the inner heart and inner man."

We must balance our subjective feelings with objective doctrine, which is teaching of the Word of God and the principles of the Word of God. The clear statements of the Word must always judge the obscure feelings of the inner heart and inner man. Doctrine must always be our guiding force. Doctrine is the foundation for discernment. The healthy basics of doctrine are the safeguards to discernment. Direction is the focus for discernment. It asks, "Where will this truth take me?"

Discipline is the practice of discernment. Self-discipline and Word-discipline must be the practices that we function through and in when there is a season of revival. Diagnosis is the fruit of discernment. It is the ability to understand how all the parts work together with other bottom-line principles, philosophies, and doctrines to give power to the truth being preached or trend being pushed. Diagnosis takes time and a certain amount of technical skill. Diagnosis is the work of the man of God who will rightly divide the Word of God, which again is work.

During these seasons of revival, let us respond wisely. Let us watch our reactions carefully, but let us not become so gullible that we do away with sound judgment and Word-of-God reasoning. Discernment is in high order when there is a mighty moving of the Holy Spirit.

Chapter 8

TESTING THE AUTHENTICITY OF REVIVAL

*R*evival is a time of refreshing that brings a new life to the spirits of God's people and lifts up our souls. It is a time of fresh anointing where God moves by His Holy Spirit to put new oil into the hearts and lives of those who are seeking Him. Revival is a time when God heals His church.

Revival has been called a refiner's fire, rains of refreshing, watering the seed, soaking in God's love, a new liberty of the Spirit, a new spiritual oil change, and our returning to our first love. All of these describe some dimension of God moving anew upon His chosen people or His redeemed community.

During times of revival, there is a heightened sense of emotions and different kinds of physical manifestations in response to God's presence. As people soak in God's love and their hearts soften before Him, there could be the shedding of tears and, at times, physical manifestations such as shaking, twitching, falling, or just being in a sleep-like state. None of these really prove there has been a life change, only that the person is being touched by the awesome presence of God. John Wesley recorded some people's responses to the power of God in his journal.[1]

Some unusual things can happen during revival, and this is why we in the body of Christ must pay attention to see that what occurs is truly of the Holy Spirit.

Unfortunately, revival is usually accompanied by excesses and a general lack of wisdom and discernment. Most people are not as concerned about what is biblical as they are with receiving more of what is happening. There are some who believe that everything in revival is from God and that nothing should be checked—the more spectacular, the better. But left unchecked, emotional manifestations can become extreme emotional outbursts that bring ridicule or criticism to the work of God.

During the Great Awakening, Jonathan Edwards was appalled by certain extremes and set out to correct these excesses. He was scheduled to speak at the commencement service at Yale University and decided to take the opportunity to gather his thoughts on the problems of the awakening. He spoke on "The Distinguishing Marks of a Work of the Spirit of God." As you can see from the title of his message, he was dealing with the same revival struggles and tensions that we deal with during revival today.

The two groups that Edwards had to deal with were the Extremists and the Traditionalists. The Extremists were unbalanced, emotional enthusiasts who were so fanatical that many people saw them as superficial and unruled by the Spirit of God. The Traditionalists, on the other hand, were doctrinally and theoretically anti-revivalists, and they were called the Old Lights, the Old School, or the Regulars.

These two camps of opposing views caused great emotional outbursts during revival, which raised important questions during Edwards's time, just as they raise questions in our time. It was evident that a mighty work of the Spirit was being done then, just as is evident the Spirit is seeking to do a mighty work in our time. But equally evident was the extreme emotion that was obviously humanly engineered.

We must learn to recognize excesses during times of revival, and we must know how to bring balance to them without quenching the Spirit or adopting a judgmental attitude when we see those excesses.

But what are the true distinguishing marks of a work of the Spirit of God? How would we know if we were being moved by our emotions or minds, by crowd control or manipulation, and not by the true work of the Holy Spirit? Where do we draw the line? How are we to know what is really of God and what is not of God?

If we rely on feelings and emotions, we may react negatively to things that really are the Spirit of God moving. If we go by our traditions, we might be tempted to unfairly judge something that is new to us, but truly is of God.

TEST ALL THINGS

In 1 Thessalonians 5:21, the apostle Paul tells us to test the authenticity of revival: "Test all things; hold fast to what is good." One translation says, "By all means use your judgment and hold on to whatever is good."

> "It is our responsibility as believers to test all things to make sure they are from God."

It is our responsibility as believers to test all things to make sure they are from God. But how do we test? By what criteria do we test?

First, let us examine the word test as it is used in both in the Old and New Testaments. There are several Hebrew words for test used in the Bible, and they all can be applied to the concept of "testing all things."

"Test" in the Old Testament

"Nasah"-This word indicates the attempt to prove the quality of someone or something. Often, a time of pressure and difficulty constitutes the test (see Exodus 20:20; Deuteronomy 8:16).

"Then the Lord said to Moses, 'Behold, I will rain bread from heaven for you. And the people shall go out and gather a certain quota every day, that I may test them, whether they will walk in My law or not' " (Exodus 16:4).

"So that through them I may test Israel, whether they will keep the ways of the Lord, to walk in them as their fathers kept them, or not" (Judges 2:22).

"Sarap"-This means to smelt or refine, and it refers to the process by which gold or silver is refined. This illustrates the purification process of God's people. Visitation is a time to purify what God has exposed, to refine and burn out that which is impure (see Psalm 26:2; Isaiah 48:10).

"I have set you as an assayer and a fortress among My people, that you may know and test their way" (Jeremiah 6:27-30).

"You have tested my heart; you have visited me in the night; you have tried me and have found nothing; I have purposed that my mouth shall not transgress" (Psalm 17:3).

"Bahan"-This means to test specifically in the spiritual realm with a focus on some quality, such as integrity. This

word has the sense of examination designed to prove the existence of the quality sought. Visitation is a time to test our level of spiritual maturity and our responses to God's dealings (see Psalm 7:9; Proverbs 17:3; Malachi 3:10-11).

"In this manner you shall be tested: By the life of Pharaoh, you shall not leave this place unless your youngest brother comes here" (Genesis 42:15).

"I know also, my God, that You test the heart and have pleasure in uprightness. As for me, in the uprightness of my heart I have willingly offered all these things; and now with joy I have seen Your people, who are present here to offer willingly to You" 1 Chronicles 29:17.

"That You should visit him every morning, and test him every moment?" (Job 7:18).

"Test" in the New Testament

"Dokimazo, dokime, and dokimos"- These are New Testament words that emphasize that the test is designed to display the authenticity of what is tried. This is a test to make certain that something is accepted as trustworthy and acknowledged as authentic.

"And do not be conformed to this world, but be transformed by the renewing of your mind, that you may prove what is that good and acceptable and perfect will of God" (Romans 12:2).

"Each one's work will become clear; for the Day will declare it, because it will be revealed by fire; and the fire will test each one's work, of what sort it is" (1 Corinthians 3:13).

"But let each one examine his own work, and then he will have rejoicing in himself alone, and not in another" (Galatians 6:4).

"Beloved, do not believe every spirit, but test the spirits, whether they are of God; because many false prophets have gone out into the world" (1 John 4:1).

> **"God does not expect us to stop using our minds."**

"Anakrino"- This word means to examine, to investigate, to search or enquire carefully (see 1 Corinthians 10:25-27).

"These were more fair-minded than those in Thessalonica, in that they received the word with all readiness, and searched the Scriptures daily to find out whether these things were so" (Acts 17:11).

"My defense to those who examine me is this" (1 Corinthians 9:3).

SCRIPTURAL PRINCIPLES OF TESTING

In the early church there was a surging life of the Spirit that brought its own perils. There were so many diverse spiritual manifestations that some kind of test was needed to ensure that they were from the Spirit of God. So the early church had to use the Word of God, hold it supreme, and test all experiences and all fruit.

When God reveals new truth—truth that is not new to

God or to the Scriptures but to the generation discovering the truth—there is usually a tendency to reject it at first. This rejection comes out of the discomfort we can have with things that are not birthed by those we are familiar with, or simply because we have never heard the new truth before. We can also feel uncomfortable because new truth will demand of us something that we are not ready to give, not necessarily because our hearts are hard, but because it is so new that we're not comfortable moving into that new truth.

The testing process necessitates that we use our minds to examine closely the basic theologies that undergird spiritual claims and subjective experiences. God doesn't expect us to stop using our minds. He has filled us with the Spirit of wisdom and understanding. We do not have to negate intellect, and therefore inadvertently fall into gullibility.

The testing process I will be laying out in this chapter will help us to keep the good and discard the useless in times of revival. It will also keep us from discarding the good and keeping the useless.

The principles of testing revival by the written Word of God, by the scriptural fruit that revival produces, and discerning a shift in focus are three very safe, basic principles to use.

TESTING BY SOUND DOCTRINE

During seasons of revival, God's people must be every sensitive to doctrine, which is simply the teaching of the Word of God. The Word is the basis for all movings of the Holy Spirit. All that is going to happen in the Kingdom of God will be brought about through the preaching and the teaching of the Word of God.

In Mark 1:21-28, we see doctrine and revival type activity partnered together, as Jesus taught with authority and cast out the unclean spirit by the power of the Holy Spirit. We must do exactly as Jesus did and seek both the authority of Scripture and the power of the Holy Spirit as we test revival (also see Luke 4:32; John 7:16-17; Acts 13:11-12).

The written Word of God, the final authority on everything concerning our life in the Spirit, tells us the importance of doctrine:

"For I give you good **doctrine**: do not forsake my law" (Proverbs 4:2).

"Whom will he **teach knowledge**? And whom will he make to understand the message? Those just weaned from milk? Those just drawn from the breasts?" (Isaiah 28:9).

"That we should no longer be children, tossed to and fro and carried about with every wind of doctrine, by the trickery of men, in the cunning craftiness of deceitful plotting" (Ephesians 4:14).

"Take heed to yourself and to the **doctrine**. Continue in them, for in doing this you will save both yourself and those who hear you" (Timothy 4:16).

The Bible establishes the benefits of sound **doctrine** and exhorts the redeemed community to take heed. Sound doctrine does the following:
- It gives substance to our faith.
- It stabilizes us during times of testing and contradiction.

- It equips us to detect and confront error.
- It becomes a spiritual filter to remove ungodly fears and superstitions.

We must be careful not to espouse the anti-doctrine attitudes that characterized many of the revival movements of the past. We must see the importance of keeping Scripture—that is, sound doctrine—and experience together, and not allow experience to be separated at any point. Richard Lovelace states: "For the purity of a revival is intimately related to its theological substance. A deep work cannot be done without the sharp instruments of truth. Unless revival involves the issues as in theological reformation, its energy will be contained and its fruit will not last."[2]

Establishing Sound Doctrine

Martyn Lloyd Jones, one of the greatest twentieth century exporitors in all of England and pastor of the famous Westminster Chapel, spoke of the dangers of fanaticism, and what he said bears quoting here: "Fanaticism is a terrible danger which we must always bear in mind. It arises from a divorce between Scripture and experience, where we put experience above Scripture claiming things that are not sanctioned by Scripture or are perhaps even prohibited by it. There is a second danger, and it is equally important that we should bear it in mind, the second is the exact opposite of the first as these things generally go from one violent extreme to the other. The second danger then is that of being satisfied with something very much less than what is offered in the Scripture and the danger of interpreting the Scripture by our experiences and reducing its teaching to the level of what we know and experience. I would say that the second is the greater danger of the two at the present time."[3]

We must not establish doctrine by our personal experiences or by our personal words or rhemas (personal, spoken words). Doctrine or teaching is established by interpreting the whole of the logos, the written Word of God. All experiences and ideas must conform to the written Word of God, not to the idea of the Word of God, but to the actual written Word of God itself.

"That by two immutable things, in which it is impossible for God to lie, we might have strong consolation, who have fled for refuge to lay hold of the hope set before us. This hope we have as an anchor of the soul, both sure and steadfast, and which enters the Presence behind the veil" (Hebrews 6:18-19).

We need to be very careful, especially during times of revival, that we honor the written Word of God, that we give the Word its proper placement in our personal lives, in our judgments, and in our decisions. Revival is a time when subjectivity is heightened, so we must have the objectivity the Word of God gives us in testing.

The Bible tells us to hold the written Word of God supreme in order to avoid any possibility of deception in the things that happen during revival seasons:

"For thus says the Lord of hosts, the God of Israel: Do not let your prophets and your diviners who are in your midst deceive you, nor listen to your dreams which you cause to be dreamed" (Jeremiah 29:8).

"And Jesus answered and said to them: 'Take heed that no one deceives you' " (Matthew 24:4).

"Let no one deceive you with empty words, for because of these things the wrath of God comes upon the sons of disobedience" (Ephesians 5:6).

"Now the Spirit expressly says that in latter times some will depart from the faith, giving heed to deceiving spirits and doctrines of demons" (1 Timothy 4:1). (Also see 1 Thessalonians 2:4; Matthew 24:24; Romans 2:2; 1 John 4:1; Acts 2:42; 1 Timothy 5:17; 2 Timothy 4:2.)

> **"Revival activities, beliefs, and behaviors must be spiritually discerned through the written Word of God and biblical principle, not by our emotions, opinions, religious backgrounds, or personal likes or dislikes."**

Revival activities, beliefs, and behaviors must be spiritually discerned through the written Word of God and biblical principle, not by our emotions, opinions, religious backgrounds, or personal likes or dislikes. We are to test the work of the Spirit by the principles in the Word of God. These principles are an extension of God's character and convictions and are our prevailing value system for living. Principles are the laws, guidelines, or guiding forces that we use in life.

I do not want to suggest that we are not to experience all things taught in Scripture, only that what we experience be taught in Scripture. The Scripture must be the governing power by which we interpret what we are seeking to experience and are experiencing.

Loving the Word of God

Psalm 19:7-10 sums up what Psalm 119 takes 176 verses to articulate. These four verses articulate our respect and love for the Word of God:

"The law of the Lord is perfect, converting the soul; the testimony of the Lord is sure, making wise the simple; the statutes of the Lord are right, rejoicing the heart; the commandment of the Lord is pure, enlightening the eyes; the fear of the Lord is clean, enduring forever; the judgments of the Lord are true and righteous altogether. More to be desired are they than gold, yea, than much fine gold; sweeter also than honey and the honeycomb" (Psalm 19:7-10).

There are six descriptions of the Word of God in this passage, with six corresponding results of that His Word working in us:

DESCRIPTIONS OF THE WORD	RESULTS OF THE WORD WORKING
1. God's law is perfect— The Word of God is comprehensive. Nothing has been added and nothing has been taken from it. It covers completely all aspects of life.	**1. Converting the soul—** The Word transforms and permeates our souls. The word Soul is used twenty-two times to refer to our inner person.
2. Testimony is sure— God's Word is reliable and trustworthy. It is a foundation upon which we can, without hesitation, build in a world of uncertainty.	**2. Making wise the simple—** Simple speaks of a person with an open mind or an open door to the mind. It is a mind that is so open that we never know when to close it. To say "I'm open-minded" sometimes is a negative. But the Word of God makes wise the simple. It puts a screen on the door of our minds and locks it when that is needed.
3. Statutes are right— The principles of God's Word never change and they always work. They are right because they are the maps that lay out a straight course for any person who would be guided by them.	**3. Rejoicing the heart—** There is a joy of discovery in the Word of God. Joy comes from walking in obedience to the Word of God.
4. Commandments are pure— God's Word is clear. It is a product that has been purified and, thus, is unadulterated. There are no unwholesome elements in it. It is totally pure and right.	**4. Enlightening the eyes—** In the midst of life's contradictions, when there is no way to understand the darkness and confusion of life, the Word of God gives us hope and enlightens our eyes. When situations are hopeless, when innocent people are killed, when the newborn dies in the crib, when the righteous saint dies prematurely of cancer, it is the Word of God that gives us understanding.
5. Fear is clean— The Word of the Lord motivates us to have respect for and to fear the Lord and to hold His Word highly. The fear of the Lord is clean; it is morally right. It has been purified like metals that have gone through the fire.	**5. Enduring forever—** All things will pass away, but the Word of God endures forever. Experiences are for a season, ideas are for awhile, everything in life is temporal, but the Word of God lasts for eternity.
6. Judgments are true— God's Word pronounces a verdict on many different issues and so speaks with final authority. Judgment speaks of the verdicts of God. They are true in their utter dependability.	**6. Righteous altogether—** God's Word produces comprehensive character. It produces integrity and righteousness that will permeate every area of our lives.

To test is to use your head and think clearly. Examine closely the basic theologies and doctrines that undergird spiritual claims and spiritual teachings. Does the spirit contradict the Word of God? No revelation of the proclaimed should ever be held higher than the written Word of God (see John 15:2-8; Philippians 1:11; Hebrews 12:11).

INSPECTING THE "FRUIT" OF REVIVAL

When people are touched by the living Spirit of God, their lives can be impacted but not necessarily changed. In order for us to test revival, we must see fruit in people's lives. But what should be the fruit of people touched by revival?

> **"We must make sure that all experiences and manifestations during revival produces long-lasting fruit."**

The word fruit, as it is used in the New Testament, speaks of the works or deeds of the individual, of the visible expression of the power of the Holy Spirit working inwardly and invisibly in that person. The quality of the fruit is evidence of the character of the power producing it.

"You will know them by their fruits. Do men gather grapes from thorn bushes or figs from thistles?" (Matthew 7:16).

"You did not choose Me, but I chose you and appointed you that you should go and bear fruit, and that your fruit should remain, that whatever you ask the Father in My name He may give you" (John 15:16).

Testing fruit in the revival context means to test new things by how they affect the character and behavior of people. Spiritual phenomena from God have certain distinguishable characteristics that are called the fruit of the Spirit. We must test all spiritual experiences and manifestations by how they affect people. We must make sure that all experiences and manifestations during revival produces long-lasting fruit.

The Fruit of Holiness

Revival should always produce a sense of holiness because the Holy Spirit visits our inner worlds and changes our character and behavior.

The word holiness means set apart, separate, a cut above, morally blameless, separated to God with conduct befitting one who is separated. Holiness is living a life in conformity to the moral precepts of the Bible and in contrast to the sinful ways of the world. Holiness consists of that internal change or renovation of our souls, whereby our minds, affections, and wills are brought into harmony with those of God (see Romans 6:19; Psalm 139:1-4; 1 Samuel 16:7; Proverbs 23:7; Philippians 4:8; 1 Corinthians 6:12).

If a person is walking in the flesh, he will have the evidence of that walk. The fruit or the works of the flesh are listed for us and we can examine a person's life according to the evidence.

"Now the works of the flesh are evident, which are: adultery, fornication, uncleanness, lewdness, idolatry, sorcery, hatred, contentions, jealousies, outbursts of wrath, selfish ambitions, dissensions, heresies, envy, murders, drunken-ness, revelries, and the like; of which I tell you beforehand, just as I also told you in time past, that those who practice such things will not inherit the kingdom of God" (Galatians 5:19-21).

But the next two verses in the fifth chapter of Galatians list the fruits of the spirit: "But the fruit of the Spirit is love, joy, peace, longsuffering, kindness, goodness, faithfulness, gentleness, self-control. Against such there is no law" (Galatians 5:22-23).

Holiness means that we realize that there are certain habits that are permissible, but that we should not be mas-tered by anything. It means that we realize that certain things are allowable but not beneficial for others we influ-ence. We must ask ourselves if what we do causes another person to be weakened. This is the question of those who are experiencing a true revival spirit, who desire to live in holiness. Certain life activities are acceptable, but do they bring glory to God?

The Fruit of Perseverance

The Bible speaks of another kind of fruit in 1 Peter 1:5-7: "who are kept by the power of God through faith for salvation ready to be revealed in the last time. In this you greatly rejoice, though now for a little while, if need be, you have been grieved by various trials, that the genuineness of your faith, being much more precious than gold that perishes, though it is tested by fire, may be found to praise, honor, and glory at the revelation of Jesus Christ."

This fruit is that of perseverance. This passage describes a testing of our faith through the trials that grieve us. These are trials that God allows to prove the authenticity of our faith.

DISCERNING A SHIFT IN FOCUS AND PERSPECTIVE

A third principle in testing the authenticity of revival is observing a shift in focus and perspective of those who take part in revival activity.

A shift comes when we begin to focus on ourselves, our experiences, our rhemas, or on externals more than the objective Word of God and what it says to us. Especially during revival, we must discern if there has been a shift in focus and perspective concerning Christ and His Word.

> "A shift comes when we begin to focus on ourselves, our experiences, our rhemas, or on externals more than the objective Word of God and what it says to us."

The shift comes when we interpret intensity as a sign of supernatural spirit or revival. Intensity is not an infallible sign of revival. We can be intense about a lot of things in life, things such as recreation, relationships, and work. Atmosphere can become intense at an opera or an athletic event of any kind. We can become intense when disciplining a child or when speaking to someone about a belief that we have.

The Bible demonstrates a shift in focus in Matthew 17:17, the account of Peter, James, and John accompanying Jesus on the Mount of Transfiguration. Peter had an intense supernatural experience, and his response was, "let us stay here!"

Peter's shift in focus went from extending the kingdom of God, healing the sick, delivering the demon-possessed, helping the poor, and preaching the gospel to "let us stay here! Do we have to go back down? Do we have to face the widows again? Do we have to extend the kingdom of God any more? Why can we not just stay here? This is a very intense experience!"

Another intense spiritual experience in the Bible that had a different result. In Acts 2:1-4 we have the Upper Room experience at Pentecost and the responses of those who had undergone an awesome filling of God's Spirit. What was their response? "Let us go! Let us preach! Let us build! Let us give ourselves to the extending of the kingdom of God!"

Spiritual experiences result in kingdom fruitfulness when they are absorbed and then channeled as a force to launch the person or church away from passivity and into dynamic spiritual activity. This is a principle we can use to discern the authenticity of our response to the true work of the Holy Spirit. If the working of the Holy Spirit gives us a desire only for more experiences, then we must doubt the track we are on.

The Holy Spirit does not come that we might just stay on the Mount of Transfiguration or in the Upper Room. The Holy Spirit rests upon us that we might become salt and light, kingdom builders who extend the message of the gospel of Jesus Christ. A Holy Spirit visitation focuses us on the fact that there are many nations yet to hear the gospel, there are more than 16,000 people groups not evangelized and groups of people who do not have a Bible in their language, the poor are here to be fed and that their are cities here to be ministered to.

THE FOCUS OF JESUS

When Jesus received a supernatural revelation in God's presence, what was the result? What did it do for His focus? Did He have a shift in focus? No! The Lord Jesus Christ in Matthew 17 simply said, "Let us go down from this mountain." He knew that waiting at the foot of the mountain were people in need. He knew that He could begin to minister immediately through the power of the Spirit that came upon Him when He was on top of the mountain.

We cannot become so absorbed with our experiences that we become spiritually passive and miss the whole purpose of the moving of the Holy Spirit. When we have biblical focus, we are not just concerned with what we can experience. A biblical focus is a Jesus focus. He was and is the perfect model for all believers.

> "We cannot become so absorbed with our experiences that we become spiritually passive and miss the whole purpose of the moving of the Holy Spirit."

If we have a Jesus focus, we will respond the same way Jesus did: "Let us go down from this mountain. Let us leave this room. Let us go back into the city." Like the apostle Paul and all the great leaders in the church world, spiritual experiences should not cause people to become passive, but to become dynamic and aggressive.

Today we are experiencing and want to experience more of the outpouring of the Holy Spirit. We will have many kinds of experiences that will flood our lives and minds as Jesus fills us more and more with His awesome anointing. But as He fills us, let us keep our direction clear. Let us keep our focus right. Let us identify with the biblical mandate that is already upon us.

The power of the Holy Spirit has come upon us so that we might become witnesses both in Jerusalem and Judea and all the uttermost parts of the earth (Acts 1:8). Our responsibility is to go up the mountain and receive from God's empowering presence, and then strategically come down to minister.

"Now as they came down from the mountain . . ." (Matthew 17:9).

"And when they had come to the multitude . . ." (Matthew 17:14).

NOTES

1. John Wesley's Journal, July 7, 1739: "He (Whitefield) had an opportunity of informing himself better, no sooner had he began to invite all sinners to believe in Christ than four persons sunk down close to him almost at the same moment. One of them lay without sense or motion. A second trembling exceedingly. The third had strong convulsions all over his body but made no noise unless by groans. The fourth equally convulsed, called upon God with strong cries and tears. From this time I trust we shall allow God to carry on His own work in the way that pleases Him."

2. Richard Lovelace, *Dynamics of Spiritual Life*.

3. Dr. Martyn Lloyd Jones, *Revival*, (Wheaton: Crossway Books), Chapter 4.

PART 3

INGREDIENTS FOR EXPERIENCING REVIVAL

Chapter 9

THE BENEFITS OF BROKENNESS

*A*nything that is broken is deemed by man to be unfit, and he ends up throwing it away. But to God, only that which is broken is useful. Just as flowers yield their perfume when they are crushed and grapes produce wine when they are squashed, so the vessels of God—His people—are ready for revival only when they are broken. God's vessels, the ones He uses, are broken vessels.

Revival is that spirit that reveals to us our sinfulness, the areas in our lives that need to be broken so that God can do something great with us. God's Word tells us that He draws near to us when we are broken, when we recognize where we are without His favor.

The word break in the Hebrew means to shatter, smash or crush, and describes the breaking of an earthen vessel. It also describes the breaking of a human heart.

"The Lord is near to those who have a broken heart, and saves such as have a contrite spirit" (Psalm 34:18).

"The sacrifices of God are a broken spirit, a broken and a contrite heart—these, O God, You will not despise" (Psalm 51:17).

Judges 7:19 tells us that the vessels used by Gideon were broken pitchers before the light could be seen and the trumpet could be heard. In Jeremiah 18:1-3, we have the potter's house where the marred vessel comes and is broken and made again into another vessel. In 2 Corinthians 4:7, it simply states, "We have this treasure in earthen vessels."

Matthew 21:44 simply states that whoever falls on the stone shall be broken. We see also in the twenty-sixth chapter of Matthew, the alabaster box that was taken and broken, and then the perfume filled the room. In 1 Corinthians 11:24, it says, "This is My body which is broken for you," speaking of the communion that we would partake of as a symbolic act of recognizing the redemptive work of Christ.

> "Revival spirit always deals with our hearts and usually comes to break us of our pride and carnality."

Revival spirit always deals with our hearts and usually comes to break us of our pride and carnality. When God wants to do an impossible job, He takes an impossible person and crushes him or her. In the times of Holy Spirit outpouring, not only do we feel the love of God, but we also feel the hammer of God. For God does not come to fill us up with His mercy and compassion without changing the vessel He's filling. Usually there is thirsting and a brokenness that is administered to the vessel of God before there is an infilling.

Psalm 31:12 says, "I am forgotten like a dead man, out of mind; I am like a broken vessel." This verse is true to the atmosphere of God-sent revival, the atmosphere of people being broken, tenderized, and exposed to the dealings of God so that they can change.

TRUE CONFESSION

Many people live lives of quiet habit and sin that annihilate their spiritual walk and power. Revival comes to reveal this carnality and break these people from these sins so that they might become broken vessels.

"Reproach has broken my heart, and I am full of heaviness; I looked for someone to take pity, but there was none; and for comforters, but I found none" (Psalm 69:20).

"I am feeble and severely broken; I groan because of the turmoil of my heart" (Psalm 38:8).

The first confession of a broken person is the admission of total inability to succeed without God's favor.

In Psalm 51, we have the prayer of a leader who has a broken and contrite heart after being dealt with by God. This Psalm breathes from the spirit touched with the finest sensibilities and spiritual feelings of brokenness.

David intentionally sinned against God, even after God had given him an anointing on his life. He had seen the mountain top in both the natural sense and the spiritual sense. He had claimed many natural and spiritual battles. He had delivered both his own soul and the souls of the people he led. And yet David fell into deep sin. He sinned when he relaxed his spiritual passions, when he thought he was stronger than he really was.

In Psalm 51:1, David prayed: "Have mercy upon me, O God, according to Your lovingkindness; according to the multitude of Your tender mercies."

David's prayer is for mercy, not for more anointing, for more victories, for more prosperity, and not for more promotion. He is broken, and now he needs mercy, lovingkindness, and the tenderness of God's hand. He knows that without that touch, he will be finished.

Through all of this, God used David's sin to break him...and to revive him. In failure, David experiences brokenness that is actually the beginning of greatness.

David did not try to blame-shift his problems (see 1 Samuel 15:24, 30; 2 Samuel 12:13). His confession was a confession of his own total responsibility for his failure, without which he knew there would be no true forgiveness or restoration.

We are all prone to shifting the responsibility of our sins from ourselves to other people and things. We blame the circumstances in which we are placed or we blame the temptation itself. We even blame our own lack of knowledge. But David had the right estimation of his sin. He knew that his sin was not just misdirection or the result of imperfect development. He knew that it was a violation of God's holy law. He grieves, he hates, he has deep sorrow, and he begs God for the mercy that he needs.

> "Sin and guilt for sin are not transferable. If I do evil, the guilt is my own."

David felt utterly polluted and defiled by his sin. He recognized the power of sin to destroy. He knew that sin opposes true moral relations and order. David did not see himself as the developed good person. He saw himself as conceived in sin from the first moments up to now. He saw sin as sin, and nothing but sin.

True revival always brings a true evaluation of sin and true repentance of sin. True revival does not motivate God's people to shift blame, but to confess honestly and ask God, through His mercy, to remove that which has caused the transgression.

Sin and guilt for sin are not transferable. If I do evil, the guilt is my own. This is the cry of a broken person. It is the result of a revival spirit. The cry for a deep radical, super-natural, inward change of heart.

THE NECESSITY OF THOROUGH CLEANSING

After David sinned, he cried out for the thoroughness of God's work. He did not pray for a change of state, but a change of nature. He prays: "Blot out my transgressions..." "Wash me thoroughly from my iniquity..." "Cleanse me from my sin . . ." "I acknowledge my transgressions..." "My sin is always before me..." "Against You, You only, I have sinned."

David is asking God for something that can be likened to an account of debt being wiped away or canceled by the creditor. Not only is the debt forgiven, but all the disposition to contract further debt must be eradicated. David prays for his sins to be blotted out. He prays for a purging. This is the term for what God alone can do. It is like the cleansing of the leper, like scrubbing and dealing deeply with the blemished area. It can refer to a sustained process as well as an instantaneous act. David prays for the washing and the new creation to take place by the sovereignty of God—nothing less than a miracle. David says wash me, clean me, and create in me a clean heart.

> "A clean heart carefully and habitually guards against everything that pollutes the mind."

Renewal is a moving of the Holy Spirit upon people who know the brokenness of sin, who wish to be deeply changed, who wish to have a clean heart and a fixed, habitual abhorrence of all forbidden indulgences of the flesh. All past impurities, either of heart or life, will be reflected on with shame and sorrow. A clean heart does not entertain with pleasure or delight impure thoughts and impure desires.

A clean heart carefully and habitually guards against everything that pollutes the mind. A person with a revival spirit will avoid sensuality, which has a special ability to extinguish the power of Holy Spirit thinking.

MARKS OF TRUE BROKENNESS

David cried out to God, "Do not take Your Holy Spirit from me . . . Do not cast me away from Your presence." The prayer here is begging God not to withdraw His sensible, gracious influences upon the hungry soul. This is a prayer that God will not withdraw His spiritual power, His spiritual voice, His spiritual peace. Revival spirit will motivate that kind of praying.

The identifiable marks of brokenness that revival spirit will bring can be seen in at least some of the following:

1. A broken spirit brings a quickening of conscience violation.

2. A broken spirit is a sensitive spirit. It discerns what is amiss, like your body discerns a broken bone.

3. A broken spirit is pliable, teachable and never reactionary. It is never close-minded or stubborn.

4. A broken heart is soft and easily penetrated, while a hard heart cannot be penetrated at all. You cannot

work on it.

5. A broken spirit signifies that a person is in submission to God, is obedient, easily bent to humility, and not reactionary.

6. A broken spirit has no pride. All ideas of its own importance are gone.

7. A broken spirit has no hypocrisy. It honestly reveals itself to God.

8. A broken spirit has deep sincerity.

9. A prayer from a broken heart is a real prayer, deeply felt. It is a hymn sung with deep and real feelings.

10. A broken spirit is not made by strong forceful instruction. It is not originated in any human or finite power. It is accomplished through God's dealings. We can be like a worm or a snake. A worm has no defense and does not react, but a snake, when stepped upon, strikes back and defends itself.

THE TRUE GLORY OF BROKENNESS

When God breaks us, He does so to bring us to Himself and to bring glory to Himself. The following anonymous essay gives us a beautiful, compact picture of God's desire for our brokenness:

"God uses most for His glory those people and things which are most perfectly broken. The sacrifices He accepts are broken and contrite hearts. It was the breaking down of Jacob's natural strength at Penial that got him where God could clothe him with spiritual power. It was breaking the surface of the rock at Horeb, by the stroke of Moses' rod, that let out the cool waters to thirsty people.

It was when the 300 elect soldiers under Gideon broke their pitchers, a type of breaking themselves, that the hidden lights shone forth to the consternation of their adversaries. It was when the poor widow broke the seal of the little pot of oil, and poured it forth, that God multiplied it to pay her debts and supply means of support.

It is when a beautiful grain of corn is broken up in the earth by death, that its inner heart sprouts forth and bears hundreds of other grains. And thus, on and on, through history, and all biography, and all vegetation, and all spiritual life, God must have broken things.

> "Revival is not all emotion and high feelings of exaltation. Revival will bring people down low, down to the ground, down to themselves."

Those who are broken in wealth, and broken in self-will, and broken in their ambitions, and broken in their beautiful ideals, and broken in worldly reputation, and broken in their affections, and broken in times of health; those who are despised and seem utterly forlorn and helpless, the Holy Ghost is seizing upon and using for God's glory. 'The lame take the prey,' Isaiah tells us."

THE PURPOSE OF BROKENNESS IN REVIVAL

Revival is not all emotion and high feelings of exaltation. Revival will bring people down low, down to the ground, down to themselves. Revival will bring a brokenness of heart and spirit before it brings a cry of victory and exaltation.

Let us not miss the true purpose of God's pouring out His Spirit upon His redemptive community. It is not first to receive from us the emotional acts of worship and high exaltation and praise, nor is it to move us into spiritual gifts or more boldness in our witnessing. God pours revival spirit out upon His people, first to bring us to a deep sense of our own sin, our own impurities. Then He can bring into us a spirit of humility and brokenness.

God knows that from a broken vessel there can be much light. God can renew a broken vessel, and He can fill it with whatever He would like. Then, all glory will go to Him.

The germs of the worst sin are in us all. Something in us is near to hell, and something in us near to God. In our deepest degeneration remains something good, something sacred and undefiled. It is our new nature. Revival should be a continuous flow of God's Spirit through broken vessels to the world.

Chapter 10

A PASSION FOR GOD'S PRESENCE

*A*s revival sweeps across the land and begins to arouse the hearts of people, God's first call is to bring His people into His presence. This is a call to live our whole lives, both as individuals and as a congregation, in the awesome presence of a living God. Times of refreshing from the presence of the Lord is a promise.

"Repent therefore and be converted, that your sins may be blotted out, so that **times of refreshing** may come from the presence of the Lord" (Acts 3:19).

The presence of God is to be the great passion of every believer's heart. We are called to love the presence of the Lord and to desire to live in His presence every minute of the day. In 1 Peter 2:9, we are referred to as a "royal priesthood," and as such, we are called to enter into and live in His presence.

During times when spiritual fires burn most brightly, the presence of Christ is the dominant feature in the church. When the church is functioning at its best, when it is on fire for the Lord, the presence of Christ is the focus of the corporate life. When the awesome presence of Christ evaporates from the local church congregation, or any Christian gathering, it soon becomes a mechanical, organizational group that is not accomplishing Christ's mandates.

A.W. Tozer stated: "It was God's will that we should push on into His presence and live our whole life there. Not just a doctrine to be held, but a real life experience every moment of the day."[1]

MOVING INTO TIMES OF REFRESHING

Joel Hawes, the minister of the First Congregational Church in Hartford, Conn., gives a description of revival that took place in that city in 1820:

"The whole theory of revivals is involved in these two facts. That the influence of the Holy Spirit is concerned in every instance of sound conversion, and that this influence is granted in more copious measure and in great power at some times than at others. When these factors concur, there is revival of religion."[2]

"Times of refreshing" is almost synonymous with "seasons of revival." That thought surely opens up for us a mental vista of the possibilities of blessing through seeking God's presence, possibilities often hidden by the thick clouds of our own great ignorance.

To be in the presence of the Lord is to be revived. When a community of believers is brought low before the presence of the Lord, when the very air that they breathe appears to be super-charged with the sense of His presence, then there is the beginning of revival. In fact, it is revival.

J. Edwin Orr, in his book, *Times of Refreshing: 10,000 Miles of Miracles*, wrote: "I have witnessed many revivals of God's people, both individuals and companies. The Holy Spirit working always brought a fullness of joy: cups ran over, worries disappeared. When love and joy and peace came in at the door, misery went up the chimney, and search parties failed to locate it afterwards. Delight thyself in the Lord and He shall give thee the desires of thine heart."[3]

During spiritual awakening, there is first an overwhelming awareness of the presence of God among His people. "What have been the outstanding features of this movement?" asked Dr. Cammon, who was a key leader of the Lewis Revival, in the years 1949 and 1953. He states, "First an awareness of God." Then he went on to say, "I have no hesitation in saying that this awareness of God is the prime need of the church today."

In the early 1700s, the Moravian Revival swept across England. One particular meeting, which was called the Love Feast at Fetter Lane, was a memorable one during this time of revival. Besides about sixty Moravians, there were present no fewer than seven of the Oxford Methodists, namely John and Charles Wesley, George Whitefield, Wesley Hall, Benjamin Inghan, Charles Kinchin, and Richard Hutchins, all of them ordained clergymen of the Church of England. John Wesley wrote in his journal:

> "**During spiritual awakening, there is first an overwhelming awareness of the presence of God among His people.**"

"About three in the morning, as we were continuing instant in prayer, the power of God came mightily upon us in so much that many cried for exceeding joy and many fell to the ground. As soon as we were recovered a little from that awe and amazement at the presence of His majesty, we broke out with one voice, 'We praise Thee, Oh God, we acknowledge Thee to be the Lord.' "

When the times of refreshing are released from the heavenlies, it is the sign of a season of revival. These times of refreshing are always connected to the presence of the Lord because that is the power that is able to renew minds, enliven discouraged souls, and release the river of God to bring refreshing.

Augustine wrote: "Thou hast formed us for Thyself and our hearts are restless until they find rest in Thee." There is a restlessness in the church until it finds a place where it connects with the presence of God and enters into His rest.

UNDERSTANDING THE PRESENCE OF GOD

In understanding the presence of God we must understand God Himself. Doctrinally, when we speak of defining God we must define His character and His attributes. God is unlimited and unbounded, while we human beings are finite and confined in space. God transcends everything in His creation. The biblical picture of God's infinity is frequently that of His exaltation. "In the year that King Uzziah died, I saw the Lord sitting on a throne, high and lifted up, and the train of His robe filled the temple" (Isaiah 6:1).

> "There is a restlessness in the church until it finds a place where it connects with the presence of God and enters into His rest."

God's throne is beyond the highest heavens. In 1 Kings 8:27, it says, "But will God indeed dwell on the earth? Behold, heaven and the heaven of heavens cannot contain You. How much less this temple which I have built!" God not only fills the heavens, but He also fills the earth and people's heart with His presence.

DEFINING THE LEVELS OF GOD'S PRESENCE

There are different levels of the presence of God that we must understand in defining revival and experiencing His awesome presence.

First of all, the word presence as used in the Old Testament is translated from the Hebrew word *paniym*, and is used seventy-six times. It is derived from the root word *pana*, which means to turn the face. When we speak of the presence of God, it literally means in Scripture to fill up, to pervade, to permeate, to overspread, to be under the eyes of, or in the face of. The idea of God's presence has to do with God's face being turned toward someone in acceptance and favor. This word means to be sufficient, to be able to sustain or support. When God is present, He is sufficient to sustain and support what He energizes.

The three understandable aspects of the presence of God are the omnipresence of God, the manifest presence of God, and what could be called the felt, released, personalized presence of God.

The Omnipresence of God

The omnipresence of God simply means that God is everywhere all the time and His presence fills all. This points to the presence of God in every place and to every person. God is present in the whole created universe. In Isaiah 66:1, God declared, "Heaven is My throne and the earth is My footstool."

In Jeremiah 23:24 it says: " 'Can anyone hide himself in secret places, so I shall not see him?' says the Lord; 'Do I not fill heaven and earth?' says the Lord." This declaration emphasizes the presence of God in the whole universe. God fills Heaven and earth. God is here, and all of creation is alive with His presence.

"Such knowledge is too wonderful for me; it is high, I cannot attain it. Where can I go from Your Spirit? Or where can I flee from Your presence? If I ascend into heaven, You are there; if I make my bed in hell, behold, You are there" (Psalm 139:6-8).

"Then Jacob awoke from his sleep and said, 'Surely the Lord is in this place, and I did not know it' " (Genesis 28:16).

God is all-present, unlimited by space or time. God is present even beyond space and fills all things. Finite space depends upon Him for its existence. Yet people, and even the church, may at times not experience or acknowledge that God is present. But this does not subtract from or change God's presence. Whether we acknowledge it or not, God is everywhere and fills everything. He is as much present to a single atom as to the most distant star. There is no place where God is not.

The presence and manifestation of the presence is not the same. If we cooperate with Him in loving obedience, God will manifest Himself to us and that will ruin us for anything else.

The Manifest Presence of God

There is the second aspect of God's presence, which could be called the manifest presence of God. This is when God reveals Himself, usually by sovereign means and ways. This is the presence of God that can be felt, even when we are not seeking God or practicing the spiritual disciplines—prayer, repentance, and other truths that Scripture defines as an approach to the living God—that allow us to experience the presence of God. There are times when God chooses to manifest Himself apart from our initiation, simply because He is God and He is sovereign.

"So that they should seek the Lord, in the hope that they might grope for Him and find Him, though He is not far from each one of us; for in Him we live and move and have our being, as also some of your own poets have said, 'For we are also His offspring' " (Acts 17:27-28).

God does not have His being in us, but our lives and activities—our very existence—are in Him. At every moment, in every situation, we are involved with God. A person may have turned from God, gone spiritually far away from God and, therefore, God is far from that person. But this does not change the fact that God is always immediately at hand.

> "Whether we acknowledge it or not, God is everywhere and fills everything. He is as much present to a single atom as to the most distant star."

"And they heard the sound of the Lord God walking in the garden in the cool of the day, and Adam and his wife hid themselves from the presence of the Lord God among the trees of the garden" (Genesis 3:8). This is a manifest presence of God that can be felt. It is a presence that can penetrate the human being. "Then Cain went out from the presence of the Lord and dwelt in the land of Nod on the east of Eden" (Genesis 4:16). In the same way that Adam and Eve felt the presence of God in the garden, Scripture says that Cain left the presence of the Lord. The omnipresence of God is everywhere, all the time, so Cain could not evade the presence of God. But he left the manifest presence of God, that presence that surrounded the garden and could be felt.

Leviticus 22:3 states: "Say to them: "Whoever of all your descendants throughout your generations, who goes near the holy things which the children of Israel dedicate to the Lord, while he has uncleanness upon him, that person shall be cut off from My presence: I am the Lord.' " This verse simply states that a person may be cut off, not from the omnipresence of God, but from the manifest presence of God.

At times, a strange sense of God can pervade a building, a community, or a district. Many people have written articles or testified to feeling this awesome, sovereign presence of God at different times, in different places.

In 1858, during the American revivals, as ships drew near the American ports, they seemed to come under the influence of God's Spirit. Ship after ship arrived in America with the same accounts of sudden conviction and conversion. This was the sovereign presence of God being manifested in a situation or a circumstance where God Himself has initiated His presence upon people.

The Personalized Presence of God

The third aspect of the presence of God is what we will call the felt, revealed, personalized presence of God. This is the presence of God that is available to God's people as they follow a biblical pattern of prayer, worship, and seeking of God.

There is a slight difference between the manifest presence of God and the felt, revealed, personalized presence. The manifest presence of God can come about by a sovereign act of God without any human initiation. God Himself can instill His presence into, say, an industrial area where people work or to someone walking down a street. This is a miracle, a sovereign act of a holy God. But the Scripture also speaks of how we can seek God to be in His presence, how we can fast, pray, worship, and exert ourselves in spiritual disciplines that allow us to live our lives in the very presence of the living God. This is the presence that we can touch that abides with us not only in our individual lives, but also in our corporate lives.

Psalm 22:3 says, "But You are holy, enthroned in the praises of Israel." There is a connection between the audible praises of God's people and the presence of God being revealed. As that presence is released in a worship service or a prayer time, we experience a different level than just the omnipresence or the manifested sovereign presence of God.

"Do not cast me away from Your presence, and do not take Your Holy Spirit from me" (Psalm 51:11).

"You will show me the path of life; in Your presence is fullness of joy; at Your right hand are pleasures forevermore" (Psalm 16:11).

"**There is a connection between the audible praises of God's people and the presence of God being revealed.**"

"You shall hide them in the secret place of Your presence from the plots of man; you shall keep them secretly in a pavilion from the strife of tongues" (Psalm 31:20).

"Let us come before His presence with thanksgiving; let us shout joyfully to Him with psalms" (Psalm 95:2).

As we seek this third level of God's presence, we have the responsibility to actively seek, pray, believe, and enter into the presence of God with sacrifices of praise and worship, prayer and fasting, and to believe that His presence will be there.

"And it came to pass when the priests came out of the Most Holy Place (for all the priests who were present had sanctified themselves, without keeping to their divisions), and the Levites who were the singers, all those of Asaph and Heman and Jeduthun, with their sons and their brethren, stood at the east end of the altar, clothed in white linen, having cymbals, stringed instruments and harps, and with them one hundred and twenty priests sounding with trumpets—indeed it came to pass, when the trumpeters and singers were as one, to make one sound to be heard in praising and thanking the Lord, and when they lifted up their voice with the trumpets and cymbals and instruments of music, and praised the Lord, saying: 'For He is good, for His mercy endures forever,' that the house, the house of the Lord, was filled with a cloud" (2 Chronicles 5:11-13).

In this passage, we see once again that God's presence is available to His people. The worship and praise of the priests compelled God to manifest His presence in a felt, revealed, personalized way. The priests themselves were so convicted by the presence of God that they could not stand and continue their work and ministry on that given occasion.

A PASSION FOR GOD'S PRESENCE

Revival is a time when the presence of God moves from the omnipresence to the manifest presence to the felt, revealed, personalized presence of God.

There are times when God chooses to release His presence in such a sovereign way, that people are in awe. They may come to revival meetings out of curiosity or because they want to feel the manifested presence of God or see His manifested miracles. But the key to the longevity of revival is that we walk in the presence of God, that we walk in the Spirit. It is one thing to be slain in the Spirit, but it is another thing to walk in the Spirit. It is one thing to have a curiosity for the presence of God, but another to have a hunger and a discipline to walk in the presence of God. As revival spirit is released in our time, our desire should be to walk in God's presence and to enjoy the manifested, felt, released presence of God.

Indeed, we need to understand that the presence of God is uniquely present through the Spirit's indwelling of the people of faith. In John 14:17, Jesus said this about the Holy Spirit: "The Spirit of truth, whom the world cannot receive, because it neither sees Him nor knows Him; but you know Him, for He dwells with you and will be in you."

> **"It is one thing to be slain in the Spirit, but it is another thing to walk in the Spirit."**

Paul later attested to the Gentiles in Ephesians 2, verses 12 and 22, "that at that time you were without Christ, being aliens from the commonwealth of Israel and strangers from the covenants of promise, having no hope and without God in the world . . . In whom you also are being built together for a dwelling place of God in the Spirit."

The indwelling of the Spirit of God is a wondrous fact known in Christian experience. Omnipresence thereby becomes vivid presence. No hope without God, in the sense of being blind to God's presence, changes to fullness of hope and the experience of God's compelling reality. The omnipresence of God is a fact. God is everywhere, and is present in every person. But the personal knowledge of that fact and the experience of that presence is what finally really counts.

NOTES:

1. A.W. Tozer, *The Knowledge of the Holy* (San Francisco: Harper and Row Publishers, 1961), n.a.

2. Joel Hawes and Edward A. Lawrence, *The Life of Joel Hawes* (Hartford, Conn.), 113.

3. J. Edwin Orr, *Times of Refreshing: 10,000 Miles of Miracles*, n.a.

Chapter 11

THE POWER OF REVIVAL – THE TRANSFORMATION OF LIVES

*T*here was a time in human history when craftsmanship was highly esteemed. This was a time when items were hand-crafted originals in which the craftsman had invested his time, energy, creativity, and even something of his own personality.

But in the early 1900s, assembly line production came into existence. As a result, products that had previously taken days, weeks, or months to produce could be mass produced in hours. Unfortunately, while the quantity increased, the quality often decreased.

I believe it is that way in our churches today. We mass produce believers, and while we may claim hundreds or thousands in church attendance, often the quality of the end product is diminished. While seeing hundreds or thousands of people saved and into the fellowship is certainly a worthwhile goal, we must make sure that what we produce is a biblical product.

But the questions that arise are: What should the end product resemble? What process should we use to produce the end product? Has God given us a biblical pattern to follow? What part does revival play in this process? How do we balance emotions, experiences, and personal revelations of what God is saying to a person about change with what Scriptures say about change?

The need for revival in the church is usually because there is potential for a spirit of lukewarmness. That happens when Christians stagnate in their growth and in their love toward God. This is the time when God needs to move in, by His Holy Spirit, to bring new life.

THE NEED FOR CHANGE

A.W. Tozer once asserted, "It is change, not time, that turns fools into wise men and sinners into saints."

God does not want us as believers to live in eternal childhood. God desires to change us, to bring us to maturity in our faith in Him. It is the need for change, the need for bringing maturity in Christ, that is our focus. Our goal should be to bring every believer into full maturity according to biblical process and biblical standards.

> **"Revival atmosphere is a time of highly intensified emotions and affections as people are touched by the moving of the Holy Spirit."**

In Colossians 1:28, Paul states this goal and vision: "Him we preach, warning every man and teaching every man in all wisdom, that we may present every man perfect in Christ Jesus."

EXPERIENCE VERSUS MATURITY

Revival atmosphere is a time of highly intensified emotions and affections as people are touched by the moving of the Holy Spirit. During these times when people feel changed, transformed, and delivered and feel they have received something from God, they can make great confessions, but this can quickly turn into disillusionment if the confession does not turn into reality.

We need to thoroughly discuss the scriptural mandate for believers to become mature disciples in Christ. The question to be asked is, can a revival atmosphere produce a disciple? Can an experience at the altar with flowing tears and high emotions produce a mature saint? Obviously, the surface answer to these questions would be "no." People need more than a trip to the altar or an experience in a revival meeting to be transformed deeply in their habits and lifestyles and to become mature believers in Christ.

On the other hand, there are times when people encounter God in such a way that their lives are changed immediately, on the spot, never to return to the old way. They then begin to add to their experience the disciplines of reading the Scripture, prayer, and the breaking of habits, so that they can become all that God had called them to become.

Most of the time, though, people who embrace a revival experience need also to grasp a biblical process for becoming a disciple. True maturity is never automatic. Change can be automatic. The breaking of a habit can be automatic. But maturity in Christ requires more than leaving something behind and breaking an old pattern. Maturity in Christ involves becoming like Christ in character, in spirit, and in attitude. This is a process.

THE ULTIMATE GOAL: CHRISTLIKENESS

Most of us would agree that at the center of our resolve is what we call Christlikeness. Because God has planted His own life in our personalities, it is our destiny to be like Him. We are predestined to be confirmed to the likeness of His Son.

Obviously, the maturity level is not the same in every believer, and neither is the maturity process. But the standard of what we are to become is the same for every believer because the Word of God becomes the measuring rod.

Maturation is a developmental word. It refers to becoming fully developed, fully grown, and brought to fruition.

Each of us has our own personal criteria for what constitutes a spiritually mature person. But we do not define maturity culturally or individually. We define maturity according to the context of Scripture. We realize that the transformation into the likeness of Christ is the work of the Holy Spirit. Revival is an intensified moving of the Holy Spirit upon believers that should result in the start of an intensified process whereby believers become more mature in Christ.

> **"...we do not define maturity culturally or individually. We define maturity according to the context of Scripture."**

MATURITY REQUIRES A RECOGNITION OF NEED

Revival atmosphere brings us to our knees, to a place of humility as we recognize how much we need God. The prayer of people touched in revival is usually, "Give me more, Lord. I want more of You, more of the Spirit, more of the Word. I want to be more submissive. I want to be filled with God."

Richard Halverson, in *Treatment of Maturity*, emphasizes the awareness of our own inadequacy:

"One of the clearest evidences of Christian maturity is an increasing awareness of one's need, an increasing lack of self-confidence and an increasing sense of one's dependence upon the Holy Spirit. Christian growth is accompanied by an increasing sense of the futility of human effort in its utter inadequacy at its very best. But this sense of need is always more than balanced by a growing realization that Christ has made ample provision and the need is the door to spiritual fulfillment."

These are great prayers and desires, and all of them must be translated and transformed into the reality of character development so that a believer can become mature.

A SCRIPTURAL BLUEPRINT FOR MATURITY

To define the true biblical product of maturity so that we have a standard that all can use, I will lay out a survey of Scripture, taking it in blocks.

I will point out, first of all, the biblical product in creation, followed by the biblical product under the Old Covenant, under the New Covenant, as seen in the Book of Acts, then as taught in the Epistles. Then I will give a practical list of characteristics of a mature Christian who has been in the atmosphere of the presence of God and has developed the character of Christ.

THE BIBLICAL PRODUCT IN CREATION

The first thing we must understand if we are going to grasp the concept of a scriptural product of maturity is that God created man according to a specific standard with specific goals in mind.

Genesis 1:26-28 gives us an account of God's final step in creation: He made us a person after His likeness.

"Then God said, 'Let Us make man in Our image, according to Our likeness; let them have dominion over the fish
of the sea, over the birds of the air, and over the cattle, over
all the earth and over every creeping thing that creeps on
the earth.' So God created man in His own image; in the
image of God He created him; male and female He created them. Then
God blessed them, and God said to them, 'Be fruitful and multiply; fill the
earth and subdue it; have dominion over the fish of the sea, over the birds
of the air, and over every living thing that moves on the earth.' "

> "God's purpose was to have a being who would rule and have dominion, which speaks of God's divine destiny for us."

God's premise in creating humans was to have a part of
creation that was "in His image." The word image involves
the two ideas of representation and manifestation. The idea
of perfection is not in the word itself, but must be sought in
the context. People were created to be a visible representation of God, a being that corresponds to the original. God's
purpose was to have a being who would rule and have
dominion, which speaks of God's divine destiny for us.

The Fall of Creation

Sin entered the picture as Adam and Eve fell. In the fall,
humans ceased to be a perfect vehicle for the representation of God. This fall drastically changed our relationship
with Him. But the fallen condition of humankind is not a
complete about face to the original image. We are still suitable in God's eyes to bear responsibility. We still have God-

like qualities, such as love, goodness, and beauty, none of which are found in mere animals.

Through the regenerative and redemptive process, God's grace in Christ will yet accomplish more than what Adam and Eve lost when they sinned. God will remake people as born-again creatures in His likeness and in His image. God will perfect us so that we become an exact replica of Him. The replica will have limitations: We will never become little gods and we will never have the essential attributes of God, such as omnipresence or omnipotence. But we will develop the moral character of God in perfect love, joy, obedience, and moral justice. These are all attributes that the Bible promises us Christ will develop in the believer.

"And have put on the new man who is renewed in knowledge according to the image of Him who created him" (Colossians 3:10).

"And that you put on the new man which was created according to God, in true righteousness and holiness" (Ephesians 4:24).

"And as we have borne the image of the man of dust, we shall also bear the image of the heavenly Man" (1 Corinthians 15:49).

A Work of Divine Grace

God has created people to bear His image and to express and represent His character on earth. The invisible God is made visible through the work of redemption in His creation, that is, redeemed man. Therefore, as a revival spirit moves upon the hearts and spirits of believers, there will be a resulting representation of Christ's character and a manifestation of God's attributes.

The word character in the Greek denotes the work of an engraving tool that is used to cut into or emboss a stamp or impression, as on a coin or a seal. An engraving tool makes an impression in the image of itself. All the features of the image correspond respectively with the instrument producing it.

In much the same way, God is going to chisel upon us His image—His character qualities—so that we will bear His mark upon our lives. As a coin would bear the mark of the tool that has engraved upon it, a touch from the Holy Spirit will mark us. Revival must result in an engraving of the virtues of God into the soul and spirit and character of His people.

> "...as a revival spirit moves upon the hearts and spirits of believers, there will be a resulting representation of Christ's character and a manifestation of God's attributes."

"He is the image of the invisible God, the firstborn over all creation. For by Him all things were created that are in heaven and that are on earth, visible and invisible, whether thrones or dominions or principalities or powers. All things were created through Him and for Him. And He is before all things, and in Him all things consist" (Colossians 1:15-17).

"Who being the brightness of His glory and the express image of His person, and upholding all things by the word of His power, when He had by Himself purged our sins, sat down at the right hand of the Majesty on high" (Hebrews 1:3).

"That I may make it manifest, as I ought to speak" (Colossians 4:4).

THE BIBLICAL PRODUCT IN THE OLD COVENANT

God's standard of godly character, which is obedience to His authority and His law, has never changed. God created humans, and even though they fell, God still has a standard for us to live up to. Under the Law, we have the Ten Commandments and numerous other exhortations that were given so that the people of Israel would become like God, both in their attitudes and in their lifestyles. God's desire was for a people of prayer and worship, so He speaks of raising up a whole nation of kings and priests who would learn how to worship Him.

"Now therefore, if you will indeed obey My voice and keep My covenant, then you shall be a special treasure to Me above all people; for all the earth is Mine. And you shall be to Me a kingdom of priests and a holy nation.' These are the words which you shall speak to the children of Israel. So Moses came and called for the elders of the people, and laid before them all these words which the Lord command-ed him" (Exodus 19:5-7).

God still desires that we be a certain kind of people, that we fulfill His purpose of resembling Him in character qual-ities and character virtues.

After the fall, God was willing to use whatever means necessary to produce people who are acceptable to Him. When Israel disobeyed, it meant that God would send other nations to rise up against them. It might result in traveling through the wilderness for forty years, or spending time in Babylon, or being under the heavy rule of a godly or ungodly king.

"He has shown you, O man, what is good; and what does the Lord require of you but to do justly, to love mercy, and to walk humbly with your God?" (Micah 6:8).

BIBLICAL PRODUCT IN THE NEW COVENANT

"And Jesus came and spoke to them, saying, 'All authority has been given to Me in heaven and on earth. Go therefore and make disciples of all the nations, baptizing them in the name of the Father and of the Son and of the Holy Spirit, teaching them to observe all things that I have commanded you; and lo, I am with you always, even to the end of the age.' Amen" (Matthew 28:18-20).

This passage states the one goal Christ has for His people. That goal is to make disciples. He wants to produce learners, people who would bear their crosses daily and become like Him, people who would not live selfishly or under the carnality of the old man, people who would put off the works of the flesh and follow Christ with a new nature and a new motive and a new lifestyle (also see Matthew 9:36-38; Luke 9:23-25, 14:25-25; John 8:31, 13:34-35, 15:7-17).

To welcome a revival spirit, we must be motivated to become disciples of Christ. We must be motivated and willing to bear our crosses daily and follow Christ in a sacrificial lifestyle. We must be committed to His teachings, His principles and His ways. We must be committed to fulfilling all that Christ commands us to fulfill. The only way we can do this is to abide in Christ. John 15:1-8 reveals to us the principles of what it means to abide in Christ.

A revival atmosphere does not necessarily equate with abiding in Christ. God wants to revive us as we abide in the wonderful, life-changing presence of Jesus Christ.

BIBLICAL PRODUCT IN THE BOOK OF ACTS

In the second chapter of Acts we have the revival of Pentecost, which was a dynamic outpouring of the Holy Spirit with supernatural signs and wonders. We see in this chapter the fire, the wind and the miracle tongues that came upon those who received the Holy Spirit. They were thought of as drunk people. They were mocked, ridiculed, and questioned, yet these people had experienced the Holy Spirit.

> "A revival atmosphere does not necessarily equate with abiding in Christ."

The disciples of Christ who had experienced the fire, the wind, and the tongues were the same people who had experienced the ten-day prayer meeting in the Upper Room, where they had been transformed into disciples and mature believers in Christ. They go on to follow doctrine, to commit themselves to praying with other believers, to ministering to the poor, and to extending the kingdom of God outside of their own cities.

Verses 30 through 42 of this chapter demonstrates for us what kind of people the Holy Spirit wants to produce. They were people who demonstrated their beliefs by their actions. They were people who repented, who turned from their old life lives, were baptized in water, filled with the Holy Spirit and joined to the people of God. They drank in the teachings of the Word of God. They loved doctrine. They had daily fellowship with the saints. They loved prayer, both private and corporate, and they took communion with the people of God. They were involved with witnessing, extending the kingdom of God, and, if need be, laying down their lives for the kingdom of God. These were people who took part in that awesome day of Pentecost, yet they were also people who did the practical, day-to-day things that Jesus commanded them to do.

> "A revival that results only in intensified emotional church services and experiences runs the risk of shallowness and a short lifespan."

It must be the same with us. Whenever revival flows with supernatural signs and wonders, it must result in practical lifestyle change and practical Christianity. A revival that results only in intensified emotional church services and experiences runs the risk of shallowness and a short lifespan. All revivals must result in true New Testament Christianity. If not, we might only be experiencing emotionalism, revivalism, or a form of Pentecostal escapism.

We should never thwart the emotions that are shown during revival times. God has made people emotional beings. There is nothing negative about crying, shouting, lying on the floor, or jumping up and down as the Holy

Spirit moves upon a person. But emotions and manifestations themselves do not make great disciples. What makes great disciples is the following of the Word of God in forms of discipline that produce a biblical product. This is what will produce a lasting, productive revival

BIBLICAL PRODUCT IN THE EPISTLES

"The mystery which has been hidden from ages and from generations, but now has been revealed to His saints. To them God willed to make known what are the riches of the glory of this mystery among the Gentiles: which is Christ in you, the hope of glory. Him we preach, warning every man and teaching every man in all wisdom, that we may present every man perfect in Christ Jesus. To this end I also labor, striving according to His working which works in me mightily" (Colossians 1:26-29).

In this passage, the apostle Paul lays out a standard for us to measure up to. His goal was a biblical product: Christ in all His glorious riches actually dwelling in the spirits, hearts and lives of all who accept Him. Christ in us!

Christ in us means that Jesus is joined with our spirits, which are beyond our physical selves. This means that the same Spirit that was in Christ is also in us. Christ in us involves receiving Christ as Lord and Savior, being born again by allowing Christ to be born in us, and surrendering our lives to Christ.

Revival atmosphere does not necessarily produce this in everybody, but we as leaders, pastors, and disciples must have this goal as we see people come to the altar during times of revival.

TWELVE CHARACTERISTICS OF A BIBLICAL PRODUCT

If I were to profile a biblical product, I would list at least twelve attributes of people who are becoming disciples of Christ. These people are:

12 characteristics of a BIBLICAL PRODUCT

1. People who are in submission to Jesus as Lord (Luke 14:25-35; 9:23-25).
2. People who are filled with and living by the Holy Spirit (Ephesians 5:17-18).
3. People who function in their spiritual gifts (Romans 12:1-6).
4. People who are committed to and supporting the local church (Acts 2:37-47).
5. People who are fervent worshipers (John 4:24; Romans 12:1).
6. People who pray faithfully (2 Timothy 2:1; Colossians 4:2).
7. People who boldly share their faith (I Thessalonians 11:8-10; Acts 1:1-8).
8. People who give generously (2 Corinthians 8-9; Malachi 3:10-11).
9. People who are family builders (Colossians 3:18-21; Ephesians 6:1-2).
10. People who serve others (John 13:34-35).
11. People who are overcoming self life (Luke 9:23-25; Romans 6:1-10).
12. People with a world vision (Matthew 9:36-38, 28:16-18; Acts 1:1-8).

BEARING BIBLICAL FRUIT (DISCIPLES)

In Matthew 28:18-20, we are called to become disciples of Christ, to allow Him to work in us in such a way that we represent His image and character here on planet Earth. We are also called to make disciples. We see in this passage that disciple making was Christ's approach to producing a biblical product. Jesus made Himself available to the multitudes, but He gave Himself to His disciples.

Making disciples—aiding others to become mature Christians—means personal involvement. It means personal interest and investment. It also involves personal emotion, personal appointments, personal association, personal commission, and personal impartation (see Mark 3:13-15; Matthew 9:35-10:5; Luke 6:12).

PAUL THE DISCIPLE MAKER

Paul established a disciple-making process that involved teaching the Word of God, prayer, authority, submission and character development.

"...disciple making was Christ's approach to producing a biblical product."

The apostle Paul stated in Colossians 1:28 that his goal in ministry was to present every man perfect. The word perfect in this verse is translated *telion*, which means complete, fully grown, mature. It suggests attainment of the proper end of one's existence: maturity in faith and character. This maturity is possible only by virtue of the believer's union with Christ. Only then will the process of maturity in Christ begin. (Also see 1 Corinthians 2:6, 14:20; Ephesians 4:13.)

PAUL'S STRATEGY FOR DISCIPLE MAKING

Paul accomplished the goal of bringing people to maturity by using proclaiming, admonishing, teaching, and presenting in his ministry.

Proclaiming is a solemn or public proclamation. It means to speak something with authority (see Acts 3:24, 4:2, 13:5). Admonishing is where we get the word counseling. It is the word *noutheteo*, which means a confrontation of sin and has to do with the will and emotions. It literally means to call to one's mind. It denotes warning (see Acts 20:31; Romans 15:14; 1 Thessalonians 5:12). Teaching is the Greek word *didasko*, which means to impart instruction. Matthew 5:2 says, "Then He opened His mouth and taught them" (also see Matthew 26:55, 28:20; Luke 11:1). The word presenting, as used in Colossians 1:28, is the word *paristemi* which means to station by one's side, to place beside (also see Matthew 26:53; 2 Corinthians 4:14, 5:10; Revelation 20:12).

Paul's dedication to this ministry of presenting people perfect is seen in the words he uses to describe his process for bringing people to maturity. Paul speaks of the labor of ministry. The word labor is *kopiao*, which means to labor excessively, to be weary, worn out with the toil of the task, to exert all strength available in reaching the goal.

THE DIFFICULTIES OF DISCIPLE MAKING

I am sure all of us would like to believe that a trip to the altar, a series of revival meetings, or even a year of revival could change people forever. If that were true, our jobs as disciple makers would be a lot easier.

Well, revival atmosphere does make our work easier. Revival atmosphere, when the Holy Spirit is released in a fuller measure, leads people into maturity and change. But, as I pointed out earlier in this chapter, revival does not complete the process of maturity in Christ. Revival is a wonderful time of life-changing visitation by the Holy Spirit. But we must still be diligent in the labors of ministry we are assigned to. The result of these labors to us personally—to be weary and worn out—is not something that we hold as a high goal in our lives and ministries, but it is the goal in Scripture.

Paul says, "I struggle." *Aganoizomai* is the Greek word for struggle, and it literally means to agonize. It is a word from the athletic arena that suggests an intense exertion or strenuous activity. The powers that wrestled with Paul for the ruin of his work were real and resolute. Therefore, he had to meet with them, foot to foot, face to face. He had to struggle with them.

> "Revival is a wonderful time of life-changing visitation by the Holy Spirit. We must be diligent in the labors of ministry we are assigned to."

Disciple Making Requires Using God's Strength

Just as Paul's ministry was a labor and struggle, so is ours. There are times when we as disciple makers must spend time in the renewing presence of God so that we will have the strength to properly minister to people the truth of God's Word.

Laboring and struggling does not mean we must burn out. That happens when we labor in our own strength. But when we labor and struggle in the power of the Holy Spirit, we do not lose our fire. Instead, we become revived in our toil.

The secret of productive ministry is to be energized by the Holy Spirit, as Paul says in Colossians 1:29: "To this end I also labor, striving according to His working which works in me mightily." This verse speaks of an energizing. This tells us that the struggle and challenge of ministry are not to be carried out by natural powers, but by the supernatural power at work within all of us who are involved in the labor and struggle of bringing people to maturity.

Paul was most himself when he was least dependent upon his own resources. We are not to rely on our own energy, but upon Christ's energy, that presence that works mightily in us. This is why revival is a wonderful time when we drink deeply of the Holy Spirit and become energized within our own hearts and minds. Revival comes to remind us that there is power available, there is grace available, there is energy available. Do not do it on your own strength. You will fail and become exhausted at the same time (see 1 Corinthians 12:11; Ephesians 3:20).

Disciple Making Requires Intercessory Prayer

Paul's ministry of intercessory prayer is seen in all of his epistles because he knew that without God's strength he would have become discouraged in his labors to bring people to maturity. Therefore, he gave himself more to intercessory prayer for the church than to anything else. When Paul was in prison, he had plenty of time to combat his opponents through intercessory prayer. This kind of praying caused him to exert himself strenuously. Paul's praying was focused praying (Collossians 1:9), tireless praying, unselfish praying (Collossians 1:10-11). (Also see Collossians 1:3l; Collossians 4:3l; Ephesians 6:18l; Romans 8:26; Philippians 1:4,9; Thessalonians 1:2; Thessalonians 1:11.)

God expects us to intercede and agonize for each other as part of our labor to bring people to discipleship. This kind of prayer is a sacred privilege, but it is also a duty and an obligation (see Ephesians 1:16; Romans 1:9; Collossians 3:14).

QUALITY OVER QUANTITY

We must not allow the quantity of disciples to be a substitute for quality in disciples. We must allow the Word of God to set the standard for biblical product, not other churches' trends or cultures or man-made programs. We must proclaim the message of New Testament lordship. We must proclaim that godly character is as important as charisma and spiritual discipline is as meaningful as spiritual gifts.

Experiences at church services or revival meetings do not necessarily produce mature believers. Maturity comes through a process, through structure. The process toward biblical product comes by focusing on people individually through small groups, hands-on counseling, and discipleship groups.

> "We must not allow the quantity of disciples to be a substitute for quality of disciples."

We must encourage ourselves and others in revival experiences. We must encourage people to experience emotions, subjective visions from the Lord, and revelations that come to their minds and hearts concerning what God wants to do in their lives.

But we must not let them rest only in that pool of under-standing. We must direct them into a life of discipleship. We must direct them toward becoming a biblical product. We must stay sensitive to the ministry of the Holy Spirit because He is the One building a spiritually mature church.

We must be people of the Word of God through a disci-plined manner of attaining Word knowledge. We must involve a love for doctrine, a love for theology and a love for history in our study.

Let us pursue heartily the spirit of revival and the pres-ence of Christ in our midst. Let us not shrink back from the ever-energizing, awesome presence of God in the midst of His people. Let us not discourage people from experiencing God with their minds, wills, emotions, and bodies. Let us take what happens in these revival settings and translate it into maturity through the disciplines of the Word of God and Christian living.

$\mathcal{I}$NGREDIENTS FOR SUSTAINING REVIVAL POWER

Chapter 12

THE MYTH OF
THE "MAN OF GOD SYNDROME"

*R*evival seasons cultivate an atmosphere for prayer and personal ministry to other people. As people become saturated with God's Spirit and God's presence, they receive more easily and more deeply of the things of God. Who they receive from becomes less of an issue during true revival seasons.

There has always been different philosophical and doctrinal views of who should do the ministering to people during revival type meetings.

In the 1940s and 1950s, the highly publicized and promoted evangelist was the man of God who would come to an area to minister the anointing of the Holy Spirit with signs and wonders following. People flocked by the thousands to receive from this man of God. He was God's voice, God's hands, God's vessel to bring revival.

This image went to extremes at times as these humble, anointed servants were sometimes not so humble and not so anointed. With clever promotion and a knowledge of crowd manipulation and control, they were seemingly successful. But some of these men were not manipulators at all. They had a gift of God, a call to do what they were doing, and exceptional integrity. Their revival meetings were wonderful for one week, two weeks, even ten weeks. But reality soon set in. The meetings had to end. The evangelist had to move on to bless, heal, and deliver others.

What happened then? What did the pastor do to bridge the gap between highly intensified faith meetings and a typical Sunday church service? And what about the perspective of the congregation? The people certainly could not see their pastor—and for sure not Brother Smith or Sister Jones—moving in the supernatural the way the evangelist did. They knew them too well. They bought their food at the same grocery store and worked with them at the same factory. Sister Jones was known for her gossip, and Brother Smith for his lack of patience with his children. Obviously, there was no possible faith to receive from those normal, run-of-the-mill saints. They needed the man of God back.

MOVING AWAY FROM THE "MAN OF GOD SYNDROME"

This scenario represents a historical past for a large segment of the body of Christ. But more than that, it represents a faulty theological stronghold that hinders the church from functioning as the Bible says it should.

The Old Testament offers the man of God, the prophet, coming out of the cave or wilderness to work miracles, give a word from God, and then back to the cave. But the New Testament offers a radically different model for ministry: the idea that all of us in the body of Christ are priests and kings.

"You also, as living stones, are being built up a spiritual house, a holy priesthood, to offer up spiritual sacrifices acceptable to God through Jesus Christ. But you are a chosen generation, a royal priesthood, a holy nation, His own special people, that you may proclaim the praises of Him who called you out of darkness into His marvelous light" (Peter 2:5-9).

"And has made us kings and priests to His God and Father, to Him be glory and dominion forever and ever. Amen" (Revelation 1:6).

"And have made us kings and priests to our God; and we shall reign on the earth" (Revelation 5:10).

The New Testament established the value of each individual having the glory of God in his or her life. Each person has the potential to develop his or her own spiritual gifts with a promise of power, authority, and influence.

MOBILIZED FOR MINISTRY: A CALL TO ALL

Ephesians 4:12-16 clearly states that all of us should do, not just know, the ministry. We must make room for everyone in the body of Christ to take the burden of ministry within revival contexts and revival seasons. Every saint should minister grace and impartation of strength to all who need it. We must encourage all people in the body of Christ to discover their capacities, aptitudes and abilities for the work of the ministry and then help them refine their skills. We must develop a theology of impartation that begins with a proper respect for all members and their gifts in the body of Christ. The apostle Paul in 1 Corinthians 12:12-27 offers basic foundations for developing a body-of-Christ mentality.

> "We must encourage all people in the body of Christ to discover their capacities, aptitudes, and abilities..."

Revival should not be tied to one minister, one man or one gift. God is not limited to one gifted leader; He is committed to the whole body of Christ. The church must never deify certain ministries because of their particular gifts or charisma. Revival seasons are given to the whole body of Christ for the whole body of Christ.

"From whom the whole body, joined and knit together by what every joint supplies, according to the effective working by which every part does its share, causes growth of the body for the edifying of itself in love" (Ephesians 4:16).

> "Revival should not be tied to one minister, one man or one gift. God is not limited to one gifted leader; He is committed to the whole body of Christ."

OVERCOMING THE "MAN OF GOD SYNDROME"

The "Man Of God Syndrome" is brought into proper perspective when the whole body of Christ is properly esteemed and released.

The problem with some leaders is, the control factor: when authority becomes an issue of control, not release and delegation. The theology of impartation irritates controllers or ego-laden leaders. They fear letting go of the glory, the image, the place on the pedestal. This creates the attitude of "The more I do the more I'm loved and needed, so therefore I do everything."

This kind of leadership insecurity hinders the releasing of the whole body to do the whole work of ministry. David Watson, who wrote a book on the subject of the laity, articulates the problem well: "Most Protestant denominations have been as priest-ridden as the Roman Catholics. It is the minister, vicar or pastor who has dominated the whole proceedings. In other words, the clergy-laity divisions have continued in much the same way as in pre-Reformation times, and the doctrine of spiritual gifts and body ministry have been largely ignored."

John Stott, a leading British theologian, states: "Laity is often a synonym for amateur as opposed to professional, or unqualified as compared to expert."

Layperson is a scriptural word filled with dignity and honor. The word *laos* refers to a larger grouping of people linked by relationships that give them unity and identity. *Laos* portrays a sense of specialness. It is used 143 times in the New Testament alone. In the following Scriptures, the Greek word *laos* is translated as people:

"For you are a holy people to the Lord your God; the Lord your God has chosen you to be a people for Himself, a special treasure above all the peoples on the face of the earth" (Deuteronomy 7:6).

"I will walk among you and be your God, and you shall be My people" (Leviticus 26:12).

"But you are a chosen generation, a royal priesthood, a holy nation, His own special people, that you may proclaim the praises of Him who called you out of darkness into His marvelous light" (Peter 2:9).

"Who gave Himself for us, that He might redeem us from every lawless deed and purify for Himself His own special people, zealous for good works" (Titus 2:14).

The first reformation put the Scriptures into the hands of the laity. The second reformation, taking place now, is putting the ministry into the hands of the laity. Elton Trueblood lifts the trumpet of laity also: "If the average church should suddenly take seriously the notion that every lay member, man or woman, is really a minister of Christ we could have something like a revolution in a very short time."

A layperson is nothing less than a new humanity, the vanguard of the future, the prototype of the kingdom of God not yet completed, a person of the future living in the present. Next time you hear someone say, "I'm just a layperson," say, "That's more than enough." The theology of impartation is brought to a practical application when this philosophy reigns supreme.

> "The faulty concept of placing our reliance on high-powered leaders has cost the body of Christ dearly."

The faulty concept of placing our reliance on high-powered leaders has cost the body of Christ dearly. The biblical emphasis is not on the omni-competent leader, but a multi-gifted body. Exalting one gift or ministry above others in the body of Christ will negate the beauty and variety of a gift-working body of people. Pastors, prophets, evangelists, apostles, teachers and all the ascension gift ministries have a specific function, but it doesn't include being the superstar, the elite chosen one of God. If the church exalts superstars, then the church becomes an audience, not a body.

The theology of impartation is best nurtured when there is a proper focus on the biblical model of all believers as priests and kings, as responsible, gift-bearing people. The theology of impartation will be rightly developed when the ascension gift ministries do what they are called to do: Equip! Equip! Equip!

"And He Himself gave some to be apostles, some prophets, some evangelists, and some pastors and teachers, for the equipping of the saints for the work of ministry, for the edifying of the body of Christ, till we all come to the unity of the faith and of the knowledge of the Son of God, to a perfect man, to the measure of the stature of the fullness of Christ" (Ephesians 4:11-13).

WORD PICTURES DESCRIBING THOSE WHO EQUIP

The word equip is taken from the Greek word *katartismos*, which means to prepare someone, to train, repair, adjust, or impart. This simply means that we move people from being spectators to participators, from watching from afar to actually taking part and becoming active as a functioning part of the body.

Here is a list of words and how they describe those who equip:

1. Trainers of the soldiers in army of the Lord.

2. Restorers of those in the body of Christ.

3. Framers of the boards of God's house.

4. Exercisers of the muscles in Christ's body.

5. Shapers of the stones in the temple of the Lord.

6. Healers of the breaches in the hedges of God's garden.

7. Liberators of those who are bound.

8. Adjusters of those who are out of joint.

9. Menders of those whose bones are broken.

10. Placers of God's people.

11. Organizers of the Lord's Kingdom.

12. Molders of God's clay vessels.

13. Seers of potential for God's service.

God designed the body of Christ to function at its best when each and every member is doing his or her part—through the empowering of the Holy Spirit—to minister to others. Each of us has been given the capacity to serve in some way.

UNDERSTANDING THE
MINISTRY OF IMPARTATION

*T*he theology of impartation must be built upon a theology of the body of Christ. What does the Scripture state concerning impartation? That the ministry of impartation is to be accomplished through all of God's people ministering one to another. Revival seasons are times of receiving and imparting. We must believe that by faith we can pray for, lay hands on, and impart something good to someone else.

Let us examine biblical words that fit into the impartation family:

"Give" *(metadidomi)*: To give a share of, to give or release something of value to someone else (Romans 1:11; Luke 3:11; 1 Thessalonians 2:8).

"Impart" *(prosanatithemi)*: To hand over, to confer, to place into (Galatians 1:16, 2:6; Romans 1:11).

"Deposit" *(paratheke)*: To put with, to give of some thing to another, to deposit something into another (2 Timothy 1:12; 1 Timothy 6:20).

"Communicate" *(koinoneo)*: Used in two senses. (1) To have a share in (Romans 15:27; 1 Timothy 5:23; Hebrews 2:14). (2) To give a share to, to distribute (Romans 12:13; Galatians 6:6).

"Commit" *(epitrope)*: Denotes a turning over to another, a referring of a thing to another, a committal of full powers (Acts 26:12).

God imparts something into the life of the individual that can be imparted to others. This impartation is obviously relevant to who is doing the imparting and who is doing the receiving.

IMPARTATION IN THE OLD TESTAMENT

In Deuteronomy 34:9, we see a scriptural model for impartation: "Now Joshua the son of Nun was full of the spirit of wisdom, for Moses had laid his hands on him; so the children of Israel heeded him, and did as the Lord had commanded Moses."

> **"Please let a double portion of your spirit be upon me."**

Through the laying on of hands, Moses imparted wisdom into the life and ministry of Joshua. This impartation was based upon what Moses had to give and what Joshua eagerly desired to receive.

In 2 Kings 2:9, we have another biblical model of impartation. We have two men—Elijah and Elisha—one who desperately needed what the other could impart to him:

"And so it was, when they had crossed over, that Elijah said to Elisha, 'Ask! What may I do for you, before I am taken away from you?' Elisha said, 'Please let a double portion of your spirit be upon me.' So he said, 'You have asked a hard thing. Nevertheless, if you see me when I am taken from you, it shall be so for you; but if not, it shall not be so' " (2 Kings 2:9-10).

"He also took up the mantle of Elijah that had fallen from him, and went back and stood by the bank of the Jordan. Then he took the mantle of Elijah that had fallen from him, and struck the water, and said, 'Where is the Lord God of Elijah?' And when he also had struck the water, it was divided this way and that; and Elisha crossed over. Now when the sons of the prophets who were from Jericho saw him, they said, 'The spirit of Elijah rests on Elisha.' And they came to meet him, and bowed to the ground before him" (2 Kings 2:13-15).

The mantle that rested upon Elijah—a mantle of God's Spirit for working miracles, healing, and prophetic power in the words he spoke—was now upon Elisha. This was a double portion impartation. When the other prophets saw Elisha, they simply said: "The spirit of Elijah rests on Elisha." The mantle was Elijah's spirit, and that spirit could be imparted.

IMPARTATION IN THE NEW TESTAMENT

In the New Testament, the apostle Paul speaks of impartation when he writes to the church at Rome:

"For I long to see you, that I may impart to you some spiritual gift, so that you may be established" (Romans 1:11).

Paul does not explain exactly how he will impart those spiritual gifts to these believers, but he states without hesitation that he will. He states that these spiritual gifts will work toward helping that which he established. We read in 1 Corinthians 12 (also Paul's letter) that gifts are distributed by and through the Holy Spirit.

"But one and the same Spirit works all these things, distributing to each one individually as He wills"
(1 Corinthians 12:11).

This does not negate impartation from one believer to another, for we can only minister by the Spirit and with the Spirit. All impartation is under the government of the Holy Spirit. Nevertheless, as we minister, we can by faith impart strength, encouragement, wisdom, and more of the anointing of the Holy Spirit. In James 5:14, the sick are to call for the elders to anoint them with oil and pray the prayer of faith for healing. Impartation will be powerfully administered when there is faith to impart and receive.

> "...as we minister, we can by faith impart strength, encouragement, wisdom, and more of the anointing of the Holy Spirit."

THE PROPER USE OF SPIRITUAL GIFTS

Revival atmosphere usually necessitates a great deal of personal ministry, which in bible based churches could be a renewed usage of the gifts of the Spirit. The gifts of words of knowledge, words of wisdom, prophecy, healing and counseling are powerful gifts.

When people experience a new touch of the Holy Spirit during revivals, emotions and excitement may reach a newer, higher level. In that case, some may overstep the scriptural guidelines for personal ministry to others when using the gifts of the Spirit.

Most revival type ministry is geared to personal ministry of edification, exhortation and comfort, but some may lean toward correction, direction and deliverance. If this occurs, impartation may be abused without proper over-sight and special sensitivity.

We need to develop some ministry guidelines for the use of these powerful gifts before people are injured or misguid-ed. We want to encourage the usage of all gifts by all believ-ers with practical wisdom and biblical guidelines.

We need to encourage insightful praying over people as we receive insight from the Holy Spirit, but refrain from using prophetic language or giving prophetic words. We need to give encouragement without direction and without giving people future-focused words that could confuse them as to whether they have received direction or not. When praying for people, we need to ask more questions as we pray and not rely too heavily on words of knowledge or words of wisdom. It is not unspiritual to probe, ask ques-tions and use the natural mind with the Holy Spirit to make sure our ministry is accurate.

GIFTS OF THE SPIRIT ARE FOR EDIFICATION, EXHORTATION, AND COMFORT

All gifts used in public worship services, or any gather-ing of the congregation, should be governed by love and edification (see 1 Corinthians 14:3,26,28,30).

SPECIFIC WORDS SHOULD BE JUDGED BY THE LEADERSHIP

Gifts of the Spirit, or utterances under the influence of the Holy Spirit, such as prophecy, words of knowledge, exhortation, or words of counsel, if done personally from one believer to another, should be kept general and not specific, and should seek to edify and exhort the believer being ministered to. If there is a specific word, there should be another there to judge or help discern the validity of such a word. It would be wise to involve the leadership of the church, depending on the nature of the word (see 1 Corinthians 14:12, 24-25, 29, 32).

Minister faith and pray in faith, but do not presume. When ministering to others who are in need of physical or emotional healing, we should minister in faith without pronouncing a person healed or delivered. We should pray in faith, believing for recovery, believing what the Scripture says, and then leave the working of it in the hands of God.

> **"This makes each person in the body of Christ an initiating center for ministry."**

We who administer the gifts God has wisely deposited within us, must be careful and responsible to those we minister to. We must respect their privacy, their personhood and their stand before God. If they have received healing or deliverance, let them verify this by using the proper channels. After it is verified, then let that person proclaim their miracle. If we proclaim by faith before we see the fact of the miracle, it may cause confusion, disillusionment, and discouragement if it never happens.

EMBRACING GOD'S PROMISE FOR REVIVAL

The church is fundamentally a charismatic community, for the charismata (grace gifts) have been distributed to each of us. This makes each person in the body of Christ an initiating center for ministry.

Let us believe God's promise for revival, and let each of us in the body of Christ be willing and ready to use that which God has imparted to us as we minister during these times of Holy Spirit outpouring.

Chapter 14

THE HISTORY OF HEALING

*D*uring a genuine revival that took place in the days of King Hezekiah, the king prayed for God to visit his people. In 2 Chronicles 30:20, it says: "And the Lord listened to Hezekiah and healed the people."

When the Holy Spirit moves upon hungry hearts during times of revival, there is a deepening work of faith and expectation in the awesome God of Scripture. Revival restores the sense of God's power and His willingness to break in upon our natural circumstances.

This is why revival is so very important to the lives of God's people—particularly the young. Revival allows us to see the supernatural works of God along with the written Word of God. That way, our faith becomes more tangible. Faith in a living God who can break into our world becomes an electrifying faith.

In expecting God to move in the supernatural, there is usually a release of the gifts of the Spirit, most vividly the gifts of healing and miracles. Revival nurtures a belief in faith healing, which is the spiritual process whereby physical, mental, and emotional illnesses can be cured by a supernatural intervention of God when we pray a prayer of faith.

REVIVING FAITH IN GOD'S HEALING

When the church becomes lukewarm or loses its power to expect God to do anything, the ministries of healing and miracles seem to subside. The prayers of believers can become faithless prayers of people who do not really expect God to break in and do any supernatural works in their day.

But the ministry of healing is not dead, and it should not be forgotten. Divine healing has been established throughout the Bible as being part of Christ's ministry as well as ministries of the apostles and the early church. Not only did they experience the ministry of healing, but they also passed it on to their followers. And it is being revived by the Holy Spirit and taken up by a new breed of leadership that is not only strategically moving in the Holy Spirit, but is also theologically sound. We need a host of people who understand the doctrine of divine healing, who have the faith to embrace it and impart it to the many congregations throughout the world, especially in America.

> **"We need a host of people who understand the doctrine of divine healing, who have the faith to embrace it..."**

We need to pray that God will break forth in miracles and holy gifts today so that people will see that He is still the living God in the midst of dead people. When people see that, they will be quickened to a resurrection. They will see that God can still do something and that He has liberty to work by His Spirit. God still hears the prayers of people, and He can still help them triumph in dark hours. God can break the bondage of sin and sickness in people's lives. He can still fulfill all His promises in the Scripture. This is what builds great expectation in the hearts of people to believe by faith for God to work.

DIVINE HEALING IN HISTORY

To fully understand the scriptural doctrine of healing, it is important to understand that throughout the years, we, in our Christian history, have always had doctrines of supernatural healing.

As early as 1672, during his missionary journey to America, George Fox, the founder of the Society of Friends, reported that he had prayed the prayer of faith for the physically sick and that they were healed. Fox recorded healing during his ministry in America and Britain, and related details of more than 150 of these healings in a book entitled, *Book of Miracles*.

The faith healing movement has been a very important part of Pentecostal history. The faith healing with signs and wonders ministry provided an atmosphere necessary to make other Pentecostal behaviors acceptable to the multitudes.

In tracing the healing ministries as far back as the year preceding the Civil War, we quote from Horace Bushnell, who spoke of the troubles in Christianity in his day. Horace Bushnell was a pastor in Hartford, Conn. Bushnell, who died in 1876, was a spokesman on the nature of discipleship and maturity as a balance to revival evangelism. As the natural continued to take priority over the supernatural, Bushnell observed that Christian souls were, "falling into a stupor of intellectual fatality. Prayer becomes a kind of dumbbell exercise. Good as exercise, but never to be answered. The word is good to be exegetically handled but there is no light of interpretation in souls. More immediate, all truth is to be second-hand truth, never a vital beam of God's own light. Expectation is gone. God is too far off and too much imprisoned by laws to allow expectation from Him."

The Christian world has been visibly gravitating toward this vanishing point of faith for centuries, and especially since the modern era of science began to shape the thoughts of man through scientific methods alone. Religion has fallen under the domain of mere intellectual under-standing, and so it has become a kind of wisdom to believe much, but expect little.

As far back as the 1800s, there was a longing of the church for the supernatural to be released. Within a segment of the church, the expectations for a livelier, more apostolic church were developing. As it was then, so it is now.

In the early nineteenth century in Europe, Edward Irving insisted that the power of miracles must either be speedily revived in the church, or there would be a universal dominion of the mechanical philosophy, and faith would be almost extinct. To give the law of cause and effect the center plat-form would continue to push the control-ling philosophies of society in the opposite direction of Christianity. Irving preached with power the long silent and forgotten voice of God, which was overshadowed by the philosophies of his day. His services had as many as 12,000 to 13,000 people. He preached and prayed for the supernatural to take place, and there were many signs and wonders and healings in his meetings.

> "The purpose of faith homes was to prepare people spiritually to accept biblical promises literally with a childlike faith."

The Faith Homes

The healing faith homes lasted for about 100 years in the American culture. The purpose of faith homes was to pre-pare people spiritually to accept biblical promises literally with a childlike faith. For this reason, much time was spent in the homes studying the promises of the Bible regarding salvation, sanctification, and healing. Frequently, accounts of the healing of others were communicated so as to increase the sufferers' faith in God.

One of the famous homes was run by Dorothea Trudel, her ministry was in a little Swiss village around 1851. She was quite simple in her belief that power from her results came only from prayer, the laying on of hands, and the anointing with oil. The emphasis was not placed on methodology, nor was the method used presented as an infallible cure. Samuel Zeller, her successor, held that the results of prayer were left to the sovereign will of God. In some cases the result was immediate, but in others it was slow. In still others, there was no change. Trudel and Zeller made no promises or guarantees and they did not blame for want of faith.

Otto Stockmeier

One of the most famous people to influence the faith healing movement was Otto Stockmeier, who was referred to by one of the leading American advocates of divine healing, A.J. Gordon, as a theologian of the doctrine of healing by faith. Stockmeier's initial introduction to faith healing came on Easter of 1867, when Samuel Zeller laid hands upon him and prayed for his healing. Stockmeier later opened a healing home in Switzerland, where he employed the same methodology as used by other faith healing homes.

Stockmeier's book, *Sickness and the Gospel*, and his frequent attendance at early Keswick conventions made his ministry and teaching familiar to both British and American audiences. His basic presupposition of divine healing is one that could be used as a basic statement for all churches to move into divine healing ministry. Stockmeier said that the soul is the life of the body and that God did not intend for His saving and sanctifying ministry to stop with regeneration and renewal of the soul. Since man is created for the glory of God, he is to do God's will and fulfill God's purpose. To accomplish this objective, man needs the members of his body, as well as the powers of the soul, totally free and at the absolute disposal of God. The members of man's body should not be bound by sickness, nor should his spirit be exposed to the oppression which sickness in its various forms can bring.

The Holiness Movement

The Holiness Movement, which dated from the mid-nineteenth century, also greatly influenced the area of the outpouring of the Holy Spirit with signs and wonders and miracles. This movement held that the average Christian life is grievously destitute of real spiritual power and is often essentially carnal. The Holiness Movement emphasized perfection as the obtaining of spiritual power and the infilling with the Holy Spirit.

Andrew Murray

Andrew Murray was born in South Africa in 1828. After receiving his education in Scotland and Holland, he returned to South Africa and spent many years as both pastor and missionary.

Having received healing himself, Murray was one of the great apostles of the faith. He said that divine healing accompanies the sanctification by the Spirit, that it takes place wherever the Spirit of God works in power. Murray, who wrote the books, *Sanctification, Be Perfect, The Second Blessing, and The Two Covenants,* suffered from what was diagnosed in his day as a relapsed throat because of his extensive preaching. He did not receive any help through the medical world, so he sought divine healing. A pastor in South Africa, Murray traveled to America and sat under the ministry of William Boardman and his staff for three weeks at a healing home, where Murray himself received his complete and total healing. After his healing, Murray wrote several books, one of which was entitled *Divine Healing.* That book greatly influenced people's thinking concerning the ministry of healing, and it is used to this present time as a resource book for the subject of healing.

The Healing Movement

> "An important facet of the Faith Healing Movement's holiness heritage was the emphasis and prominence given to the laity."

An offspring of American perfectionism, the divine Healing Movement inherited or adopted many of the characteristics and methodologies of its parent. The Healing Movement also structured camp meetings that not only emphasized holiness, but also included special faith healing services specially done by visiting ministries.

Dr. Charles Cullis, a medical doctor from Boston, Massachusettes is said to have done more to progagate faith healing than any one individual. Dr. Cullis was a vital link between The Holiness movement and The Healing Movement. He has been named by many as the apostle of Divine Healing in America, and through his ministry up until his death in 1892 was a true pioneer.

An important facet of the Faith Healing Movement's holiness heritage was the emphasis and prominence given to the laity. A dominant characteristic for both movements was the claiming of biblical authority and experiential authentication with their particular teachings.

> "The healing ministry has been with us since the beginning of creation, was extensively used by the Lord Jesus Christ and the apostles..."

CATEGORIES OF SICKNESS

Throughout the healing ministries our nation has seen, sickness has been broken down into three categories. First, there were afflictions that were caused by the evils that people brought upon themselves by committing such sins as pride, envy, temper, intemperance, vices, and so on. The second category of sicknesses were sent by God for the purpose of bringing families to a sense of total dependence upon Him, or to remind them that without sanctification, no human would see God. Thirdly, there were the mysterious illnesses of body and mind that had to be borne, such as the one the apostle endured in 2 Corinthians 12.

THE SIGNIFICANCE OF HEALING IN HISTORY

Divine healing first found acceptance in Europe and then within the more radical sections of Protestant churches of America, especially in the Holiness Movement, where it found a larger acceptance in American culture. At a time when America faced the tensions and stresses of internal military and political conflict (and the recovery from such), when science was seemingly dethroning God by destroying the simple world of yesteryear, when criticism of the Bible was threatening its true meaning, and when industrialization was reforming people's lives, there rose a deep desire within many Americans to see and experience again the supernatural intervention of God in their daily lives. There was a desire for God's miraculous intervention, which would show His supernatural power over sin, sickness, and human inabilities.

As we trace the doctrine of healing and the healing ministries throughout history, we can see that many of the principles that worked since the times of Christ will also work today. If we will put into practice just what the faith homes were doing in the mid-1800s, we would probably see more healing throughout the church.

The history of healing should help give us faith that we are not moving into some obscure doctrine when the Holy Spirit performs the miraculous and the supernatural in our gatherings. The healing ministry has been with us since the beginning of creation, was extensively used by the Lord Jesus Christ and the apostles, is recorded in church history, and has been a part of Christian heritage for centuries.

For these reasons, it is vitally important that we have a theology of healing established so that faith can be nurtured with sound doctrine.

Chapter 15

THE BIBLICAL FOUNDATION OF HEALING

"Then He called His twelve disciples together and gave them power and authority over all demons, and to cure diseases. He sent them to preach the kingdom of God and to heal the sick" (Luke 9:1-2).

When revival sweeps into a nation and people begin to expect God to do the miraculous, a theology of healing is very important. If there is no clear theology established, then there may be extremes and excesses because of a lack of proper understanding concerning the Scriptures and the principles of divine healing and the supernatural.

It is vital during times of revival that we establish and nurture a belief in the supernatural and in healing itself. It is during these times that many people will be seeking after the supernatural because of the atmosphere of expectation and faith that accompanies revival. Our altars will be filled with people seeking healing-body, soul, and spirit.

DEFINING HEALING

Divine healing can be defined as the process by which God supernaturally imparts life, health, and strength to afflicted souls and bodies. Healing and health may be received as part of our salvation package.

The Hebrew word for heal means to sew together, to mend, to bring healing to a wounded person's soul, spirit, or body. It means to bring total restoration. The Greek word for healing means to heal or bring wholeness, to save thoroughly. It means to bring to a place of completion and cure. It denotes the idea of being made healthy and sound.

We are called to minister not just to the spirit and soul of people, but also to their bodies. We must believe, even in the face of unbelief. We must take God at His Word that He is able to heal and desires to heal completely. We must believe for the healing of marriages, the healing of the tormented, the healing of the mentally deranged, and the healing of sick and twisted bodies. We must believe that people will to be put back together, mended, and totally restored.

C. Peter Wagner, professor of Church Growth at Fuller Seminary, states in his book, *How to Have a Healing Ministry in Any Church*, "My dream is that by the end of the century, overt and front ministries of praying for the sick will be as common in church across the board as Sunday school is now."[1]

There are many, many people who need the healing that Professor Wagner wrote about. This is why we see strange and unexplainable physical responses to the presence of God during times of revival. Many times during these seasons of ministry, people are seeking a touch of the living God so that their bodies can be touched, so that bitterness can be broken, and so that resentment can be removed, so that there can be actual physical healing. People need to be mended and restored, and sometimes this does not happen with the person lying still or just standing upright, not making a sound. Sometimes, there is an immediate response to God when He begins to heal a person.

HEALING DEMONSTRATES GOD'S GOODNESS

One of the Old Testament names for God was *Jehovah Rapha*, which means, "The Lord is my Healer." The word *Rapha* in the Hebrew means restoring to normal.

God heals because He is a good God. The Psalms speak of the overwhelming goodness of God expressed toward his people, and one of the expressions of His goodness is healing. Because God is good, He desires to touch not only the spirits of people, but also their minds and bodies.

"Good and upright is the Lord; therefore He teaches sinners in the way" (Psalm 25:8).

"The Lord is near to those who have a broken heart, and saves such as have a contrite spirit" (Psalm 34:18).

"Truly God is good to Israel, to such as are pure in heart" (Psalm 73:1).

> **"He desires to touch not only the spirit of people, but also their minds and bodies."**

"For You, Lord, are good, and ready to forgive, and abundant in mercy to all those who call upon You" (Psalm 86:5).

"Praise the Lord! Oh, give thanks to the Lord, for He is good! For His mercy endures forever" (Psalm 106:1).

"You are good, and do good; teach me Your statutes" (Psalm 119:68).

The Hebrew word for good means the power to preserve and support, in contrast with evil, which spoils and destroys. The Israelites found renewed reason for praising God as the One who is God. Everything that comes from Him is good, favorable, pleasing, and pleasant.

God wants to be gracious and considerate, to show favor to His people. Part of the favor He shows is power to heal our bodies, souls, and spirits. He extends pardon and shows mercy to those who are bound in sin. He shows generosity to all through His grace and His power to touch the human heart. It says in Psalm 103:2: "Forget not all of his benefits who healeth us from all of our diseases." The benefits of God are anything contributing to an improvement in a condition or rewards that He brings to us. God compensates for our lack Himself by being strong and full.

> "The benefits of God are anything contributing to an improvement in a condition or rewards that He brings to us."

OUR RESPONSE TO GOD'S GOODNESS

"What shall I render to the Lord for all His benefits toward me?" (Psalm 116:12).

Having recovered from an illness and being overwhelmed by God's goodness toward him, the psalmist asked what he should return to God for such benefits. He then answers himself: dedication, sacrifice, and the keeping of vows. He was so moved by the goodness of God and the power of healing that he wanted to repay God for what He had done.

Obviously, we cannot repay God for all that He does for us, but we should have hearts full of gratefulness for God's willingness to heal our frail bodies and confused minds. We are to bless the Lord with thanks for all of His benefits. We are to remember we have received providential mercies and special seasons of divine blessings in abundance.

We should praise God for the possessions of life, for the continuance of bodily life and enjoyment, for protection from numerous dangers, and for the constant meeting of our needs. We should praise God because He truly is a good God.

There are distinct spiritual advantages in recollecting divine goodness that will convince us of God's providential care for us at all times. This revelation will preserve us from undue despondency under the adverse trials of life and help us connect thoughts of God with every detail of everyday life.

We have been redeemed from undesirable conditions in body, soul, and spirit. God delivers us from all destruction! These conditions may be the work of the devil against us or brought on by serious disobedience toward God and His Word (see Job 2:7; Deuteronomy 28; John 10:10; Luke 13:16).

The word redemption in its basic use has to do with deliverance of persons or properties that have been sold for debt. It indicates some intervention or substitution that effects the release from an undesirable condition and has a foundation theologically in understanding the doctrine of healing.

The word destruction expresses an idea of complete annihilation. The enemy has sought to corrupt us, spoil us, ruin us, or mar us. The enemy seeks to mar anything good, anything that can be corrupted or spoiled. "The thief comes to steal, kill and destroy," it says in John 10:10.

NOTES

1. Dr. C. Peter Wagner, *How to Have a Healing Ministry in Any Church*.

Chapter 16

CHRIST THE HEALER: THEN AND NOW

*T*hroughout the New Testament, we can see the consistent affirmation of the prophetic role of Jesus Christ as not just our savior, but our healer.

Isaiah 53 is probably one of the greatest Old Testament prophecies concerning the coming Messiah. Verse 5 of this chapter states: "But He was wounded for our transgressions, he was bruised for our iniquities; the chastisement for our peace was upon Him, and by His stripes we are healed." Isaiah 53 refers to the healing ministry of the Lord Jesus Christ. It says that the Messiah will come with the power to do signs and wonders, smiting the curse of sickness upon the human body, which will result in wholeness. That was part of the message of the Lord Jesus Christ.

Matthew 8:17 quotes from Isaiah: "That it might be fulfilled which was spoken by Isaiah the prophet, saying, 'He Himself took our infirmities and bore our sicknesses.' " This is one example of the New Testament establishing and confirming the Old Testament's prophecy of Christ being not only the Messiah who would save people from sin, but also the Messiah who would heal people from sickness (also see Mark 2:1-12; John 5:35-42; Matthew 20:29-34).

Another passage in the book of Isaiah gives us another beautiful messianic prophecy concerning the role of Christ as our healer:

" 'The Spirit of the Lord God is upon Me, because the Lord has anointed Me to preach good tidings to the poor; he has sent Me to heal the brokenhearted, to proclaim liberty to the captives, and the opening of the prison to those who are bound; to proclaim the acceptable year of the Lord, and the day of vengeance of our God; to comfort all who mourn, to console those who mourn in Zion, to give them beauty for ashes, the oil of joy for mourning, the garment of praise for the spirit of heaviness; that they may be called trees of right-eousness, the planting of the Lord, that He may be glorified.' And they shall rebuild the old ruins, they shall raise up the former desolations, and they shall repair the ruined cities, the desolations of many generations" (Isaiah 61:1-6).

This Scripture is fulfilled and quoted by the Lord Jesus Christ:

"So He came to Nazareth, where He had been brought up. And as His custom was, He went into the synagogue on the Sabbath day, and stood up to read. And He was handed the book of the prophet Isaiah. And when He had opened the book, He found the place where it was written: 'The Spirit of the Lord is upon Me, because He has anointed Me to preach the gospel to the poor; he has sent Me to heal the brokenhearted, to proclaim liberty to the captives and recovery of sight to the blind, to set at liberty those who are oppressed; to proclaim the acceptable year of the Lord' " (Luke 4:16-19).

The atonement of Christ lays the foundation equally for deliverance from sin and for deliverance from disease. Complete provision has been made for both. As we see in Luke's eight-fold description of Christ's ministry, healing and deliverance rank first mention:

ℰight-fold Description of CHRIST'S MINISTRY

1. To heal the broken-hearted.
2. To deliver the captives.
3. To heal the blind.
4. To set free the blind.
5. To set free the bruised.
6. To comfort the mourning.
7. To give beauty for ashes.
8. To give the garment of praise for the spirit of heaviness.

In Matthew 8:1-17, we read the accounts of the healing power of Christ as he heals the leper, the centurion's servant, Peter's mother-in-law, and the multitudes. Matthew 8:17 records the reason for these healings: "that it might be fulfilled which was spoken by Isaiah the prophet saying, 'He Himself took our infirmities and bore our sickness.' " Matthew 9:35 says, "Christ in His preaching of the Gospel, healing every sickness and every manner of disease." In Matthew 10:1 it says, "He gave them power to heal all manner of sickness and all manner of diseases." Jesus, at times, rebuked the spirit of infirmity or cast out demons (see Matthew 12:22; Mark 9:22-24, 5:1-20).

SALVATION: THE FOUNDATION FOR HEALING

The basis for all belief in divine healing is that God is supernatural. God, who created humans, knows us in every way and, by His power, may do all that is necessary to restore us to wholeness, and to redeem us to Himself (see Luke 1:37; Jeremiah 32:17; Acts 26:8). The Bible declares that Christ came that He might redeem all men from the curse and the bondage of sin. Christ's redemptive work upon the cross is available to all who believe and extend their hearts toward Him in faith.

> "The basis for all belief in divine healing is that God is supernatural."

The word salvation is the Greek word *sozo*, which means to save, deliver, or protect. Salvation is also defined in the Greek to mean to heal, to preserve, or to make whole. The word *sozo* is translated in Matthew 9:21, "to be made whole." In Luke 8:36, it says, "all those who are possessed of devils were healed." In Acts 7:25, it is translated, "by His hand would deliver them." In Acts 27:34 it says, "For this is for your health."

We can see in all these Scriptures that the word *sozo* is translated as wholeness, healing, deliverance, and health. So in its fullest work, salvation is to be understood as not only healing the soul from sin, but also the availability of God's power to heal the body from sickness.

CHRIST HEALED ALL DISEASES

Jesus ministered healing to those with blindness, deafness, dropsy, dumbness, fevers, hemorrhages, hunched backs, epilepsy, lameness, leprosy, lunacy, and palsy. He healed the maimed, the terminally ill, and those with withered arms. He restored deaf ears.

The Lord Jesus Christ ministered healing through a number of different ways:

- He laid hands upon people and prayed for them, calling upon the power of His Father to heal the sick (Mark 5:23, 6:5, 8:3; Luke 4:14, 13:13).

- He spoke the word of faith and the word of healing. Sometimes He spoke the word in the sick people's presence, other times in their absence, sending it to them by the Spirit of God (Luke 4:32, 36, 7:7).

- He rebuked infirmities and diseases and the devil, thus bringing in a supernatural healing (Matthew 17:18; Mark 1:25, 9:25; Luke 4:35, 9:42).

- People were healed through touching Jesus or His clothing, as the woman who had the sickness for so many was healed by touching hem of His garment (Matthew 9:21, 14:36; Mark 5:28, 6:56, 8:22).

- He said many times "thy faith had made thee whole" (Matthew 9:9, 22, 29; Mark 2:5, 10:32; Luke 5:20, 8:48, 18:42).

We see different ways that the Lord ministered this beautiful gift of healing as He removed sickness from the bodies of those who were tormented. The Scripture also says that He healed the people for a number of reasons.

First of all, Matthew 14:14 says He healed people to show compassion to them. Matthew 8:16-17 tells us that He healed people to fulfill prophecy. John 5:36 says He healed people to prove God had sent Him. In 1 John 3:8 we see that He healed people to destroy the works of the devil.

HEALING IS FOR THE WHOLE PERSON

Humans are born into sin. Therefore, we are born with a disease. Not just a disease of our bodies, but a disease of our understanding, our wills, our affections, and our minds. Jesus came to heal the whole of this disease.

> **"The Holy Spirit will allow light, life, and healing to come into our understanding..."**

Disease of Incapable Understanding

Christ came to heal us from the disease of incapable understanding. It says in 1 Corinthians 2:11-15: "Our natural understanding is totally incapable of comprehending spiritual things." The Holy Spirit will allow light, life, and healing to come into our understanding so that we can see and understand the secret things of God.

Disease of the Will

Jesus also came to heal the disease of the will. Isaiah 53:6 simply explains that "Our wills are naturally stubborn." We are inclined to turn to that which is opposed to God, yet through the blood of Christ and through the Holy Spirit, our wills are healed. Then, we are able to have a will that is obedient to the Holy Spirit and one that is bent toward doing the will of God instead of our own selfish wills.

Disease of the Affections

Christ came to heal the disease of our affections. Colossians 3:2-3: "The affections of the heart can be alienated." God, through the Holy Spirit, communicates an impulse to the soul whereby the poisonous influences are destroyed and our affections are restored to God.

Disease of the Mind

Romans 8:6 tells us that Christ came also to heal the disease of our minds. Our minds are bent, bogged down, and bombarded until they are sick. Our minds need the healing of the Holy Spirit.

Disease of the Body

Christ also came to heal the disease in our bodies. Isaiah 53 states, "By His stripes we are healed." Everything can be taken to God in prayer so that the healing power of Jesus is released in our bodies. We can believe God for healing right now.

HEALING IS FOR TODAY

"I am the Lord, I change not!" (Malachi 3:6). God always was the healer. He is the healer still and will ever remain the healer (see Mark 16:16-18; Luke 9:1-2; 1 Corinthians 12:8-12; Isaiah 35:4-6).

Hebrews 13:8 states: "Jesus Christ is the same yesterday, today, and forever." This is a very important verse when considering the theology of healing.

Healing has not changed since the beginning of time, when God moved upon the lives of people to heal their bodies, souls, and spirits. We can see this personified in the life and the ministry of the Lord Jesus Christ as He touched many people with the power of healing.

The Sadducees did not accept Christ because they were the modernists—the liberals—of that day. They did not believe in angels, in spirits, in the resurrection, or in any supernatural manifestations. Therefore, the Sadducees were passed by. When the supernatural took place, they were not involved.

So it is today. We have our modern-day Sadducees who do not believe in the supernatural, who preach against the power of the Holy Spirit. We also have modern-day Pharisees. In the New Testament, the Pharisees were those who went by the letter of the Law and the letter of the Old Testament, yet they missed the power and spirit of the new covenant. The modern-day Pharisees are the fundamentalists who believe that miracles, the appearance of angels, and resurrections took place in Moses' day, but that these things are not for our age. They believe that God worked in opening the Red Sea and healing people in the Old Testament, but that He does not work that way anymore.

Christ has come to heal, not just yesterday, but today and forever. There are many promises of healing in the Word of God that we must preach, teach, and believe because the Bible states it.

"God is not a man, that he should lie; neither the son of man, that he should repent: hath he said, and shall he not do it? Or hath he spoken, and shall he not make it good?" (Numbers 23:19).

"For ever, O Lord, thy word is settled in heaven" (Psalm 119:89).

"Then said the Lord unto me, Thou hast well seen: for I will hasten my word to perform it" (Jeremiah 1:12).

"Christ hath redeemed us from the curse of the law, being made a curse for us: for it is written, Cursed is every one that hangeth on a tree" (Galatians 3:13).

We need to place our faith in the Word of God and rely on the promises concerning the healing that Christ made available to us through His atonement.

> "We should believe for the signs that Jesus talked about, to follow the church today."

"Ah Lord God! Behold, thou hast made the heaven and the earth by thy great power and stretched out arm, and there is nothing too hard for thee" (Jeremiah 32:17).

"These signs shall follow them that believe" (Mark 16:17).

We should believe for the signs that Jesus talked about to follow the church today. Our theology of healing is based fully on the patterns that we see in Scripture. It should be built upon the solid foundation of the biblical premise for healing and upon an attitude of faith that we nurture in the community of the redeemed. We must have faith in the healing power of God in our day.

F.F. Bosworth, a healing evangelist in the '40s and '50s, said, "Do not doubt God. If you must doubt something, doubt your doubts, because they are unreliable, but never doubt God or His Word." D.L. Moody echoed this sentiment when he said, "Is there any reason why you should not have faith in God? God has never broken one of His promises. I defy any infidel or any unbeliever to place his finger on a single promise God has ever made and failed to fulfill. The devil is the liar. He always lies, he never tells the truth about the Word of God."

> **"Disease and sickness are not from God. We must renounce and confess our trust in God and His Word."**

STEPS TO RECEIVING HEALING

We Must Believe that Healing is Ours

Healing is part of the atonement that God has worked for our lives. God has already provided healing for us all, if we put our faith in the atonement (see 1 Peter 2:24; Isaiah 53:1-3; Matthew 8:17; Psalm 103:2).

We Must Have Faith

Disease and sickness are not from God. We must renounce them and confess our trust in God and His Word. Our faith is in God's Word, not in our own reasoning, intellect, or experience. We must have faith in the never-changing Christ and the never-changing Word of God (see Matthew 9:29; James 1:6; Mark 6:1-6).

We are to Ask for the Anointing With Oil

This is to be administered by the elders in the local church. James 5:14 says: "If any are sick among you, ask for the anointing with oil." Many times, sick people never ask for healing. They never ask for prayer or for the anointing oil. We must ask so that we might receive.

We Need to Lay Hands on the Sick

We must obey the Scripture when it says to lay hands on the sick. Mark 6:18 says to "lay hands on the sick and they shall recover." Luke 13:13 says, "Jesus laid His hands on her and she was healed." Acts 28:8 says, "Paul laid his hands on him and healed him." We need to believe that the laying on of hands will result in God working with us. We need to do this even if we are sick ourselves or if those who are sick do not believe.

LOOKING TO JESUS

In Numbers 21:8, we read the story of Moses lifting up the serpent on a pole so that all who would look at it would be healed. Jesus quoted this Scripture in John 3:14 where He says, "As Moses lifted up the serpent in the wilderness, so the Son of Man shall be lifted up." Here we see the Christ as both Savior and Healer.

Looking steadfastly to Christ is not looking to lying vanities. Looking means to be occupied and influenced by what we are looking at. It is the equivalent of Abraham refusing to consider his own body and waxing strong in faith and looking into the promises of God.

Looking at or being occupied and influenced by our feelings or symptoms is the opposite of what God requires. Looking means we give attention to the Word of God and His provision. That means we live with expectation that God, being a mighty God, can do mighty works in our bodies and in our circumstances. Looking means a steadfast fixation. This is not a glance, but a faith staring that allows us to begin to grow in faith so that God can do unto us what He has already done in the cross.

The Bible is trustworthy. God honors certain principles and acknowledges people for their confessions of faith and their ability to respond to His spirit. Faith and believing for healing can be hard at times, but God will work mightily if we will pray mightily.

PART 5

HINDRANCES OF REVIVAL

Chapter 17

ATTITUDES THAT QUENCH REVIVAL

*A*s we discussed earlier, we in the body of Christ must test everything that occurs in revival to make certain that it is of the Holy Spirit. But there is another responsibility we have during times of revival. It is to make certain that we do not do anything that will quench the Holy Spirit.

In 1 Thessalonians 5:19-21, the apostle Paul exhorted the church in Thessalonica to do the things that would allow a continuance of the moving of the Holy Spirit: "Quench not the Spirit, despise not prophesying. Prove all things and hold fast that which is good." The Thessalonians were given this teaching because they were a church that experienced revival. First, for the sake of context, we will briefly sketch what a church in revival looks like by viewing the Thessalonians as the example, then we will examine Paul's instructions.

Under Paul's ministry, the church experienced the moving of the Holy Spirit and established a strong foundation for a continuing work of God. There are at least nine characteristics of a church in revival as seen in the Thessalonian church:

1. The church experiences the power proclamation and demonstration of the gospel (1 Thessalonians 1:5-6).

2. The church resists the continuous infiltration of an idolatrous culture (1 Thessalonians 1:9).

3. The church is not shaken by faith's apparent contradictions (1 Thessalonians 3:2-3, 5).

4. The church makes personal holiness a serious objective, especially sexual purity (1 Thessalonians 3:13; 4:1-8).

5. The church encourages true spirituality as seen in a person's work ethic (1 Thessalonians 4:9-12).

6. The church wisely follows proven leadership (1 Thessalonians 5:12-13).

7. The church clearly pursues biblical wholeness for each individual in a defined biblical process (1 Thessalonians 5:23-24).

8. The church establishes doctrine as its foundation, not religious trends, emotional spiritual experiences, or charismatic personalities (2 Thessalonians 1:5-12; 2:10-11).

9. The church guards against spiritual gullibility that creeps in when subjective experiences are exalted above objective truth (2 Thessalonians 2:9-17).

QUENCH NOT THE HOLY SPIRIT

The Holy Spirit was moving in the Thessalonian church and Paul wanted the people in the church to guard against quenching what God was doing in their midst. We must also be careful in our day not to quench, suppress, or extinguish the fire of the Spirit.

What does Paul mean when he says, "Quench not the Spirit" in 1 Thessalonians 5:19? Different translations of this same verse could help clarify what he was saying:

- "Quench not the manifestation of the Spirit." (CON)
- "Do not put out the light of the Spirit." (TCNT)
- "Do not extinguish the Spirit's fire." (BER)
- "Do not stifle the utterance of the Spirit." (KNOX)
- "Do not stifle the inspiration of the Spirit." (NEB)[1]

The word quench in the Greek means to extinguish, quench, suppress, subdue, stifle, snuff out, stamp out, or cause something to dry up (see Matthew 12:20, 25:8; Mark 9:34-48; Ephesians 4:16; Hebrews 11:34). In Scripture, the Holy Spirit has been likened to fire, and fire can be extinguished, stifled, or snuffed out (see Matthew 3:11; Acts 2:3; 2 Timothy 1:6).

QUENCH NOT AND TEST EVERYTHING

Let us deal with the attitudes that could quench revival. First, let us divide the attitudes into two sections and put them into a diagram. This scale will represent the balance between "quench not" and "test everything."

Balanced Response
to Revival

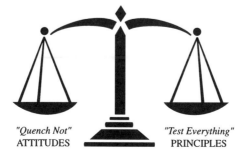

"Quench Not"
ATTITUDES

"Test Everything"
PRINCIPLES

1 Thessalonians 5:19-21

The balance approach to a church in revival is to quench not and yet test everything. "Quench not" represents to us the attitudes we need to continue in revival, having discernment of the attitudes that quench revival. "Test everything" alludes to the attitudes we need to guard the moving of the Holy Spirit and to make sure that we do not go into any kind of extremes.

"Principles, on the other hand, are convictions that conquer us and become our value system for living."

Attitude, in this context, refers to a mind set or willingness. It speaks of our single-heartedness. It speaks of our passions, our emotions, and our desires to be right with our perspectives toward God, His Word, and especially, in this case, towards revival itself.

Principles, on the other hand, are convictions that conquer us and become our value system for living. Principles are our laws, guidelines, guiding forces, or comprehensive and fundamental laws. They are the doctrines we follow. The principles that we have arise out of the unchangeable Word of God and are simply an extension of God's character. For a church to continue in revival, it needs a balance of attitudes and principles.

Our responsibility is to have an attitude toward the things of God, that will neither stifle, nor snuff out the moving of the Holy Spirit. We must be very careful to have an attitude that will not quench the revival atmosphere in our lives or in the congregation.

Now let us take a look at some Spirit-quenching attitudes that are laid out for us in the Word of God. This section deals with the attitudes of the Pharisees and Jesus' response to those attitudes.

SPIRIT-QUENCHING ATTITUDES OF THE PHARISEES

During Jesus' earthly ministry, the Pharisees had attitudes that would quench the moving of the Holy Spirit. The Spirit-quenching attitudes of the Pharisees could be likened to attitudes toward revival today.

As we examine the Pharisees and their attitudes, we can discern what caused them to quench the moving of the Holy Spirit.

The Pharisees were a dedicated group of people who at one time were well respected as leaders in Israel. In fact, the Pharisees were the most respected and influential group in all of Judaism. The word Pharisee itself means "the separated ones" or "God's loyal ones" (see Ezra 6:21, 9:1, 10:11; Nehemiah 9:2, 10:29).

Originating in 135 B.C., the Pharisees were a committed fellowship of men determined to follow, in exact detail everything required by the Mosaic Law. As the most conservative leaders and followers of the Judaistic teachings of their day, the Pharisees believed in the resurrection, in angels, and in Satan. They looked for the Messiah and rejected the idea that force should be used to win freedom.

Essential to pharisaism was to represent the pure community and the true people of God and prepare themselves for the coming of the Messiah by complete adherence to every minute detail of the Law.

In pharisaism, Jesus met Israel as it strove for true faith in obedience to God but had become totally hardened in formalism, thus barring itself from precisely what it was searching to do, to please God and to prepare itself to receive the coming Messiah.

Pharisees multiplied minute precepts and distinctions to such an extent that, upon the pretense of maintaining the Law intact, the whole life of Israel was hemmed in and burdened on every side by instructions so numerous and trifling that the Law was almost, if not wholly, lost sight of.

The Pharisees did anything possible to avoid any contact at all with the heathen lest they themselves should thereby be defiled. They avoided all possible contact with non-Pharisees because the latter was to them included in the description of the unclean Israelite.

The four Gospels tell us that the Pharisees found fault with the free association of Jesus with publicans and sinners as He entered with them into their houses (Mark 2:14-17; Matthew 9:9-13; Luke 5:27-32). This attitude was in keeping with the pharisaism I am describing.

According to the Talmud, the Pharisees' commentary on Scripture, there were seven kinds of Pharisees.

- The Shechemite Pharisee who simply keeps the Law for what he can profit from it, just as Shechem submitted to circumcision to obtain Dinah (Genesis 34:8-19).
- The Tumbling Pharisee who, to appear humble, always hangs down his head.
- The Bleeding Pharisee who, in order not to see a woman, walks with his eyes closed and thus often meets with wounds.
- The Mortar Pharisee who wears a mortar-shaped cap to cover his eyes in order that he might not see any impurities and indecencies.
- The What-Am-I-To-Do-Yet Pharisee who, not knowing much about the Law, as soon as he had

done one thing, asked "What is my duty now and I will do it?" (Mark 10:17-22).

- The Pharisee From Fear who keeps the Law because he is afraid of future judgment.
- The Pharisee From Love who obeys the Lord because he loves him with all his heart.

SIGNS OF PHARISAIC ATTITUDES

Every group of followers of Christ—every movement, any denomination, any organization—has the potential of developing pharisaic attitudes. When life in the Spirit and the power of God dies out, and function becomes a ritual, pharisaism will most certainly arise.

Obviously, it is our responsibility to not allow a spirit of pharisaism to surface in our hearts or in our congregations. Nevertheless, this spirit can creep in slowly and overtake our hearts and attitudes, causing us to become so hemmed in and burdened by the traditions of our own ways that we lose all sight of pleasing God and doing those things that are different than what we are used to.

"Every group of followers of Christ has the potential of developing pharisaic attitudes."

What are some of the signs of growing pharisaic attitudes? How can we discern these attitudes in our personal lives and in the lives of those we might be responsible for?

The Lord Jesus Christ speaks to and about the Pharisees continually in the Gospels. One chapter that stands out as the pilot Scripture for studying the Pharisees is Matthew 23, where we have the seven woes given by the Lord Jesus Christ. In this chapter, He warns the people and His disciples not to imitate the conduct of these leaders, because in several respects they failed to practice what they preached.

This chapter falls into three categories: Verses 3-12 is a description of the sins of the Pharisees; verses 13-36 lists the seven woes pronounced upon the them; and verses 37-39 is Christ's lamenting prayer over Jerusalem.

In addition to Matthew 23, I will also be citing other Scriptures that address pharisaic attitudes that we should watch for in ourselves.

Sign One: Resistance to Anything New

"But woe to you, scribes and Pharisees, hypocrites! For you shut up the kingdom of heaven against men; for you neither go in yourselves, nor do you allow those who are entering to go in . . ." (Matthew 23:13).

The Pharisees expected that Judaism would develop and flower along the lines they themselves had already charted, that the Messiah would be a "Super Pharisee" who would resolve all disputes by brilliant interpretations of the Talmud.

The Pharisees had a resistant attitude that labeled others as heretics, an attitude that led the way to resistance to all that Christ taught, and kept people from discovering the great truth and freedom that He brought. They opposed Christ in their teaching by proclaiming the doctrine of work-righteousness. Their many rules and regulations were directly contrary to Christ's teachings of grace and freedom in Him. The Bible says in Luke 11:52 that by such teaching the Pharisees took away the key of knowledge (also see Hosea 4:6).

The attitude of resistance to anything that is new or different to us is a very dangerous one. It not only hinders individuals from taking part in revival, but it also hinders those who might otherwise have enjoyed the moving of the Holy Spirit, but are trapped with the same attitude.

Sign Two: Negative Power or Influence on People's Lives

"Woe to you, scribes and Pharisees, hypocrites! For you travel land and sea to win one proselyte, and when he is won, you make him twice as much a son of hell as yourselves" (Matthew 23:15).

On the positive side, the Jews were marked by missionary activity that was carried out against the pagan idolatry and immorality of the day. They proselytized, both by means of the open synagogue with its translation of the Hebrew Old Testament into Greek and by the very life and habits of the devout Israelites. The Gentiles had been greatly blessed by the Jews' songs and testimonies. Many of them turned away from their former wicked practices and superstitions and had begun to attend the synagogues.

This Scripture describes the activities of the devout Jews. They would go over land and sea to make one single proselyte. They did not lack in fervor or focus, but lacked in the quality of disciples they produced. Their disciples would become just like them, but worse.

The proselytes did not accept the Jewish religion "hook, line and sinker." Some were called "worshipers," simply because they became proselytes who now worshipped the living God. They had given up their heathen practices and had become sufficiently sympathetic toward the religion of the Jews, and they probably would attend the synagogue meetings.

Other proselytes proceeded much further in changing from paganism to the religion of the Jews. Although it was impossible for them to become Jews by race, they became Jewish in religion and often more Jewish than the Jews themselves. In fact, some changed their ways to such an extent that—by means of baptism and the bringing of the sacrifice and, in the case of men, by being circumcised, and by promising to submit to all the commandments, including all the rabbinical regulations— they were accepted into the Jewish community as proselytes of righteousness, and called new men and new women. At times, they were even given new names.

> "Discipling people into hypocrisy, legalism, wrong focus, criticism, a judgmental attitude, or exclusiveness are all signs of having negative influence on people's lives."

It was not the purpose of the Pharisees merely to change a Gentile into a Jew, so he might become a full-fledged legalistic, ritualistic, hair-splitting Pharisee filled with fanatical zeal for his new salvation-by-works religion. Soon this convert would even out-Pharisee the Pharisee in bigotry. The new converts frequently outdid themselves in becoming fanatically devoted to the new faith. This was what Jesus was referring to when He said they would make the Pharisees' converts twice the child of hell as they were. These were very strong words. A "son of hell" is a typically Hebrew way of describing a person belonging to, worthy of, and bound for hell.

When Jesus saw in the Pharisees the annulment of God's sovereignty and the enthronement of a man-made righteousness, He, as the obedient servant of God, could only speak in truthful assessment of what they were doing to themselves and their converts among the Gentiles.

Discipling people into hypocrisy, legalism, wrong focus, criticism, a judgmental attitude, or exclusiveness are all signs of having negative influence on people's lives. We must make certain in our time of revival that we concentrate on bringing people into proper focus, and that is God's grace and mercy that is shown through the works of Christ.

Sign Three: Narrow and Rigid Formalism

"Woe to you, blind guides, who say, 'Whoever swears by the temple, it is nothing; but whoever swears by the gold of the temple, he is obliged to perform it.' Fools and blind! For which is greater, the gold or the temple that sanctifies the gold? And, 'Whoever swears by the altar, it is nothing; but whoever swears by the gift that is on it, he is obliged to perform it.' Fools and blind! For which is greater, the gift or the altar that sanctifies the gift? Therefore he who swears by the altar, swears by it and by all things on it. He who swears by the temple, swears by it and by Him who dwells in it. And he who swears by heaven, swears by the throne of God and by Him who sits on it" (Matthew 23:16-22).

The Pharisees' hair-splitting distinctions as to which oaths were binding and which were not, perverted the understanding of people's relationship to God as creator and governor of the universe. This Scripture could refer to the rabbis who fought against the abuses of vows among the unlearned mass-es. This is doubtless, but the way they fought them was by differentiating between what was binding and what was not. In that sense, they wittingly or unwittingly encouraged evasive vows and, therefore, lying. Jesus cut through these complexities by insisting that people must simply tell the truth.

In their narrowness, the Pharisees had added to the Law and changed much of people's understanding of the Law. They determined that the Law had 613 commandments, 248 positive and 365 negative. They developed an interpretation of the Law, adding thirty-nine acts that were prohibited on the Sabbath day alone. They had thirty-one customs and traditions to be strictly obeyed at all times, and getting around these was very difficult and complex.

> "During this time of revival, it is important that we not be like Pharisees by becoming so narrow and formal that we lose sight of God's incredible grace and mercy."

The Pharisees' focus on the fulfillment of the Law became a fixation, and they became more narrow as time progressed. The Pharisees began to fence in the truth and demand things that God never demanded. They built clear, rigid laws for all to follow that were simply human-ordained and not God-ordained. They became so intensely narrow and rigid in their formalism that, to them, fulfillment of the Law was more important than loving God or even knowing God.

During this time of revival, it is important that we not be like the Pharisees by becoming so narrow and formal that we lose sight of God's incredible grace and mercy. God has given us His written Word that we may know Him and His ways. We must make sure we never inadvertently add to what He has already told us.

Sign Four: A Focus on Non-essentials

"Woe to you, scribes and Pharisees, hypocrites! For you pay tithe of mint and anise and cumin, and have neglected the weightier matters of the law: justice and mercy and faith. These you ought to have done, without leaving the others undone. Blind guides, who strain out a gnat and swallow a camel!" (Matthew 23:23-24).

The Pharisees' lack of understanding of God's will was exemplified in their caring about the trivia of ritual practices while minimizing the great moral precepts that were meant to be practical and practiced, such as mercy and faith.

No doubt, the Pharisees scrupulously observed the tithes and ordinances of Leviticus 27:30-33 and Deuteronomy 14:22-29. In fact, as was usual with them, they overdid it by giving the Lord the tenth portion of the small, aromatic herbs that they grew in their gardens and by requiring their followers to do likewise. This would be like us tithing upon the salt and pepper on our tables.

The Pharisees required that the sweet-smelling mint, the dill, and the small seeds of cumin—all used to flavor food—be tithed upon, even though nothing was mentioned in the Law concerning tithing upon these flavorings and spices. Yet the Pharisees again went beyond the Law by adding more strict rules and regulations that did not pertain to righteousness or to fulfilling the moral law of God.

The Pharisees were into tithing, which is a great mark of maturity and loyalty to God. But to take it and extend it beyond its intended truth was to pervert the truth. They would not even eat at someone's home if it could not be proven that the person had tithed upon all the food in the house. They began a reproach to hospitality.

The Pharisees stressed human regulations at the expense of divine ordinances. It is upon this point that all the emphasis is placed here in these two verses. Even though they could get people to tithe on mint, dill, and cumin, they themselves were not encouraging people to be involved with the weightier matters of the Law, such as justice, mercy, and faithfulness.

The Scribes and Pharisees always illegitimately overstretched the Law. Was that not exactly what they did

"...we too can become hung up with things that are really non-essentials."

with respect to fasting, hand-rinsing, and Sabbath day observance, by adding many other precepts to the Law?

Micah 6:8 states "He has shown you, O man, what is good and what does Jehovah require of you but to do justly and to love mercy and to walk humbly with your God?" So interpreted, we see that the combination of justice and mercy means the exercise of fairness and helpfulness with help to our neighbors. This was exactly opposite to the attitude that the Pharisees had to the common people.

In our time, we too can become hung up with things that are really non-essentials. Like the Pharisees of Jesus' time, we can see these things as signs of spirituality or essential parts of fulfilling the righteousness of God.

We must be on guard that we do not focus on things that God is not focused on. When we do that, we become fixated on fulfilling traditions and laws that are not God-ordained. In our day and age, things that are not essential are things such as our dress and hairstyles, make-up, earrings, and different kinds of customs and traditions in the church.

Sign Five: Externalizing Spirituality

"Woe to you, scribes and Pharisees, hypocrites! For you cleanse the outside of the cup and dish, but inside they are full of extortion and self-indulgence. Woe to you, scribes and Pharisees, hypocrites! For you are like whitewashed tombs which indeed appear beautiful outwardly, but inside are full of dead men's bones and all uncleanness. Even so you also outwardly appear righteous to men, but inside you are full of hypocrisy and lawlessness" (Matthew 23:25-28).

Here we see that the Pharisees' scrupulous attention to the externals of religion led to ignorance concerning their own inner perversions. Their outward conformity of appearance, which was to be seen of men, often concealed the inner corruption of moral defilement. Within themselves, they remained full of greed and self-indulgence. The Pharisees were so focused on and occupied with external religion instead of the inner person that they did not know how to beautify what was inside them.

To be fixated on external religion is to focus on behavior, prescribing for each person in detail each acceptable and non-acceptable activity. When a church becomes externalized in its spirituality, all it will ask for is what appears to be righteous and spiritual. In that case, there is no real focus on the inner person or the inner heart or on trying to read the fruit of the Spirit. The focus becomes more on works and accomplishments and how much is produced through the person. Consequently, people can hide their failures of

> **"To be fixated on external religion is to focus on behavior."**

character behind works of religion and activities in pro-grams in the church. Externalizing religion usually is some-thing that young people will not do. Therefore the young people will begin to suffer more quickly than others.

Jesus simply calls the Pharisees blind and exhorts them to the priority of faith in God: First, deal with the inside, and the outside will take care of itself. He taught that out-ward conformity to the tradition of the elders—in the case of this Scripture, that was the thorough cleansing of the outside of the cup and dish—will never bring about inner purity of heart. Jesus was telling them that, by the grace of God, the inner person must be purified first. When that has been done, one need not bother about outward ceremonial cleansing. Jesus was telling the Pharisees that their failure to see this was because they were blind, and willfully so.

Jesus' reference to the whitewashed tombs is another illustration of how the Pharisees were inwardly polluted, perverted, and filled with unrighteousness. Passover was just around the corner. This meant that pilgrims would be streaming into Jerusalem from every direction and would see hundreds and thousands of white-washed tombs. The tombs would be powdered with limestone dust to make them look as neat and trim as possible before the Passover. They had to be made conspicuous so that none of the pil-grims would bump into the tombs and inadvertently be defiled. But inside the tombs, there were dead men's bones and all manner of dirt and debris. "Similarly," says Jesus, "You too outwardly seem to be people full of righteousness, but inwardly you are full of hypocrisy and lawlessness."

The hidden character of the Pharisee does not here encourage internalized piety but is in need of total moral renewal in terms of justice, mercy, and faithfulness. The outside, the external, the bits of religious observance easily seen by men, will then take care of itself.

Sign Six: Willful Blindness to Your True Spiritual Condition

"Woe to you, scribes and Pharisees, hypocrites! Because you build the tombs of the prophets and adorn the monuments of the righteous, and say, 'If we had lived in the days of our fathers, we would not have been partakers with them in the blood of the prophets.' Therefore you are witnesses against yourselves that you are sons of those who murdered the prophets. Fill up, then, the measure of your fathers guilt." (Matthew 23:29-32).

> "Pharisees actually thought they were the cutting-edge movement of leadership in their day and age, that they were only ones who were truly dedicated and loyal to the purposes of God..."

Pharisees actually thought they were the cutting-edge movement of leadership in their day and age, that they were the only ones who were truly dedicated and loyal to the purposes of God in fulfilling all the laws that had been set out since Moses to the time they were living in. They thought they were actually protecting the religion against apostasy and paganism. Pharisees had been on the cutting edge of Judaism during the reign of a pagan Greek government. But now, their pride in scholarship and private interpretations had actually perverted their perspective to a point where they were not even aware of their own spiritual condition.

In truth, Pharisees could not be told what the condition of their spirits were. Because of their position, they had canonized their own opinions and attitudes. They felt they could judge anyone and everyone, and all would have to submit to their own spirituality. After all, they were the standard of everything that was truth.

Pharisees had built large, elaborate tombs indicating the places where the prophets had been buried. These tombs were at the same time monuments and memorials to the dead. They had created huge structures to remind people of the faith of the prophets. Yet they themselves were never obedient to the prophets or in the spirit of the prophets. Some people believe that the tomb of the prophet Zechariah, at the base of the Mount of Olives, was being built during Christ's earthly ministry. In that case, then at the very moment Jesus was denouncing the Pharisees for their attitudes toward present truth, they were in the act of building another tomb to another prophet. David's tomb was being kept in honor is clear from Acts 2:29.

Pharisees once again were fulfilling the letter of the Law as they could see it, and yet they were occupying themselves with the task of honoring dead prophets. At the same time, they were making plans to murder the greatest prophet of all, the Lord Jesus Christ, the Word become flesh. "If we had lived in the days of our fathers," the Pharisees said, "if we had been there, this would have never happened. We would never have been involved with persecuting or slaying the prophets sent to the people of God." But they would not accept the Word and they, in their spiritual condition, would actually become the murderers who would put Christ on the cross through lying and manipulation in order to stop

His teaching and preaching and His power ministry that He used to bring a word of truth to that nation.

Pharisees would not accept their spiritual condition because they had beautiful synagogues, great building programs, beautiful monuments, and tombs that were elaborately decorated. Millions of dollars of that day were probably put into the different synagogues, monuments, tombs, and their religion. The Pharisees could not understand how anyone could see them as being out of touch with God or the with fulfilling of the Word of God. But because they were so externalized and focused on non-essentials themselves, they could not see their own true spiritual condition. In truth, they were not on the cutting edge. They were not even in the game.

Jesus speaks very harsh words to this group of people who could not see their spiritual condition. In verse 33, He says, "You snakes, you offspring of vipers, how are you going to escape being sentenced to hell?" Jesus ends this particular rebuke by saying, "I am sending you prophets and wise men and scribes and yet you are going to fulfill the baseness of your heart in that you will reject the prophets and wise men, reject the ambassadors of God and bring upon yourselves the judgments and condemnation of Jehovah Himself" (also see Luke 11:49; Jeremiah 7:25-29; John 3:7).

"God brings revival time to bring to our attention our true spiritual conditions."

God brings revival time to bring to our attention our true spiritual conditions. We must not be like the Pharisees and concentrate on what is on the outside while ignoring what needs to change on the inside.

Sign Seven: Spiritual Emptiness

"See! Your house is left to you desolate; for I say to you, you shall see Me no more till you say, 'Blessed is He who comes in the name of the Lord!' " (Matthew 23:38-40).

In Matthew 24:1, we read that Jesus left the temple and was walking away when the disciples approached to call His attention to the buildings of the temple. He answered them, "Do you see all this? I solemnly assure you there shall not be left here one stone upon another that shall not be thrown down."

The Lord Jesus Christ, who was the fullness of the glory of God, the fullness of grace and truth, is leaving the temple. And once His glory leaves the temple, there is no purpose for it.

When a river leaves the river bed, there is no longer any purpose for the riverbed. And once a fire leaves the fireplace, there is no longer any purpose for the fireplace. Likewise, Jesus is now leaving them with a dead temple, a dead religion, and an empty house.

Matthew's inclusion of this lament shows that Jesus' prophecy concerning the temple was not given in a spirit of vindictiveness. His lament over Jerusalem frames the laments of woe and love. He, of course, transfers the rejection of the prophets to Himself. He weeps over Jerusalem. He says He would have gathered them like a hen gathers her chicks under her wings. He no doubt was recalling Isaiah 31:5 where Yahweh proposed to overshadow Jerusalem to protect her. "But you were not willing" is the sad statement of judgment given at the very time that Jesus was leaving the temple. This is very close to the same picture that Ezekiel gives us of the glory departing from the temple in Ezekiel 11.

A Pharisee is one who restricts spiritual flow and spiritual experiences until religion becomes a purely intellectual and theological exercise. The Pharisee does not accept or recognize spiritual emptiness, but it becomes reality. It becomes fact.

We must be careful that we do not become spiritually empty, even as we move into times of revival. We must make sure that we are filled with the fullness of Christ's glory, with the true empowerment of His Holy Spirit. God is willing, and we must respond to Him.

Sign Eight: Lip Service Without Heart Service

"These people draw near to Me with their mouth, and honor Me with their lips, but their heart is far from Me. And in vain they worship Me, teaching as doctrines the commandments of men" (Matthew 15:8-9).

"A Pharisee is one who restricts spiritual flow and spiritual experiences until religion becomes a purely intellectual and theological exercise."

The Pharisees continually honored God with their mouths, as is clear from passages such as Matthew 6:5 and Luke 18:11. Yet their hearts were corrupt and far removed from the One they were praising with their lips.

The Pharisees appeared to be something other than what they really were. They were actually enemies of the cross and of the message of God, yet they knew what to say. The Pharisees had learned how to live out their religion so people would think they were really fulfilling it in their hearts. But their worship was vain and futile, neither honoring God nor benefiting themselves or others in any way. It was only lip service.

When our hearts are estranged from God's Word, they become hardened and filled with mere human traditions. Revival time is an opportunity for us to make sure that our hearts remain near God and His Word. We must make sure that we fill our hearts with His presence.

Sign Nine: Hardness Toward People's Problems

"Then He said to them in His teaching, 'Beware of the scribes, who desire to go around in long robes, love greetings in the marketplaces, the best seats in the synagogues, and the best places at feasts, who devour widows' houses, and for a pretense make long prayers. These will receive greater condemnation' " (Mark 12:38-40).

This same denunciation of the Pharisees can be paralleled in other Scriptures, such as Matthew 23:6-7 and Luke 20:45-47. Jesus gives this harsh profile of the Pharisee who is more concerned with appearances than with God's people.

Obviously, Jesus was not saying that all Pharisees were this way. But He had seen enough in the religion to know that this was a prominent characteristic in some Pharisees. They were proud, selfish, insincere, and untrustworthy. Jesus exhorted people to be on their guard against them so they would not be influenced or come under their condemnation.

Jesus said these men relished parading about in long, flowing robes, putting on airs as they walked around like kings or priests about to perform official functions. They were so formal in their responses in the marketplace that scarcely a friendly word could be spoken to them or about them without them returning a formal salutation. The Pharisee was always looking not for a token of friendliness, but for a demonstration of respect and a public recognition of his prominence.

The Pharisees had no heart for people. Christ came to die for people, to minister to those who were hurting and needed healing of spirit, soul, and body. The Pharisees could not be bothered with religion that could be so involved with people, that they did not have time to fulfill their laws or to walk around saying formalities, thus demanding admiration and recognition.

The Pharisees loved having the chief seats in the synagogue. These were the seats in front of the raised platform on which stood the prayer leader and the reader of the Scripture. It was considered the best seat to be near the person leading or reading the prayer, and it also faced the congregation, thus giving the Pharisee the ability to see everybody. Being ushered to such a seat was regarded as a mark of honor. The Pharisee loved sitting in these seats, ones that everyone would recognize and seats where he would have a prominent place to speak words that would require respect. At the banquet, he would also seek the best seat. This seat was usually next to someone who was rich or in a position of higher authority, politically or religiously. Yet the Pharisee would tell the poor man to stand or to sit on the floor near someone's footstool.

The Pharisees were professionals. They had learned all the rules of the book and the rules of the game. They knew how to get what they wanted without being flatly denounced as being perverted in their motives or in their inward men.

Yet Jesus, being the Son of God, pronounced exactly what He saw. He pronounced them as being dead professionals, men who had no heart for people or for the purposes of God. Their only heart was for authority that they could use or position they could somehow obtain.

> ## "The Pharisees were professionals. They had learned all the rules of the book and the rules of the game."

We must be on guard for the pharisaic attitude that makes us care more for how we are perceived by others than for the people who are around us. We must be careful that we are not caught up with our position in our churches, or with the way we dress, talk, sit, or walk, or with how people treat us.

Revival time is a call to servanthood, a call to minister to the sick, the weak, the poor, and the lost. It is a time for us to move in ministry to what God cares about most: His people.

Sign Ten: Exclusiveness

"As Jesus passed on from there, He saw a man named Matthew sitting at the tax office. And He said to him, 'Follow Me.' So he arose and followed Him. Now it happened, as Jesus sat at the table in the house, that behold, many tax collectors and sinners came and sat down with Him and His disciples. And when the Pharisees saw it, they said to His disciples, 'Why does your Teacher eat with tax collectors and sinners?' When Jesus heard that, He said to them, 'Those who are well have no need of a physician, but those who are sick. But go and learn what this means: "I desire mercy and not sacrifice." For I did not come to call the righteous, but sinners, to repentance' " (Matthew 9:10-13). (Also see Mark 2:16; Luke 5:30.)

Exclusiveness is a terrible sin that keeps people in their own circles without ever reaching out. The Pharisees had this attitude to the extreme, as they criticized Jesus for doing what He came to do: reach out to sinners. By doing this, Jesus short-circuited the Pharisees' Talmudic systems of theology, rabbinical authority, and proper origins and pedigrees.

People who have an attitude of exclusiveness judge others they feel are of a lower class by their own feelings of superiority. They feel shamed or put down if someone of a lesser degree is even around them. Therefore, they can never be a servant. They can never teach someone who they think is in a lower class because they must maintain their status and their exclusive reputation. They only run in crowds of people who look, act and talk like them. They must be of the same financial base, drive a similar car, and live in the same type of home, in order to join in fellowship. They want to prove that they are important.

> "Revival time is a call to servanthood, a call to minister to the sick, the weak, the poor and the lost."

The attitude of exclusiveness also causes people to judge all ministries by their pedigrees. They will classify all other people in ministries according to their own ideas and perspectives, and not on the basis of the Word of God.

Someone with this kind of pharisaic attitude might say, "My denominational theology is perfect. Anything unusual or new cannot be of God unless we initiated it, unless we teach that it is of God, and unless we somehow put our stamp on it." The problem with that is that even if God approved something different or new, someone with this attitude would not even recognize it.

A Pharisee will be very critical and judgmental toward other ministries and toward movements of the Holy Spirit, thus becoming isolated and insulated from any new movement. Rather than discerning good and bad fruit from within a movement of the Holy Spirit, Pharisees will make up their minds about a movement and then seek out evidence from the fringes of the movement to condemn it. They use the extremes, the fanaticism, and the immaturity they see to justify their already bad attitudes. This is a sure way to miss revival in our day.

> "We need to repent of any attitudes of exclusiveness that may creep into our personal lives or church bodies."

We need to repent of any attitudes of exclusiveness that may creep into our personal lives or church bodies. We must be willing and ready to do just as Jesus did: minister to those inside and outside our circles.

REPENTING OF PHARISAISM

As we move into times of revival, it is vital that we individually and corporately repent of any pharisaic attitudes in our midst. We must discern if any of these evils are lurking in us that might cause us to quench the moving of the Holy Spirit.

In His Word, God has given us examples of these attitudes. It is our responsibility to deal with them, to root them out, and dispose of them. Then we will be sure not to put out the fire of God's Spirit.

NOTES

1. "CON" is The Epistles of Paul, N.J. Conybeare.
   "TCNT" is the Twentieth Century New Testament.
   "BER" is the Berkeley version of the New Testament.
   "KNOX" is the New Testament translation of
   Monsignor Ronald Knox.
   "NEB" is the New English Bible.

Chapter 18

COMBATTING SPIRITUAL NEGLIGENCE

*I*n the last chapter we saw the apostle Paul's exhortation in 1 Thessalonians 5:19: "Do not quench the Spirit." We have the responsibility to avoid attitudes that quench the moving of God's Spirit, but we also have an obligation to make sure we do not fall into spiritual negligence, which can also cause us to miss the fullness of a Holy Spirit revival.

We do not want to quench in any way the revival that God might want to send us in our day and in the days to come. To quench the Spirit is to neglect the biblical principles that develop spiritual life and hunger within us.

REVIVAL CAN BE DESPISED

In 1 Thessalonians 5:20, the apostle Paul says, "Do not despise prophecies." Prophesying refers to a message inspired by the Spirit and given in a present situation for the awakening and conviction of listeners. Prophesying refers to an openness to the Holy Spirit, to the receiving of the inspired Word of God that strikes a note in the spiritual man to move and be motivated by the Spirit. Prophesying can also be seen as a power and a force that moves and drives the people of God, like wind drives a huge ship. Likewise, we are moved by the Holy Spirit. We are impelled by the Holy Spirit. Yet we are warned by Paul not to despise this move of God.

We must be careful that we do not reject or despise what God Himself is initiating. We must not set something aside as having no real value or importance until we have tested it scripturally with a heart of humility and receptivity.

The New Testament uses the word despise twelve times (see Mark 9:12; Luke 18:9, 23:11; Acts 4:11; Romans 14:3, 10; 1 Corinthians 1:28, 6:4, 16:11; 2 Corinthians 10:10; Galatians 4:4; 1 Thessalonians 5:20). This word in the Greek means to ignore, reject, or become complacent toward something. It denotes an attitude of being unconcerned or of treating something with contempt. The apostle is saying, "Please, do not ignore, despise, or make little of those things that God has established as being important."

"It is possible to despise revival. We can react against it or actually speak against what God is trying to do in our midst."

It is possible to despise revival. We can react against it or actually speak against what God is trying to do in our midst. We have that choice. Why has God chosen to work this way? Would it not be more effective for the work of God to progress quietly and steadily without the excitement and upheaval that is produced in seasons of revival?

God wants us to understand that there are times when He does things outside of our reasoning and comfort zones. We must understand that God knows best how to bring us into a season of revival, and we must never despise the holy movings of God's Spirit.

Revival Counters Spiritual Decline

The Holy Spirit moves on His people with revival to battle spiritual decline and then to create spiritual momentum.

Throughout church history, there has always been the tension between the decline and degeneration, which works against the spiritual health of the God's people, and the moving of the Holy Spirit, which brings spiritual life and momentum.

The revival principle is that of a concentration of force to create momentum. In military terms, concentration of force is where an army concentrates its efforts on one point so that it can break through at that point and create military momentum. In the same way, God desires to create momentum in the life force of the church. He does this by the moving of the Holy Spirit upon the hearts of people so that there will be a spiritual momentum and life created in the midst of God's people.

IDENTIFYING THE SOURCE OF REVIVAL

In 1832, three years before Charles Finney's ministry as a revivalist became prominent, an American Presbyterian minister and writer by the name of Calvin Colton wrote that genuine revivals could be classified into two different types:

1. **The old**, he wrote, which came mysteriously and unexpectedly, directly from the presence of the Lord with overwhelming effect, were, until a few years past, the more ordinary character of revivals.

2. **The new**, he believed, were the same in character and nature, but they had only begun to occur in recent years because previously, people had not learned how, as instru-

ments, to originate and promote revivals.[1]

There are many different ways that revival can happen, but who or what is the source of revival? Who initiates revival? Does God initiate, or do we? Can an outpouring of the Holy Spirit occur only by the sovereignty of God's giving, or can we obtain it by the use of biblical principles, patterns, and application of divine disciplines? There are two extremes that attempt to answer these questions.

The extreme attitude concerning the sovereignty of God says that if God wills to send revival, it will come. Nothing we can do or say will change this. This extreme absolves us of any responsibility to seek revival or to prepare for it. It says that all we have to do is just wait around and see if God will initiate a move of His Spirit. And since it is all God's responsibility to bring revival, if He does not initiate a move, then it is His problem, not ours.

The other extreme says that we can have revival whenever we want it, that basically, God is at our beck and call. We have all the keys and principles, and all we need to do is apply them. But this extreme puts people in control of God's times and seasons. For us to have the ability to initiate a revival spirit any time we so desire does not seem to be scripturally sound. We are not little gods, but servants of the living God.

There is a balance between these two extremes, and God's Word gives us that balance in understanding the area of revival doctrine.

SOVEREIGNTY OF GOD   HUMAN RESPONSIBILITY

On this scale we have two sides. On one side is the sovereignty of God; that is, God initiates and God moves. On the other side we have the responsibility of people, we respond and we obey. This demonstrates the balance of how revival takes place in God's times and seasons. To put it into words, God initiates and we respond. This is spelled out for us in Psalm 110:3, where it says, "Your people shall be willing in the day of Your power; in the beauties of holiness, from the womb of the morning, you have the dew of Your youth."

God is the initiator of revival and we are the responders. God directs His purposes and guides and governs all things after the counsel of His will. He does not let anything get out of hand. Nothing happens without His initiation and power. He carries out His plans continually and consistently (see Isaiah 46:9-11).

> **"God is the initiator of revival and we are the responders. God directs His purposes and guides and governs all things after the counsel of His will."**

When God begins to move by His power, we need to respond with humility and run hard after Him. We need to do our part in humbling ourselves, praying, and preparing our hearts. As a field must be readied for the seed to be received, so we must prepare our hearts for revival. This does not put us in charge, it puts us in response.

THE POTENTIAL OF MISSING VISITATION

"How shall we escape if we neglect so great a salvation, which at the first began to be spoken by the Lord, and was confirmed to us by those who heard Him?" (Hebrews 2:3).

We can miss a Holy Spirit visitation by our own passiveness and by neglecting our responsibilities toward God's visitation. The second and third chapter of Hebrews, which records for us Israel's history, demonstrate the spiritual negligence that led to God's people missing revival in their day. How did Israel miss God's moving in its day? How may we miss God moving in our day?

By Not Hearing God's Spirit Speaking Today

"Therefore, as the Holy Spirit says: 'Today, if you will hear His voice...' " (Hebrews 3:7).

> ## "We can miss a Holy Spirit visitation by our own passiveness."

One spiritual negligence that keeps us from God's visitation is not hearing God's Spirit speaking today.

Arthur Wallis, who has written numerous articles and books on revival, states: "The spirit of revival is the consciousness of man made aware of His presence and His voice."

Revival is the ability to respond to God's voice. The Holy Spirit in us works like a telephone. When the phone rings, we can answer and receive instruction from Him. We must develop our spiritual ears. An undeveloped spirit is the main cause of spiritual deafness and spiritual neglect. We must develop a sensitivity to God's voice. Without that sensitivity, the voice of God will be muffled to us, and we will miss the day of visitation (see Revelation 2:7, 11, 17, 29, 3:6, 13; Isaiah 55:3).

"The Lord God has given Me the tongue of the learned, that I should know how to speak a word in season to him who is weary. He awakens Me morning by morning, He awakens My ear to hear as the learned. The Lord God has opened My ear; and I was not rebellious, nor did I turn away" (Isaiah 50:4-5).

If we are going to respond to revival, we must have an awakened ear every morning. The word open in Isaiah 50:4-5, in the Hebrew, means to loosen that which has bound and hindered, to unstop, to plow a field that is hardened, to break the clods of dirt. The word wakened in the Hebrew means to become alert, watchful, as opposed to both sleep and idleness. For us to enter into a spirit of visitation, we must open our ears and be awakened in our spirits.

We can grow spiritually in Christ, but we can also grow in callousness. We can become so familiar with the holy things of God that we forget how to be sensitive to the Holy Spirit. Of course, there are times when God will initiate a plowing of His people or an opening of their ears. Our responsibility is to respond in these spiritual times where God is digging out our ears so that we can respond more deeply to the visitation of God.

God has spoken to His people in the past. He has appeared in visible form, spoken through dreams and visions, spoken in a still small voice, and spoken with the voice of thunder. God has spoken through kings, priests, prophets, and angels.

God not only spoke in the past, but He is speaking today. He is no longer adding to the written Word, the canonized sixty-six books of the Bible. But through His word and through His Spirit He guides, directs, prompts, teaches, comforts, encourages, and illuminates. God speaks. It is our responsibility to listen and to respond, especially in days of revival (see Genesis 3:8-0, 6:13; Exodus 3:4-10; 1 Samuel 3:1-14,21).

Let us examine the three key words in Hebrews 3:7 that apply to the idea of listening to God's voice during revival seasons: the words today, hear, and voice.

Paul is stating in this verse that the Holy Spirit speaks today and we must hear His voice . . . today. Today emphasizes the present moving in God, hearing the Holy Spirit today. Not just in past days or in previous revivals, but now—today.

> "We must respond now, not tomorrow, not next year. God is sovereign, and His sovereignty is revealed in His timing and in the manner and measure of the Spirit's working..."

In Hebrews 3:7-10, a day denotes a whole forty years, a generation. A generation day does not merely refer to one calendar day, but to the time, whatever its length, in which God would yet speak to Israel by His grace. We use the phrase "Every generation has its day of visitation" sometimes without defining what we mean by a day of visitation. A day of visitation might last forty years or it might last twenty years. This does not speak of a twenty-four hour day, but of a time period in which God calls a generation to respond to Him.

From the beginning of creation to the present, every genuine revival is clearly stamped with the hallmark of divine sovereignty, especially in the time factor. Today becomes God's divine moment, God's divine strategy. Maybe it does not fit our schedule, but it is His day. We must respond now, not tomorrow, not next year. God is sovereign, and His sovereignty is revealed in His timing and in the manner and measure of the Spirit's working as His purposes are being carried out.

"If He withholds the waters, they dry up; if He sends them out, they overwhelm the earth" (Job 12:15).

This Scripture refers to the sovereignty of God and the timing of God in revival. Today is the day of salvation and God's moment for a generation. If we are to move into visitation and revival then we must respect God's moment.

Hebrews 3:7 also talks about whose voice we are listening to: God's. The Spirit speaks expressly in the latter days. We need to hear what the Spirit says distinctly, clearly, and specifically in the day of visitation.

In 1 Timothy 4:1, it says, "Now the Spirit expressly says that in latter times some will depart from the faith, giving heed to deceiving spirits and doctrines of demons." We need to be certain that we are hearing the distinctive voice of the Holy Spirit in the day of visitation.

Matthew 4:4 says, "But He answered and said, 'It is written, "Man shall not live by bread alone, but by every word that proceeds from the mouth of God." ' " There is life in all the words that proceed from His mouth, and a revival movement lives on His words during that season and that day. But there must also be a response to every declaration coming forth from the voice of God.

By Not Maintaining a Soft and Receptive Heart

"Do not harden your hearts as in the rebellion, in the day of trial in the wilderness" (Hebrews 3:8).

"But exhort one another daily, while it is called 'Today,' lest any of you be hardened through the deceitfulness of sin" (Hebrews 3:13).

To be hardened of heart is to literally set your heart against God. To be hardened of heart is to allow the deceitfulness of sin to settle upon your heart and to allow your heart to become closed to spiritual things.

Israel did not maintain a soft and receptive heart, and therefore they missed the day of their visitation. Israel was embittered against God, hard and unyielding, all forty years in the wilderness. Consequently, their day of visitation was turned into a day of rejection.

The same thing can happen to us today. We could miss our day of visitation if we do not maintain a softness of heart. When God, in His grace, allows us to hear His voice, we must make certain that we do not make our hearts stiff like a dried, hard branch that will not bend or yield. It is a serious mistake to think that God will go on offering His grace despite all our rejection and thinking that we may yield when we please.

Hebrews 3:13 states "any of you" can be hardened through the deceitfulness of sin. In the Greek it would read, "Lest someone out of your number." If any person falls into hardness of heart, it can ultimately affect the whole body of Christ. We must guard one another against hardness and exhort one another "while it is called today."

We must break up the hardness of heart in order for the rain of the Holy Spirit to fall upon us and to penetrate deeply into the soil of our souls. Hosea 10:12 says, "Sow for yourselves righteousness; reap in mercy; break up your fallow ground, for it is time to seek the Lord, till He comes and rains righteousness on you."

The fallow ground in this verse refers to the condition of our hearts. Fallow ground is ground that has been plowed before but has become hardened. Fallow ground is land that has yielded fruit in times past, but has become unproductive through lack of cultivation and through lying idle. This verse tells us that when a believer becomes insensitive to the sins that grieve the Holy Spirit and unresponsive to His voice, the ground of the heart becomes hard. It also tells us that we need to prepare the ground of our hearts, to make it fertile again.

But how do we rid ourselves of this hardness of heart? Only the presence of the Holy Spirit can soften a hard heart. Religious atmosphere will not change a hard heart. You can attend church, prayer meetings, seminary, or Bible training and still have a hard heart. You can be religiously deceived, thinking that doing many things and serving in many programs shows the condition of your heart. But doing works will never change your heart. This is why it is so dangerous to have a hard heart, and why the Scripture exhorts us so many times to guard our hearts. Proverbs 4:23 says that out of our hearts flow the issues of life.

> "We must break up the hardness of heart in order for the rain of the Holy Spirit to fall upon us and to penetrate deeply into the soil of our souls."

In Bible times, when land became too hard to plow with a normal plow, they would build or borrow a chisel plow. If the ground was too hard for the normal plow, the chisel plow would most certainly break through. The chisel plow had more prongs, stronger prongs that could dig deeply into the ground and begin to penetrate its hardness.

God, at times, needs to penetrate us with a chisel plow. He needs to plow deeply into the hardness of our hearts so that we will not live in a deceived fashion or in a religious spirit all the days of our Christian lives.

God also sends rain in the form of His Holy Spirit to soften our hearts and prepare them for plowing. Psalm 65:10 speaks about rain showers softening the ground. The rainy season of Canaan usually commences around the end of October with light showers that soften the ground, and then continues with heavy showers that last intermittently for two or three days through November or December.

> "When the rain came in sufficient quantities, he had to begin plowing. He may have had to plow in the face of hail and snow, storm and tempest."

The farmer depended upon the rain to render the rocklike soil suitable for plowing and sowing. When the rain came in sufficient quantities, he had to begin plowing. He may have had to plow in the face of hail and snow, storm and tempest. But plow he must, for if he does not plow and sow with the early rains, he will not reap after the latter rains (see Proverbs 20:4; Ecclesiastes 11:4).

By Not Believing God's Promises

"Beware, brethren, lest there be in any of you an evil heart of unbelief in departing from the living God" (Hebrews 3:12).

"So we see that they could not enter in because of unbelief" (Hebrews 3:19).

"For indeed the gospel was preached to us as well as to them; but the word which they heard did not profit them, not being mixed with faith in those who heard it" (Hebrews 4:2).

"Since therefore it remains that some must enter it, and those to whom it was first preached did not enter because of disobedience" (Hebrews 4:6).

"Let us therefore be diligent to enter that rest, lest anyone fall according to the same example of disobedience" (Hebrews 4:11).

We humans have a tendency to give ourselves over to prejudice, suspicion, and unbelief. But the Bible—the Old Testament and the New Testament—tells us that having these attitudes is sin. Unbelief is the sin that kept Israel from entering into the visitation that God had prepared for them. Unbelief can keep us from entering into revival or visitation in our day.

"Now He did not do many mighty works there because of their unbelief" (Matthew 13:58).

"So Jesus said to them, 'Because of your unbelief; for assuredly, I say to you, if you have faith as a mustard seed, you will say to this mountain, "Move from here to there," and it will move; and nothing will be impossible for you' " (Matthew 17:20).

The Greek word for unbelief *apeitheo*, as referred to in these Scriptures, is not just an absence of faith, but a resistance to faith, a resistance that hinders the Word of God and the word of faith sent by God from taking root in the heart. It is opposition to the divine will. It is a refusal to be persuaded. It is the obstinate, willful refusal to comply with or obey anything (see Mark 3:5, 6:52, 8:17, 16:14).

Religious unbelief is when, even though we believe in Christ, the virgin birth, and redemptive story, we do not believe all the things that God has for us. We need to develop an attitude of faith, a spirit of faith. We need to resist the spirit of unbelief.

"Now faith is the substance of things hoped for, the evidence of things not seen" (Hebrews 1:11).

REMEDIES FOR SPIRITUAL NEGLIGENCE

In order to prepare our hearts to hear the voice of God during our time of visitation, we must commit ourselves to hearing Him, to establishing and maintaining and softness of heart, and to believing Him to fulfill what He has promised. We must repair the damage done by our neglect of our spirits. Here are some things we can do to get started:

A Revised Devotional Life

The first step in repairing the damage done by spiritual negligence is to make prayer and living in the Word of God a habit and a principle in our lives. This is the ground level from which to restore responsiveness to a heart that has been hardened.

"Therefore I remind you to stir up the gift of God which is in you through the laying on of my hands" (2 Timothy 1:6).

"Do not neglect the gift that is in you, which was given to you by prophecy with the laying on of the hands of the eldership" (1 Timothy 4:14).

"And do not grieve the Holy Spirit of God, by whom you were sealed for the day of redemption" (Ephesians 4:30).

"Therefore, laying aside all malice, all guile, hypocrisy, envy, and all evil speaking, as newborn babes, desire the pure milk of the word, that you may grow thereby, if indeed you have tasted that the Lord is gracious" (1 Peter 2:1-3).

We need to rebuild the altar of devotion, an altar of prayer that cultivates a heart of honesty and sincerity.

Spiritual Reading

We can cultivate a new, revised devotional life by spiritual reading, a kind of reading that requires a primary emphasis on the devotional use of Scripture. This kind of Scripture reading is not to build messages, to solve problems, or to aid in arguments. It is reading the Scriptures mainly to spiritually feed and to build up our spiritual lives. The art of devotional reading is less a matter of technique than a matter of attitude of the heart.

In addition to the Bible, we need to choose some classics of faith and devotion from a broad spectrum of God's people. Seek a balance in your reading between modern and ancient writings. Accompany your spiritual reading with the keeping of a journal or some reflective notebook.

But recognize that spiritual reading meets with obstacles that discourage, distract, and dissuade you from persistence in your reading, both of the Word of God and of other good books that nurture your spiritual man. But whatever it takes, begin to repair your altar now, because repairing the altar will give a chance for your heart to be renewed and revived.

Personal Preparation for Renewal and Revival

We cannot just speak about revival of times past or revivals for the church of today. Revival comes to people, to individuals, one heart at a time. We can talk about taking thousands of people for Christ and seeing cities turned in a revival setting, but cities are turned one person at a time. Each of us must prepare individually for revival.

> *"...begin to repair your altar now, because repairing the altar will give a chance for your heart to be renewed and revived."*

"And Joshua said to the people, 'Sanctify yourselves, for tomorrow the Lord will do wonders among you' " (Joshua 3:5).

"Righteousness will go before Him, and shall make His footsteps our pathway" (Psalm 85:13).

Here are some steps we can take to prepare our hearts for renewal and revival:

Personal Purity

Revival means there are seasons when God comes to cleanse us from our sins that have long hindered the blessings that are ours by right. He comes to expose our sins so that we can confess and He can do the work of cleansing and forgiving.

The Scripture is very clear that God desires to commune with us, to visit us in a mighty way. One of the problems that we must take care of is the problem of sin and iniquity in our own lives (see 2 Corinthians 7:9-10; 1 John 1:9).

"Behold, the Lord's hand is not shortened, that it cannot save; nor His ear heavy, that it cannot hear. But your iniquities have separated you from your God; and your sins have hidden His face from you, so that He will not hear" (Isaiah 59:1-2).

Reconciliation and Restitution

There comes a time in every revival season where we must move into the ministry of personal reconciliation and restitution so that we can prepare for a deeper moving of the Holy Spirit.

Jonathan Edwards, who has written volumes on revival, spoke about the revival that took place when he was pastoring his own local church: "Abundance has been lately done at making up differences, confessing faults one to another and making restitution. Probably more within these two years than was done in the last thirty years before."

You may have wronged someone by some deceitful or unkind act. You may be bitter and wounded, or you may be the bitter, wounding person that has spoken negatively to or about others. It may be that you have harshly criticized others, secretly pulling their character to pieces, exaggerating their apparent faults, or presenting them in the worst possible light. It may be that you are refusing to forgive from the heart someone you feel has wronged you. You have a spirit of envy, bitterness, or malice that has dominated your thinking in relation to that person. If so, your responsibility is to make certain you have a clear conscience and a clear heart toward all those you walk with and know.

"Therefore if you bring your gift to the altar, and there remember that your brother has something against you, leave your gift there before the altar, and go your way. First be reconciled to your brother, and then come and offer your gift" (Matthew 5:23-24).

> "You need to learn how to pray with a prevailing prayer spirit."

"For if you forgive men their trespasses, your heavenly Father will also forgive you. But if you do not forgive men their trespasses, neither will your Father forgive your trespasses" (Matthew 6:14-15).

"This being so, I myself always strive to have a conscience without offense toward God and men" (Acts 24:16).

If there are any roots of bitterness or resentment in your life, dig them out, chop the tree down, and get rid of the bad fruit by getting rid of the bad root.

Personal Prayer

The pure heart becomes a reconciled heart, which becomes a praying heart. You need to learn how to pray with a prevailing prayer spirit. You need to learn how to pray your way into full faith, emerging with assurance that your prayer has been accepted and heard so that you become assured of receiving—by firmest anticipation and in advance of the event—the thing for which you have asked. You need to learn how to pray in the Spirit (Jude 20; Ephesians 6:18). You must personally prevail in the spirit of prayer.

"My eyes overflow with rivers of water for the destruction of the daughter of my people. My eyes flow and do not cease, without interruption, till the Lord from heaven looks down and sees" (Lamentations 3:48-50).

"So I sought for a man among them who would make a wall, and stand in the gap before Me on behalf of the land, that I should not destroy it; but I found no one" (Ezekiel 22:30).

"And there is no one who calls on Your name, who stirs himself up to take hold of You; for You have hidden Your face from us, and have consumed us because of our iniquities" (Isaiah 64:7).

Brokenness and Humility

When our hearts are sensitive, responsive, and impressionable to the movement of God, we are on our way to brokenness. Brokenness is not revival, but a vital step toward revival. Brokenness is a matter of personal choice and personal attitude. Brokenness is a matter of hunger for God to do more in us and then more outside of us.

"For thus says the High and Lofty One who inhabits eternity, whose name is Holy: 'I dwell in the high and holy place, with him who has a contrite and humble spirit, to revive the spirit of the humble, and to revive the heart of the contrite ones' " (Isaiah 57:15).

"Better to be of a humble spirit with the lowly, than to divide the spoil with the proud" (Proverbs 16:19).

"But He gives more grace. Therefore He says: 'God resists the proud, but gives grace to the humble' " (James 4:6).

BEING PREPARED FOR REVIVAL

God desires to visit our generation with a day of revival. He is initiating a time of Holy Spirit visitation. Now is the time for us to prepare to hear His voice and prepare ourselves, to hear His voice, to break up the hard ground of our hearts, and to believe His promise of renewal.

NOTES

1. Ian H. Murray, *Revival and Revivalism* (Banner of Truth Publishers), 374-375.

Chapter 19
SPIRITUAL STRUGGLES DURING REVIVAL

*T*he third chapter of Matthew gives us the account of Jesus receiving the fullness of the Holy Spirit upon His perfect human nature. As He was baptized in water, the heavens were opened and He received the coming of the Holy Spirit upon Him. Immediately after that, in Matthew 4:1, is another account: "Then Jesus was led up by the Spirit into the wilderness to be tempted by the devil." In Luke 4:13, the doctor adds another angle to the wilderness testings: "Now when the devil had ended every temptation, he departed from Him until an opportune time."

What does the Bible tell us about how Jesus answered Satan's temptations? "It is written . . ." He answered the devil with the written Word of God. Jesus knew exactly what to do when Satan came at Him like a flood: answer his lies with truth.

We need to take special notice of how Jesus handled temptation. Jesus was and is the God-man, fully God and fully man, and He knew that the devil had no counter-attack for the truth of God's Word. The same principles of speaking the truth of the Word that Jesus used, still work for us today.

REVIVAL STRUGGLES

That Jesus faced temptation immediately after receiving the fullness of the Holy Spirit is a model for our experiences today. New encounters with God are always accompanied by new levels of testings and temptations. We need to expect spiritual battles during times of Holy Spirit visitation. We could call these "revival struggles," and they have been seen in renewals past, and they will be seen in every future visitation.

Revival involves spiritual struggle in which every advance of renewal involves conflict, both with our fallen human natures and with the powers of darkness. If we are going to take part in revival, we must be prepared for a renewed and redoubled effort on the part of Satan to thwart God's visitation.

As we experience the moving of the Holy Spirit upon our hearts, we must keep in mind that periods of renewal are times of great spiritual agitation. And when this agitation comes, all believers must know how to handle the battles with the enemy, with carnal natures, and with bad habits. If all believers are not properly instructed in how to handle these struggles, some might become discouraged during the moving of the Holy Spirit.

> "Revival involves spiritual struggle in which every advance of renewal involves conflict."

Revival spirit penetrates the heart and soul of the believer to provoke change. Change is never easy, and it will never come without some wrestling with the flesh. Revival must be sustained through the discipline of walking in the Spirit and the Word. Revival calls people to a higher level of spiritual sensitivity to sin, self, and culture.

SATAN'S STRATEGIES TO HINDER REVIVAL

During times of revival, the devil will redouble his efforts to thwart what the Holy Spirit wants to do in the lives of God's people. The good news is that the Bible tells us that the enemy was defeated at the cross. If we are aware of his strategies, we will be equipped to hand him his defeat by speaking words of truth.

The Devil May Plant Lies in the Believer's Mind

Satan wants to distort the revival experience. He wants us to reject this work of the Holy Spirit as superficial carnality, excessive emotionalism, or some kind of psychological power of suggestion.

The enemy always works to distort truth, to lie about what God desires to do in us. In John 8, verses 44 and 55, Jesus talks about who Satan is and what his tactics are: "You are of your father the devil, and the desires of your father you want to do. He was a murderer from the beginning, and does not stand in the truth, because there is no truth in him. When he speaks a lie, he speaks from his own resources, for he is a liar and the father of it . . ." "Yet you have not known Him, but I know Him. And if I say, 'I do not know Him,' I shall be a liar like you; but I do know Him and keep His word" (also see Romans 3:4; 1 Timothy 1:10; Titus 1:12; 1 John 2:4, 2:22, 4:20, 5:10).

> **"Satan wants to distort the revival experience."**

The Devil May Set Leaders Against One Another

The enemy tries to thwart revival by causing division among the people of God, particularly in the leadership. This is evidenced in books, articles, and television and radio programs that speak against the moving of the Holy

Spirit. Sometimes this opposition is out of ignorance, other times out of jealousy or out of a matter of control.

Acts 5, verses 35 and 38-39 addresses this issue: "And he said to them: 'Men of Israel, take heed to yourselves what you intend to do regarding these men . . ." "And now I say to you, keep away from these men and let them alone; for if this plan or this work is of men, it will come to nothing; but if it is of God, you cannot overthrow it—lest you even be found to fight against God."

These Scriptures offer some wise counsel to those who may speak too soon concerning a move of the Holy Spirit. We should always be slow to judge a work of God's Spirit, lest we be found fighting against God.

The Devil May Push the Immature Into Overbalance

Overzealousness on the part of some in the body of Christ can quickly runs off into extremes. In most revival movements, it is usually not the extreme actions of leaders that cause most of the trouble, but those of immature converts of the movement.

The Devil May Use Condemnation and Guilt

People compare their experience with others they see or hear about, and this results in discouragement, followed by a withdrawing from the moving of the Holy Spirit.

This is human nature at its best and worst. The Adamic nature in us always leans toward comparing ourselves with other people. But God's Word warns us against doing this in 2 Corinthians 10:12: "For we dare not class ourselves or compare ourselves with those who commend themselves. But they, measuring themselves by themselves, and comparing themselves among themselves, are not wise."

INDIVIDUAL STRUGGLES

Receiving more of God into our whole person is a necessity for us to keep our first love alive and well, and this is part of revival. But revival seasons can be a time of what I call "spiritual moodiness." Revival seasons are times of spiritual highs and lows. Revival seasons usually result in emotions. This does not need to be negative, as God gave us our emotions and has redeemed them. But as people experience emotional blasts, so to speak, as they experience the powerful presence of God, they are also candidates to experience emotional lows.

> **"Especially during times of revival, we need to keep in mind that our relationship to God is not built on emotions, but on truth."**

This is where doctrine becomes the stabilizing factor in seasons of revival. Every believer must understand the doctrine of the atonement and the benefits of the atonement. All the provisions of the atonement—God's forgiveness, His grace and mercy, and His buying us back out of the slave market of sin—arise out of God's awesome grace. We stand in grace, not in works.

Especially during times of revival, we need to keep in mind that our relationship to God is not built on emotions, but on truth. What is that truth? That Christ took my sin to the cross, suffered pain, died, was resurrected on the third day, and ascended into heaven to be seated at the right hand of the Father. This is not emotion, but truth. Whether I feel good, bad, or indifferent toward Christ's work on the cross makes no difference, for it stands sure. My stability in revival times is in my position in Christ. My position in Christ is in my understanding of the Word of God concerning my union with Christ.

We need not struggle with our understanding of what it means to be in union with Christ, which is an understanding of redemption as experienced in our justification with God. All movements must proclaim justification, the awesome work of the cross. All seasons of revival must be carried along with sound doctrine.

"As you have therefore received Christ Jesus the Lord, so walk in Him, rooted and built up in Him and established in the faith, as you have been taught, abounding in it with thanksgiving" (Colossians 2:6-7). (Also see Colossians 2:10-15.)

The Struggle For Personal Holiness

The struggle with our own lack of personal holiness, the sin nature and active sin pattern in our lives, hinders us from moving into a more powerful relationship with Christ and with the Holy Spirit, and must be dealt with personally.

Holiness and the modern-day culture are destined to clash in every way possible. The changes that have taken place in today's value system have been mega-shifts. The humanistic philosophy of our American and world culture have eroded the belief in almost all moral value systems. We now face a new culture, a culture separated from God and His Word.

Barring a sovereign move of God to bring a radical paradigm shift, our cultural and moral conditions are being transformed into the following:

Current Cultural & Moral PARADIGM SHIFTS

- There are no God-given moral laws.
- There are no objective moral laws.
- There are no timeless moral laws.
- There are no laws against laws.
- There are no restraints to pleasures.
- There are no restrictions to individual choices.
- There are no absolutes or principles to live by.

Revival seasons certainly are needed to combat such a degeneration in the moral arena of our culture. The challenge of today's church is to practice holiness, to embrace holiness without becoming legalistic or harsh. Revival seasons usually come to deliver the church from the spirit of worldliness and to provoke the church through a spirit of grace to a godliness and a New Testament type of holiness. Revival spirit equips the church to confront an ungodly nature and an ungodly culture.

"Revival spirit equips the church to confront an ungodly nature and an ungodly culture."

During revival seasons, the Holy Spirit penetrates our hearts and makes our spirits and souls more sensitive to sin. But there can be satanic condemnation that moves our hearts because of that sensitivity. We must protect our hearts with truth and not allow the devil to accuse us or put us under undue condemnation. Rather, we must allow the Holy Spirit to bring true conviction.

There is a great difference between conviction and condemnation. Conviction comes with a revelation to change us. Conviction pinpoints a sin or a flaw in our lives and then releases grace to remove that sin or flaw. On the other hand, condemnation comes to pinpoint sins and flaws without the grace to change them or to release us to deal with them.

APPROACHES TO HOLINESS

In the past, the church has dealt with holiness with many different varieties of holiness theology. Here are some of them:

Eradication

This theology says that inbred sin, the Adamic nature, has been eradicated so that it is no longer possible to sin. This, of course, is erroneous in that even after the new birth, we still have a problem with the old man, the old nature, and we are prone to sin unless we follow after righteousness.

Asceticism

Monastic isolation, celibacy, and self-crucifixion are forms of asceticism. It punishes the flesh as evil through self-denial and all kinds of extreme disciplines. Asceticism does not work to destroy the inward Adamic nature. Asceticism can only deal with outward manifestations of the flesh and with the physical body.

Legalism

Legalism earns merit by works. A legalistic person is enslaved by rules and regulations for the external, yet inwardly he or she becomes rotten and weak.

Suppressionism

Suppressionism is when, through sheer self-will and self-discipline, a person tries to suppress the sin nature and the sin principle within his or her life. The problem with suppressionism is that, after a while, Christianity becomes a religion of self-works that can never properly deal with the principle of sin.

> "We need to rid ourselves of any holiness theology that does not line up with clear scriptural teachings on how we are to deal with our flesh."

We need to rid ourselves of any holiness theology that does not line up with clear scriptural teaching on how we are to deal with our flesh. There are a variety of faulty holiness concepts. Some view holy living as that which is void of all pleasures in life, saying "Everything that is pleasant is either immoral, illegal, or fattening." Some view holy living as withdrawing from life, as enjoying isolation. This is a form of modern asceticism. Some say holiness is only for the full-time ministry, the really dedicated, the missionary types, or those who are fanatical about their religion. Some view holiness with utter discouragement. They think, "My life is too sinful, so I give up. I might as well give in to my old nature and my habits because I cannot break them anyway."

All of these attitudes and approaches to dealing with sin in our lives surface even more during revival seasons. This is why it is very important that we understand the capacity of the new birth, and that we understand our position in Christ as we walk in union with Him to deal with the old man.

New birth brings a new nature. It does not eradicate the old, nor does it split the personality. Natures are capacities for either Holy Spirit activity or for fleshly activity. We must choose, moment by moment, day by day, whom we will serve.

"That the righteous requirement of the law might be fulfilled in us who do not walk according to the flesh but according to the Spirit" (Romans 8:4).

"I say then: Walk in the Spirit, and you shall not fulfill the lust of the flesh" (Galatians 5:16).

"So I said: 'Woe is me, for I am undone! Because I am a man of unclean lips, and I dwell in the midst of a people of unclean lips; for my eyes have seen the King, the Lord of hosts' " (Isaiah 6:5).

"For I know that in me (that is, in my flesh) nothing good dwells; for to will is present with me, but how to perform what is good I do not find" (Romans 7:18). (Also see Romans 8:14; 1 Corinthians 3:16; Jeremiah 17:9; Job 42:5-6.)

The struggle with a lack of desired spiritual life-flow usually is the result of not understanding the dynamics of spiritual life. Spiritual flow is produced by the presence and empowering of the Holy Spirit, not simply the comprehension of doctrinal propositions or religious activity.

"For thus says the High and Lofty One who inhabits eternity, whose name is Holy: 'I dwell in the high and holy place, with him who has a contrite and humble spirit, to revive the spirit of the humble, and to revive the heart of the contrite ones' " (Isaiah 57:15).

PREPARING FOR THE STRUGGLE

Praying for revival is only the first step in welcoming an outpouring of God's Spirit. In addition to prayer, the fallow ground of our hearts must be prepared. The soil of our hearts must be readied for revival by plowing, pulling weeds, removing rocks, and softening the soil. After the rain is poured out on this well-prepared ground, there is still preparation to do.

We must prepare ourselves for the struggles that come during revival. We must understand that our adversary knows that revival is a defeat for him, and we must prepare ourselves to fight the battle that God promises us we will win.

PART 6

PRINCIPLES FOR LEADING IN REVIVAL SEASONS

Chapter 20

REFUSING SUBSTITUTES FOR GOD'S PRESENCE

*T*he Bible gives us a wonderful example of a man of God who understood and valued the presence of God, who would accept nothing less than His full presence in his life and in his ministry.

In Exodus 32-33, God offered Moses something less than His full presence to help him lead God's people. Moses quickly declined the offer and made one of the famous statements in the Bible concerning the presence of God.

"Then the Lord said to Moses, 'Depart and go up from here, you and the people whom you have brought out of the land of Egypt, to the land of which I swore to Abraham, Isaac, and Jacob, saying, to your descendants I will give it.' And I will send My Angel before you, and I will drive out the Canaanite and the Amorite and the Hittite and the Perizzite and the Hivite and the Jebusite" (Exodus 33:1-2).

God offered Moses the angel, which is synonymous with the supernatural manifestations that the children of Israel had experienced previously. Here is Moses' response: "And it came to pass, when Moses entered the tabernacle, that the pillar of cloud descended and stood at the door of the taber-nacle, and the Lord talked with Moses. All the people saw the pillar of cloud standing at the tabernacle door, and all the people rose and worshiped, each man in his tent door. So the Lord spoke to Moses face to face, as a man speaks to his friend. And he would return to the camp, but his servant Joshua the son of Nun, a young man, did not depart from the tabernacle . . . 'Now therefore, I pray, if I have found grace in Your sight, show me now Your way, that I may know You and that I may find grace in Your sight. And consider that this nation is Your people.' And He said, 'My presence will go with you, and I will give you rest.' Then he said to Him, 'If Your presence does not go with us, do not bring us up from here' " (Exodus 33:9-15).

Moses understood the presence of God, and he did not just want the supernatural manifestations that an angel could produce. He wanted the actual, manifested, personalized, revealed presence of the living God to be with him and the nation. Moses knew that if God's presence would abide in and saturate the people that their hearts would be changed and they would follow his leadership. He

> **"Moses knew that if God's presence would abide in and saturate the people that their hearts would be changed and they would follow his leadership."**

knew that if they saw only the supernatural manifestations and working of the mighty angels that their hearts would not be saturated and they would not ultimately follow his leadership into the land that God had promised.

MOSES' PERSPECTIVE ON GOD'S PRESENCE

Moses Knew the Blessing of God's Presence

Moses knew the blessing of God's presence from all the days that he had already walked in His presence. If we spend time in God's presence as Moses did, other people will know that we are in close relationship to God and that we have an anointing and a presence abiding in our lives.

Moses Knew the Strength of God's Presence

They did not start to build the tabernacle until Moses had interceded for the glory and for the presence to be powerful and abiding, until Moses himself was saturated in God's presence.

Moses Knew the Significance of God's Presence

Moses knew that God Himself would be there, that God and all of His attributes would be available to him. God and His name would be attached to that very building program and to his ministry. Jehovah's name means "I will be all that is necessary when the need arises."

Here, Moses is promised the gracious presence of God, which God mercifully and graciously gives to manifest in His house and to reveal to His people. "For how then will it be known that Your people and I have found grace in Your sight, except You go with us? So we shall be separate, Your people and I, from all the people who are upon the face of the earth" (Exodus 33:16).

Moses Received from God's Presence

Moses received the three-fold promise that every believer may receive in Exodus 33:14: "And He said, 'My

Presence will go with you, and I will give you rest.' " God promised that His presence would go with Moses, which means that Moses had to enter into a level of spiritual receptivity. He had to be open to God's presence. Moses himself had to cultivate and keep a new spiritual awareness. Moses had to have a bending forward, sympathetic response to the very presence of God. God's special presence distinguishes God's people from everyone else. The three-fold promise that Moses received was:

"My Presence will go with you."

This is a divine deposit. God would provide to Moses the equipping and the impartation that he needed to do the work that he was called to.

"I will give you rest."

This is divine partnership. God would enter into a partnership with Moses. He would lighten his burdens and there would be a harmony of action between Moses and God. God would actually couple with him His power and anointing in his serving.

"I have found grace in Your sight."

God gave Moses His grace. This is divine skillfulness. God would provide for Moses competency and efficiency. Grace and mercy are not only a heart attitude, but also a heart equipment. God would supply for Moses the capability to do what he was called to do, and that was to take the people into the God-given vision.

A PASSION FOR GOD'S PRESENCE

Revival should produce people who have the same passion for the presence of God that Moses had. Like Moses, we should receive God's divine deposits, divine partnership, and divine skillfulness. We should also be like Moses in his discernment in rejecting mere supernatural manifestations, realizing that the abiding presence of God is more powerful than even the working miracles of angels.

We must be a people of revival, a people who relate to God's ministering presence, a people who will lay a path for others to follow into seasons of revival that last longer than manifestations of God's miraculous, awesome presence. If we are going to be a people of passion for God's presence, we should cultivate these attitudes.

> "During times of revival, the Holy Spirit increases divine desires in our souls, and only God Himself can satisfy these cravings."

A HUNGER AND THIRST FOR GOD'S PRESENCE

During times of revival, the Holy Spirit increases divine desires in our souls, and only God Himself can satisfy these cravings. As we soak in the Holy Spirit and give ourselves to the presence of God, something in us changes. That something is usually that we thirst and hunger for more. The more we drink, the thirstier we become. Spiritual thirst may be increased by exercise or destroyed by neglect. His presence is not a sovereign and irresistible force that comes upon us like a seizure from above, but one that will abide and increase in hearts that are hungry and ready for His presence.

"O God, You are my God; early will I seek You; my soul thirsts for You; my flesh longs for You in a dry and thirsty land where there is no water. So I have looked for You in the sanctuary, to see Your power and Your glory. Because Your lovingkindness is better than life, my lips shall praise You. Thus I will bless You while I live; I will lift up my hands in Your name. My soul shall be satisfied as with marrow and fatness, and my mouth shall praise You with joyful lips. When I remember You on my bed, I meditate on You in the night watches" (Psalm 63:1-6).

> "...we may go through times of testing or dryness and still be in the presence of the Lord."

This passage is a picture of David as a thirsting soul in the wilderness. David was physically in a desert, but his soul was not in a desert. David's soul was in a thirsty land, but he knew how to stir his spirit to drink from the living waters of God's presence.

Like David, we may go through times of testing or dryness and still be in the presence of the Lord. The only satisfaction for the spiritually thirsty person is to drink in of the Spirit of the Lord through the presence of God that creates a garden in the midst of the wilderness. This thirst is essential to life, and the whole person yields to its power. Our souls must follow hard after the Lord in times of dryness. We must eagerly pursue the river of God and His presence.

"The Lord is my light and my salvation; whom shall I fear? The Lord is the strength of my life; of whom shall I be afraid? When the wicked came against me to eat up my flesh, my enemies and foes, they stumbled and fell. Though an army may encamp against me, my heart shall not fear; though war should rise against me, in this I will be confident. One thing I have desired of the Lord, that will I seek: that I may dwell in the house of the Lord all the days of my life, to behold the beauty of the Lord, and to inquire in His temple. For in the time of trouble he shall hide me in His pavilion; in the secret place of His tabernacle he shall hide me; he shall set me high upon a rock. And now my head shall be lifted up above my enemies all around me; therefore I will offer sacrifices of joy in His tabernacle; I will sing, yes, I will sing praises to the Lord" (Psalm 27:1-6).

"As the deer pants for the water brooks, so pants my soul for You, O God. My soul thirsts for God, for the living God. When shall I come and appear before God? My tears have been my food day and night, while they continually say to me, 'Where is your God?' When I remember these things, I pour out my soul within me. For I used to go with the multitude; I went with them to the house of God, with the voice of joy and praise, with a multitude that kept a pilgrim feast" (Psalm 42:1-4).

A DESIRE TO HIDE IN THE SECRET OF HIS PRESENCE

Life is busy. There are many things that can take us away from the abiding presence of God that we find in our secret place, our prayer room or our own secret praise habitation. Because of this, we need to desire the secret of His presence.

"Because You have been my help, therefore in the shadow of Your wings I will rejoice" (Psalm 63:7).

"He who dwells in the secret place of the Most High shall abide under the shadow of the Almighty" (Psalm 91:1).

"The shadow of Your wings" here refers to the Ark of the Covenant, which had two cherubim angels on top of the Covenant that looked down at the mercy seat. All of this was made of one piece of beaten gold. When the psalmist says, "I want to hide in the shadow of Your wings", he is talking about sitting on the mercy seat, a secret place of communion and the abiding presence of God.

> ## "The one pursuit that we should have in life is to hide in His presence."

"For in the time of trouble he shall hide me in His pavilion; in the secret place of His tabernacle He shall hide me; He shall set me high upon a rock" (Psalm 27:5).

The pavilion in this verse was called the royal pavilion, and it was erected in the center of the army. All the mighty men camped around it to protect the king in the event of an enemy attack.

As we hide in God's presence, we hide in His pavilion. We are in a place where God protects us, and His mighty strength is around us as the mighty men of David. The one pursuit that we should have in life is to hide in His presence. Our one affection and one discipline should be to seek after His presence, which is the best shelter in the worst of times. No enemy can come into that secret place to injure or destroy us. We have God's promise, God's divine protection.

A DESIRE TO TASTE THE PRESENCE OF THE LORD

"Oh, taste and see that the Lord is good; blessed is the man who trusts in Him!" (Psalm 34:8).

We can actually taste the presence of the Lord through our spiritual senses. When our senses are open to the Spirit of God for the first time, as in salvation, we taste of the eternal kingdom. Likewise, when we first experience deep prayer, our spirit tastes something that we then begin to desire. It is like a person who first eats his or her favorite food, and once he or she tastes, this person has to have it all the time. So it is with the presence of the Lord: "Taste and see that the Lord is good."

"For it is impossible for those who were once enlightened, and have tasted the heavenly gift, and have become partakers of the Holy Spirit, and have tasted the good word of God and the powers of the age to come" (Hebrews 6:4-5).

"If indeed you have tasted that the Lord is gracious..." (1 Peter 2:3).

To taste spiritually is to begin to seek after God in prayer and worship, especially in times and seasons of revival, when the presence of God is most available. Our taste buds need to change. We need to discipline our senses to desire the right things. In order to do this, we must drink deeply of the Spirit of God.

PREPARING PROPERLY TO ENTER INTO GOD'S PRESENCE

"Therefore, brethren, having boldness to enter the Holiest by the blood of Jesus" (Hebrews 10:19).

As we prepare to enter into the presence of God, we need to develop a pattern to follow and an understanding that God's presence is available. We should not behold from a distance, but walk in and experience His presence.

"Oh come, let us sing to the Lord! Let us shout joyfully to the Rock of our salvation. Let us come before His presence with thanksgiving; let us shout joyfully to Him with psalms" (Psalm 95:1-2).

"The mountains melt like wax at the presence of the Lord, At the presence of the Lord of the whole earth" (Psalm 97:5).

In the Old Testament, we see the tabernacle of Moses, which gives us a pattern of approach to the presence of the living God. This beautifully illustrates the interior journey of the soul from the wiles of sin into the enjoyed presence of God.

As we move from the outer court—after entering the gate past the brazen altar and the brazen laver, which were in the outer court—into the Holy Place, which had three pieces of furniture, the golden candlestick, the table of shewbread, and the altar of incense, we finally move into the Most Holy Place, which contained only the one piece of furniture, the Ark of the Covenant.

THE CROSS IN THE TABERNACLE FURNITURE

The Scripture explains to us that the Holy of Holies is where the voice of God was heard and the presence of God was felt. In the Old Testament, this presence was not available to all people all the time, but only one day of the year. That day was called the Day of Atonement, when they could actually behold the entering in of the priest into the Holy of Holies. The greatest fact of the tabernacle of Moses was that Jehovah was there, a presence waiting within the veil.

"And there I will meet with you, and I will speak with you from above the mercy seat, from between the two cherubim which are on the ark of the Testimony, about everything which I will give you in commandment to the children of Israel" (Exodus 25:22).

It says "I will commune with you." The word commune in Hebrew means to meet with and speak with, to celebrate and partner with. In the tabernacle of Moses we have a pattern of approach into the very presence of God. The Ark of the Covenant, which was in the Holy of Holies, is called the Ark of His Presence. It was the Ark of His power, the Ark of His provision and protection. The Ark was first in the order, as God gave it to Moses. It was the first of furnishings made by Bezalial. It was the first article of furniture placed in the tabernacle when it was finished, because the Ark of the Covenant was a priority to God, and He wanted it to be priority to His people.

In Exodus 29, God gave the priests a five-fold promise concerning their approach into the tabernacle of Moses as they entered into His presence. God said, "I will commune with you. I will speak with you. I will give you direction. I will show you mercy. I will confirm My covenant."

We have all these promises fulfilled today as we enter into the presence of God, as long as we find and follow the pattern that God has given us to enter into His presence. The tabernacle of Moses is a simple pattern to follow.

This simple diagram is a prophetic picture and a biblical teaching of our approach into the presence of God. There are six simple truths and insights that we can follow in approaching the presence of God:

The Tabernacle Of Moses

Ark of the Covenant

Holy of Holies

Veil

Alter of Incense

Golden
Candlestick

Table of
Shewbread

Holy Place

**Outer
Court**

Laver

**Outer
Court**

Brazen Altar

Gate of the Court

Blood: This removes my guilt through confession of sin and renewing the covenant of grace, which guarantees forgiveness and cleansing.

Water: This represents removing the dust of the world by washing my mind and spirit with the water of God's Word, thus judging myself. This is a time of taking personal, spiritual inventory, of seeing myself as I really am.

Oil: This portrays receiving the fresh oil of the Holy Spirit. This is allowing Christ, my High Priest, to trim my wick and remove all burnt parts so as to release a new powerful flow of His anointing.

Bread: Receiving my personal, spiritual nourishment by partaking of the Living Bread—Christ—and the bread of communion with the saints. In the bread, we have life, healing, divine health, spiritual nourishment, and fellowship.

Incense: Receiving the power as a conqueror by giving my incense before the throne of God: prayer and intercession.

Ark: Enjoying the presence of God with freedom of spirit, soul, and body—to worship God with zeal and receive divine deposits from His presence. His presence is a place of mercy. It is mercy seated, a place of holiness, reconciliation, communion, and the glory of God.

RECEIVING THE PROMISED PROVISION FROM HIS PRESENCE

Here are the provisions that we can believe for by faith as we enter into the presence of God:

Joy: When we enter into the presence of God, we can expect to receive a measure of joy. "You will show me the path of life; in Your presence is fullness of joy; at Your right hand are pleasures forevermore" (Psalm 16:11).

Strength: We can experience the strength of God. "Honor and majesty are before Him; strength and gladness are in His place" 1 Chronicles 16:27. "He gives power to the weak, and to those who have no might He increases strength" (Isaiah 40:29).

Liberty: We can experience the liberty of God in His presence. "Now the Lord is the Spirit; and where the Spirit of the Lord is, there is liberty" (2 Corinthians 3:17).

> "Revival is a releasing of God's presence, a heightening of His presence, a deepening of His presence."

Transformation: We can believe God for the transforming power that comes in His presence. "But we all, with unveiled face, beholding as in a mirror the glory of the Lord, are being transformed into the same image from glory to glory, just as by the Spirit of the Lord" (2 Corinthians 3:18).

Refreshing: We can believe God for refreshing in His presence. "Repent therefore and be converted, that your sins may be blotted out, so that times of refreshing may come from the presence of the Lord" (Acts 3:19).

Boldness: We can believe God for boldness as we are in His presence. "Now when they saw the boldness of Peter and

John, and perceived that they were uneducated and untrained men, they marveled. And they realized that they had been with Jesus" (Acts 4:13).

Revival is a releasing of God's presence, a heightening of His presence, a deepening of His presence. In seasons of revival, we should believe for God to commune with us, to transform us, to give us a hunger and thirst for Him, to enlarge our capacity for His Spirit. Let us become people of passion for His presence, people who understand how not just to stand far off and speak of His power and His presence, but to be saturated with that power and presence.

Chapter 21

REVIVAL LEADERSHIP: THE ZERUBBABEL PRINCIPLE

*R*evival times require renewed leadership within the body of Christ, simply because of the nature of the work we as leaders will be called to do during these times.

The study of Zerubbabel in the Old Testament yields several pertinent insights from a leader who had a tremendous vision, yet was in need of personal renewal. His need for revival was not due to personal sin, failure, or a lack of spirituality, but because God had called him to accomplish difficult work and because he was leading in a time that necessitated a very real encounter with the God who had called him.

I want to examine the historical settings and the prophetic messages that accompanied renewal in the life of Zerubbabel, the leader, at a turning point in history. The focus of this examination of Zerubbabel's leadership during revival times is the fourth chapter of book of Zechariah, a minor prophet.

THE HISTORICAL BACKGROUND OF ZERUBBABEL

Zechariah's prophetic ministry took place in the time of Israel's restoration from the Babylonian captivity, in the post-exilic period. Approximately seventy-five years had elapsed since Habakkuk and Jeremiah had predicted the invasion of Judah by the Neo-Babylonian army of King Nebuchadnezzar.

When the Hebrews completed their hard service in Babylon, God influenced Cyrus, the Persian king, to allow them to return to their homeland and rebuild their temple (see Isaiah 40:2, 44:28). After the seventy years of captivity in Babylon, King Cyrus released the remnant to return to their homeland and rebuild the city.

There were actually two different remnant releases. One was under the leadership of Zerubbabel, the other under that of Ezra. The first six chapters of the book of Ezra cover the return of the remnant under Zerubbabel to rebuild the temple and the house of God. Ezra 7-10 records the return of more of the remnant under Ezra to rebuild through his teaching the spiritual condition of the people.

The historical circumstances and conditions that Zechariah ministered under were, in general, those of Haggai's time, since their labors coincided with one another. Haggai preached four sermons in four months. Zechariah began his ministry two months after Haggai had begun his. Thus, the immediate historical background for Zechariah's ministry began with Cyrus's capture of Babylon and included the completion of the restoration of the second temple.

Zerubbabel, an apostolic leader with vision to rebuild the wall and the temple, needed and received both Haggai's and Zechariah's prophetic ministries. According to second chapter of Ezra, about 50,000 people returned under the civil leadership of Zerubbabel, who was the governor, and the religious leadership of Jeshua, who was the high priest. This group completed the first works of rebuilding the foundation of the temple, which was completed under their ministry. Several obstacles arose that slowed and finally halted the construction.

THE CALL TO ZERUBBABEL LEADERSHIP

I want to profile the leader Zerubbabel in order to demonstrate the insights that we can apply to our own lives in leadership during the revivals of our day.

A Call to Leave Familiar Ground

Zerubbabel's first step in leaving Babylon was the same one that all revival leaders must take. It is the step of leaving familiar ground, of leaving the religious, traditional surroundings and moving out in the unknown to accomplish what the Spirit of God might do.

> **"It is the step of leaving familiar ground, of leaving the religious, traditional surroundings and moving out in the unknown to accomplish what the Spirit of God might do."**

"Who is among you of all His people? May his God be with him, and let him go up to Jerusalem which is in Judah, and build the house of the Lord God of Israel (He is God), which is in Jerusalem" (Ezra 1:3).

"Then the heads of the fathers' houses of Judah and Benjamin, and the priests and the Levites, with all whose spirits God had moved, arose to go up and build the house of the Lord which is in Jerusalem" (Ezra 1:5).

Zerubbabel's first step was to leave the place that he, his family, and friends had lived in for a number of years and take the 700-mile journey to Jerusalem. They left familiar ground because of the vision they had to rebuild the house. It also says in verse five: "Their spirits were stirred up." God had moved upon them. In the Hebrew, this refers to God arousing by force. It refers to the sovereign hand of God coming upon them to stir them to leave familiar ground.

In Ezra 2:1-2, there is a list of the men who joined with Ezra to leave familiar ground with him. Not only did Zerubbabel receive a stirring of the Holy Spirit to leave his familiar ground, but he was able to stir the hearts of others so that they, with vision, could leave where they were and move into where God wanted them to be.

> "It takes a stirring of the Holy Spirit to prepare people to move from the familiar, from the traditional, to a new level of spiritual activity."

It takes a stirring of the Holy Spirit to prepare people to move from the familiar, from the traditional, to a new level of spiritual activity.

A Call to Identify Priorities

Zerubbabel had to identify ministry priorities. It says in Ezra 3:2: "Then Jeshua the son of Jozadak and his brethren the priests, and Zerubbabel the son of Shealtiel and his brethren, arose and built the altar of the God of Israel, to offer burnt offerings on it, as it is written in the Law of Moses the man of God."

The first priority of a revival leader is to rebuild the altar of God. Rebuilding the altar of God to offer the sacrifices speaks of communion with God. It speaks of covenant relationship and a realization of the source of strength and power that is needed in times of transition. Building the altar of sacrifice is building a place of trust, a place of covenant, and a place of calling on the name of the Lord.

As leaders in times of revival, our rebuilding of the altar would be the building of prayer and vigor toward our relationship to God through repentance and cleansing. That way, we will have a clean start as we begin to rebuild or build new what God has put into our hearts.

A Call to Greater Vision

In Ezra 3:4-5, there was a proclaiming of the breadth of vision: "They also kept the Feast of Tabernacles, as it is written, and offered the daily burnt offerings in the number required by ordinance for each day. Afterwards they offered the regular burnt offering, and those for New Moons and for all the appointed feasts of the Lord that were consecrated, and those of everyone who willingly offered a freewill offering to the Lord."

The Feast of Trumpets was the highlight of the year. The Feast of Trumpets, the Day of Atonement, and the Feast of Booths were the three components that made up the Feast of the Seventh Month. The Feast of the Seventh Month was a time of harvest, a time of celebration. It was a time of casting vision for the coming year.

They had not experienced a Feast of the Seventh Month, the Feast of Tabernacles, for more than seventy years. There was no harvest to take in and they had nothing to celebrate. Yet Zerubbabel had a vision for the future and an ability to move into it by faith. There were no crops to harvest, no cities to celebrate in, no new temple to sit in. All they had was the vision of what God might do in the coming years.

A revival leader is one who can see what God will do, even when nothing speaks of what God might do. Zerubbabel leaders are those who can blow the trumpet, those who can see the vision. They can gather the commitment of the people and arise and move into a new level of faith.

A Call to Build and Strengthen the Foundation

It says in Ezra 3:10-13 that Zerubbabel made the foundation building glorious: "When the builders laid the foundation of the temple of the Lord, the priests stood in their apparel with trumpets, and the Levites, the sons of Asaph, with cymbals, to praise the Lord, according to the ordinance of David king of Israel. And they sang responsively, praising and giving thanks to the Lord: 'For He is good, for His mercy endures forever toward Israel.' Then all the people shouted with a great shout, when they praised the Lord, because the foundation of the house of the Lord was laid. But many of the priests and Levites and heads of the fathers' houses, old men who had seen the first temple, wept with a loud voice when the foundation of this temple was laid before their eyes. Yet many shouted aloud for joy, so that the people could not discern the noise of the shout of joy from the noise of the weeping of the people, for the people shouted with a loud shout, and the sound was heard afar off."

Zerubbabel had the capacity to make foundation building exciting, to make it a time of celebration through the

> "Foundation building–in the natural or in the spiritual–is not usually a highly emotional time, but a time to dig deep."

rank and file of Israel. He had the ability to make this kind of work glorious by giving the people the vision of what a great foundation can prepare them for.

Foundation building—in the natural or in the spiritual—is not usually a highly emotional time, but a time to dig deep, a time to remove stones and labor hard. It is tedious, slow work, and you cannot see much of the results of your work because much of it is under the ground.

In times of revival, foundation building is an absolute necessity. This is the time that all the basic foundational building stones of the kingdom of God need to be laid to prepare for an outpouring of the Spirit. These building stones are areas such as such as repentance, water baptism, Christian living, prayer, raising the family, integrity, the breaking of habits, issues of holiness, daily living in the cross, and becoming the Lord's disciples.

A Call to Warfare

We can see in Ezra 4:1-8 that Zerubbabel expected warfare to attack the work: "The adversaries of Judah and Benjamin heard that the descendants of the captivity were building the temple of the Lord God of Israel," and they were stirred to attack. Zerubbabel knew that there would be attacks whenever a leader begins to do the work of the Lord to build and extend a vision in the people's hearts. And knowing that the attack was coming enabled him to prepare other leaders and the people for this attack.

The enemy attacks through many different avenues with the intent to destroy the work of God. As leaders, it is our responsibility to prepare ourselves for that attack, then to prepare the people.

A Call to Perseverance

Zerubbabel endured delayed and incomplete vision as he was moving the people into revival. "Thus the work of the house of God which is at Jerusalem ceased, and it was discontinued until the second year of the reign of Darius king of Persia" (Ezra 4:24).

Zerubbabel had laid a strong foundation. He had warred against the enemy as he came against the vision and what they were building. Now Zerubbabel was experiencing what all leaders experience, and that is delay when what is promised is not realized, when what is prophesied is not seen, and when what is preached is not embraced. He had laid the foundation and painted the vision for a huge temple and a beautiful city. Yet now this work was in disarray. It had come to a complete stop, and the people of God had lost heart.

> "Whenever leaders move people into a time of revival, there will be vision delays. There will be revival delays."

Vision delays are disheartening to say the least. They cause murmuring and criticism in the hearts of the people and give the enemy something to build his own work upon. Vision delays open up room for criticism of the leaders who are leading the vision, causing a loss of momentum.

Whenever leaders move people into a time of revival, there will be vision delays. There will be revival delays. We can pray and fast, believe God, and prepare for revival, yet still not immediately see an outpouring of the Holy Spirit. The people may lose heart when they do not see fulfillment, even after all the hard work in preparing foundations and casting vision.

This is where perseverance becomes so vital for revival leaders. Perseverance keeps us earnestly seeking and believing for revival, even when our vision is delayed.

A Call to Prophetic Insight

Zerubbabel knew the work had stopped, yet he believed the work would not end permanently. "Thus the work of the house of God which is at Jerusalem ceased, and it was discontinued until the second year of the reign of Darius king of Persia" (Ezra 4:24).

Zerubbabel encountered what every revival leader must encounter. That is the prophetic spirit. That happens when the Spirit of God inspires leaders and people to arise and go beyond what they physically see, when the Spirit gives them more than enough strength to accomplish what God has called them to do. The prophetic spirit actually revives the spirit of the people and prepares them to move into a revival spirit where God does miraculous things in their midst.

"Then the prophet Haggai and Zechariah the son of Iddo, prophets, prophesied to the Jews who were in Judah and Jerusalem, in the name of the God of Israel, who was over them. So Zerubbabel the son of Shealtiel and Jeshua the son of Jozadak rose up and began to build the house of God which is in Jerusalem; and the prophets of God were with them, helping them" (Ezra 5:1-2).

This is the context that allows us to understand the power of the prophetic word when it is delivered to revival leadership. When the prophet arrives, he faces the pretense of the word of God that has been stopped. When the prophet leaves, the work has started again and will be completed according to the prophetic word. This illustrates the power of the inspired prophetic word in the life of a revival leader and revival people.

There is always an "until" in every promise of God. In Ezra 4:24, it says, "The work of God ceased until . . ." The word until speaks of something that is coming, something such as a word of the Lord through a prophet, or a moving of the Holy Spirit, or an outpouring of a new revival spirit upon the people. Until God moves in by His sovereign hand and changes everything that is going on. Until God's timing is brought around and executed. Until God Himself steps in.

There is time when God starts the work and a time when He finishes the work. As revival leaders, we need to keep in mind that God will finish what He has started.

REVIVAL LEADERSHIP INSIGHTS

The words of the prophet are very important during revival times. These words come and stand alongside the leaders and aid them in accomplishing the building of the house of God and the fulfilling of the vision and the moving into a revival spirit for that day. In Zechariah 4:1-6, we have the account of the prophet speaking to Zerubbabel and Jeshua concerning their leadership and what they needed to accomplish to fulfill the vision God had given them.

"Now the angel who talked with me came back and wakened me, as a man who is wakened out of his sleep. And he said to me, 'What do you see?' So I said, 'I am looking, and there is a lampstand of solid gold with a bowl on top of it, and on the stand seven lamps with seven pipes to the seven lamps. Two olive trees are by it, one at the right of the bowl and the other at its left.' So I answered and spoke to the angel who talked with me, saying, 'What are these, my lord?' Then the angel who talked with me answered and said to me, 'Do you not know what these are?' And I said, 'No, my lord.' So he answered and said to me: 'This is the word of the Lord to Zerubbabel: "Not by might nor by power, but by My Spirit," says the Lord of hosts' " (Zechariah 4:1-6).

The main purpose of this prophetic word was to encourage Zerubbabel and Jeshua in the work God had called them to accomplish—the work of rebuilding the temple—by reminding them of their divine resources and to give them the divine energy to war against the enemies of their souls.

There are several principles in this passage concerning revival leadership in our time:

Revival Times Necessitate Awakening Sleeping Leadership

Zechariah 4:1 says: "Now the angel who talked with me came back and wakened me, as a man who is wakened out of his sleep."

The Spirit of the Lord had to shake the leader because he had become lethargic due to the pressures and discouragement he had faced in seeing that the work had stopped. The Spirit came to wake him out of his own spiritual slumber and lukewarmness.

If leadership in our time is not awakened, then the people have no chance to be awakened. If leadership is not receiving a new shaking that causes them to be aroused, how can the church put on its strength? (Also see Genesis 28:16; Isaiah 51:9, 17; Zechariah 13:7; Romans 13:11.)

Revival Leadership Must Acknowledge God's Vision for Oil-Filled Churches

Zachariah 4:2 states: "And he said to me, 'What do you see?' So I said, 'I am looking, and there is a lampstand of solid gold with a bowl on top of it, and on the stand seven lamps with seven pipes to the seven lamps.' "

The word of the Lord comes to this leader to ask him a simple question: "What do you see?" When the Holy Spirit shakes leaders during revival times, He will always pose these questions: What exactly do you see? What do you want to see? What is the vision that God has put in your heart? Is it a vision of man, or is it a vision of the supernatural, sovereign God you serve? Do you see a broken-down church? Do you see people who are unwilling? Do you see people who will not volunteer for anything? Do you see people who have lost their first loves and their servants' hearts? Do you see the people who will not give of their finances? Do you see people withholding the tithe? Do you see people who have lost the prayer spirit. Do you see people whose worship is half of what it should be? Do you see people who will not bring their neighbors to church, who will not tell their friends about Christ? What do you see when you look out at your church? What do you see when you look out at your community? What do you see when you look out at your city, your nation, and the nations of the world?

Revival leadership needs a new vision, a new eye to see what God might want to do. It needs to see the potential of the people sitting in the pews, the potential of their prayer lives, of their worship lives, and of their giving lives. Revival leadership needs to see the potential of harvest in the community.

In Zechariah 4:2, Zerubbabel simply says, "I am looking." The prophet Zechariah is receiving the word that needs to be given to Zerubbabel and Jeshua because they need to have a vision of the bowl. They do not see what God wants to do, and the prophet does not see exactly what God wants to do until the Holy Spirit comes upon him. The prophet was able to say, "There is a lampstand of solid gold with a bowl on top of it, and on the stand seven lamps with seven pipes to the seven lamps."

> "Revival leadership needs a new vision, a new eye to see what God might want to do."

The lamps speak about the church of the Lord Jesus Christ, as stated in Revelation 1. The vision of the bowl is a vision of the God who has plenty of oil for His church. A vision of a lampstand with lamps is a vision of a God who has glorious power to pour through this lampstand plenty of light because there is plenty of oil.

Revival Leadership Must Assimilate God's Prophetic Message

In Zechariah 4:6-7 it says: "So he answered and said to me: 'This is the word of the Lord to Zerubbabel: "Not by might nor by power, but by My Spirit," says the Lord of hosts. "Who are you, O great mountain? Before Zerubbabel you shall become a plain! And he shall bring forth the capstone with shouts of 'Grace, grace to it!' ' "

The message that Zerubbabel receives—and the message that all revival leadership must assimilate into their spirits—is that mountains of resistance will be leveled like a plain. There are all kinds of mountains that will come against revival. Traditionalism, theological controversies, criticism by people who are pushed out of their comfort zones, and satanic attack are a few of the many mountains of resistance that will come against revival spirit and revival leadership.

"When the word of the Lord is assimilated into the spirits of the leaders, mountains of resistance are leveled like a plain..."

When the word of the Lord is assimilated into the spirits of the leaders, mountains of resistance are leveled like a plain—not by your might or by your power, but by the Holy Spirit. They will be leveled, not by the power or intellect of the great leader, but by the power of grace, the supernatural power many of us never tap into.

"Every valley shall be exalted and every mountain and hill brought low; the crooked places shall be made straight and the rough places smooth" (Isaiah 40:4).

"Behold, I will make you into a new threshing sledge with sharp teeth; you shall thresh the mountains and beat them small, and make the hills like chaff" (Isaiah 41:15).

In order for leaders to be able to thresh the mountains of resistance and make them little hills or plains and to make the crooked places straight and the rough places smooth, there must be a spirit of strength, a spirit of grace that rests upon them. There must be a vision for revival that has caught in the spirit of the leader, and not just in the mind. Isaiah 49:11 says: "I will make each of My mountains a road, and My highways shall be elevated" (also see Matthew 17:20, 21:21; Mark 11:13; 1 Corinthians 13:2).

The second prophetic message Zerubbabel had to assimilate as a revival leader was the message that ultimate triumph and completion of the vision was certain. "Moreover the word of the Lord came to me, saying: 'The hands of Zerubbabel have laid the foundation of this temple; his hands shall also finish it. Then you will know that the Lord of hosts has sent Me to you' " (Zechariah 4:8-9).

The promise to the leader was that the work would not go unfinished, even though there would be mountains of resistance, spiritual attack, disillusionment, and discouragement that would cause the people to stop. Nevertheless, the work will not stay at that place, but will begin again and be finished.

Revival leadership must have a vision for the end result. Revival leadership must believe that the ultimate triumph—the completion of the vision—is a complete outpouring of the Holy Spirit upon every heart and every church, and that God will send revival that will accomplish its work.

Revival Leadership Must Assimilate the Small Things

Zechariah 4:10 says: "For who has despised the day of small things? For these seven rejoice to see the plumb line in the hand of Zerubbabel. They are the eyes of the Lord, which scan to and fro throughout the whole earth."

When the word is not preached with power and the people do not respond enthusiastically year after year, leadership can become discouraged at not seeing the fruit of revival. The small and slow beginnings of revival can be discouraging if we do not believe that the seed has power within it to grow into a tree. We are not to despise slow beginnings.

Reading books on revival does not bring revival. Praying for revival does not always bring revival in the time period that we are praying. Some revival leaders have laid the foundation their whole lives, only to have other leaders come in and build upon the foundation and see the results of those prayers and an outpouring of the Holy Spirit.

Do not despise the day of small beginnings or the day of slow beginnings. We are to pray, sow seed, and prepare as if revival is already here. We are to put out the plumb line of the Word of God with our hands and see through the eyes of the Lord that everything that the Word teaches will come to pass.

Revival leadership must receive the message that oil-filled leaders must continually supply the oil for the lampstands.

Zechariah 4:11-12: "Then I answered and said to him, 'What are these two olive trees—at the right of the lampstand and at its left?' And I further answered and said to him, 'What are these two olive branches that drip into the receptacles of the two gold pipes from which the golden oil drains?' " The Amplified Bible says, "Which the golden oil is emptied out . . . emptied golden oil out of themselves."

We have in this passage one of the most important insights concerning revival leadership. The vision here changes and gives special attention to the important role of the leader to be oil-filled and oil-driven. For the leader is the one who drips into the receptacles of the two golden pipes from which the golden oil drains. The two leaders, being the two olive trees beside the golden lampstands, are the pipes that actually supply oil to the bowl, and the bowl itself is dripping down into the seven lampstands.

I am not suggesting that leadership replace the bowl, as if we become the divine source to the church or to the people of God. We recognize that the source of all oil is almighty God and the Holy Spirit working in and through our lives. Nevertheless, in this vision there seems to be an emphasis on oil-filled leaders who can hold enough oil to flow from them into the lampstand, which itself becomes the golden lampstand that will reflect the glory of God.

> "Revival leaders need to have new or fresh oil poured into their lives, an oil that is new in respect to quality and sweetness."

The word oil used in this passage is the word *yishar*, which means new, fresh oil. It is oil that is new in respect to time, to quality, and to sweetness. Revival leaders need to have new or fresh oil poured into their lives, an oil that is new in respect to quality and sweetness. There are many things in the life of ministry that can cause the oil to become less than what it should be or used to be. Old oil loses its strength, its sweetness, and its quality.

Before God can pour oil into His people, He must raise up oil-filled leaders—Zerubbabels and Jeshuas—olive trees who have the ability to produce oil through their ministries and calling. These are leaders who have the grace of God upon their lives so that they can pour into the church, and the church then begins to be filled with the same golden oil. It is not that the leader is the source of oil. The leader is the conduit, the tree beside the lampstand that pours into the bowl.

"And you shall command the children of Israel that they bring you pure oil of pressed olives for the light, to cause the lamp to burn continually" (Exodus 27:20).

Revival leaders are like olive branches. Olive branches are easily broken, easily dissolved, and if stepped upon, they produce oil. It is only through their brokenness and their crushed state that they can produce oil. When we as leaders are crushed or broken, what comes forth from us is the pure, new golden oil of God, full of sweetness and the quality of God Himself (also see Exodus 29:40; Leviticus 24:2; Numbers 28:5; Matthew 25:1-10; Luke 10:34; Hebrews 1:9).

> **"Revival leaders are like olive branches. Olive branches are easily broken, easily dissolved, and if stepped upon, they produce oil."**

Leaders who move into revival must be willing to be crushed, broken, easily dissolved, even stepped upon. When leaders experience opposition, criticism, discouragement, or an attack of the enemy, they must make sure they do not get filled with resentment or bitterness. Instead, because they are filled with oil, they must experience the reviving and renewing of their own hearts.

Revival Leadership Must Acknowledge that God is Sovereign and in Control of All Matters

"Then I answered and said to him, 'What are these two olive trees—at the right of the lampstand and at its left?' And I further answered and said to him, 'What are these two olive branches that drip into the receptacles of the two gold pipes from which the golden oil drains?' Then he answered me and said, 'Do you not know what these are?' And I said, 'No, my lord.' So he said, 'These are the two anointed ones, who stand beside the Lord of the whole earth' " (Zechariah 4:11-14).

Revival leaders must see themselves standing beside the Lord of the whole earth, the God who is sovereign over all—over the opposition, the pressures, and the strange circumstances of ministry. We must see that He is in control of all situations surrounding every circumstance in our ministries, our churches, and our nations.

When revival leaders experience the word of the Lord—as Zerubbabel did—and the dealings of the Holy Spirit in their lives and ministries, the result will be a renewed leadership style. They will be filled with more of the oil of God than ever, and this oil will be poured into the golden lampstand.

Chapter 22

FINDING BALANCE
IN REVIVAL SEASONS

*A*s we embrace the moving of the Holy Spirit, we need to understand that revival activity necessitates revival-type leadership. It requires leaders who have been touched by the Holy Spirit while maintaining the balance of the Word of God.

Leadership is very important to the longevity of revival. God is sovereign, but He flows through human vessels. He uses physical things such as church buildings to touch people. Ultimately He uses people to channel the moving of the Holy Spirit. For this reason, seasons of revival must be pastored carefully and wisely.

There are different philosophies regarding the pastoral administration of renewal and the work of the Holy Spirit. Some people believe that we are not to question, confront, or put our hands on any manifestation of the Holy Spirit in a service or in a person. That, they believe, would be quenching the Holy Spirit. This philosophy says that we are not to administrate the manifestations of the Holy Spirit, that we can preach the Word and believe for activity of God, but that He is sovereign and will take care of the church service or person.

There is another philosophy that teaches that leaders are to wisely administrate the church services, that leaders are responsible to step into a situation if they feel it needs correction, simply because leaders have been given authority to administrate the church service and what goes on in it.

As revival progresses, there are many different potential outcomes in the moving of the Holy Spirit within a denomination, a church, or a movement of churches. The potential of causing lines of demarcation in churches, leaders, movements, or denominations, has been seen in past history.

There is a potential for spiritual imbalances during times of revival. Experience does not produce maturity, and we must understand that in order to avoid producing the spiritual imbalances and extremes that could come during seasons of revival. There is always the potential for spiritual fire to enslave the hearts and souls of people to the point where they become unbalanced in their

> **"...we must keep a healthy tension between the subjective and objective."**

Christian walk and depend too much on feelings or subjective activity, and not on the principles of the Word of God.

Revival has positive ramifications. There is, during revival, the potential for a new divine energy to come into the hearts of the people of God and give them a passion for the lost and to heal the hurting. There is the potential for empowering worship and releasing a new level of God's presence that could reshape our public service and give us a new passion for prayer and worship itself. There is a potential for the Holy Spirit to bring a new growth, both into the spirit of the church and into the members of the church.

Leaders Must Maintain Balance

As leaders during times of revival, we must keep a healthy tension between the subjective and objective, the long-lasting and the temporal, and between faith and experienced reality.

It is poor leadership to believe that good intent and good results relieve us of our responsibility to deal with abuses and excesses, and, in due season, this will result in more extremes and abuses. Some leaders have more openness and ease in the presence of unusual or even chaotic spiritual activity, and others have little tolerance to these things.

As leaders, we must be attentive to what is going on around us, and we must seek more sensitivity to the Spirit, so that we are not tolerant of excesses and abuses. We must ask God for more wisdom and discernment in order to be attentive to these things.

We do not want to quench the Holy Spirit, but we also do not want to encourage excessiveness during His moving upon people's lives. Neither one of these will bring us to the mature flow that we need in our churches.

FINDING BALANCE IN REVIVAL

I would like to illustrate the concept of balance in revival leadership by using three natural forces that can aptly be used to describe the moving of the Holy Spirit in our midst: fire, water, and wind.

Fire: It Can Keep Us Warm or Burn Down the House

Obviously, there needs to be a screen in front of a fireplace so that the fire does not jump out and burn down the house or start a forest fire. A fire that is confined to a fireplace can heat the house, but it also has the potential to get out of hand if it is not properly confined.

But despite that risk, would we choose to stay in a cold house, or would we build a fire and take the risk that some sparks might get out onto the carpet, or somebody might get a little too close to the fire and get burned? We would choose to build the fire, but we would build it wisely and put up a screen and watch the fire closely to see that it does not burn what we do not want it to.

Is is like that with Holy Spirit revival. As leaders, we want the warmth of God's presence during these times, but we must use the screen of the wisdom of God's Word to make sure that the fire stays in the fireplace.

The Holy Spirit is likened to fire, and revival is a faith encounter with the Holy Spirit (see Isaiah 4:4; Matthew 13:11).

- Fire has the power to refine.
- Fire has the power to consume.
- Fire has the purging, purifying force.
- Fire has the zeal of God in the believer.
- Fire has the power to melt everything that needs melting.

Water: It Can Create Power or a Flood

When a dam holds back a certain amount of water in a river, it can be a great source of power that can be put to good use. Though, when water overflows the dam, it becomes a flood that can destroy homes, take lives, and devastate all in its path.

Again, it works that way during revival. There are some leaders that will just release all the water in the dam, and it flows down, causing great damage. Obviously, that is a misuse of the water. We do not have to abuse the waters of revival. We can build a proper dam that will produce abundant, useful water for the city and for the church of God.

Wind: It Can Move a Sailboat or Destroy it

In the hands of an experienced sailor, wind provides the power to move a sailboat swiftly and safely on the water. The experienced sailor knows how to adjust the sails to keep the boat under control. But without that experience and wisdom, that same wind can destroy the boat.

We need to know how and when to adjust our sails to make sure we handle the winds of revival so that they give us power to move the boat and not create a disaster.

- Wind is invisible in its working (John 3:8).
- Wind is directed in its glory (Psalm 148:8).
- Wind is effective in its presence (Ecclesiastes 1:6).
- Wind is varied in its operation (1 Kings 19:11; 1 Corinthians 12:4,11).
- Wind is powerful in its employment (Acts 2:2; James 3:4).

Fire, water or wind. Any of these can be a source of destruction or a source of divine energizing. That depends upon the leadership that flows in times of revival with wisdom. We must use principles in the Word of God as foundations for everything we do.

BOUND TO THE WRITTEN WORD

As revival leaders, we are to be bound to the written Word of God for all instructions regarding the building of God's house. All experiences in revival must submit to the Word of God. We must be careful in using the metaphorical language of Scripture to validate extra-biblical manifestations. Using Scripture to give prophetic or eschatalogical meaning to people's experiences is dangerous and could be in error of Scripture.

Leaders of God's people are responsible to clarify the difference between living by the subjective and living by the objective. The objective is the written Word of God, which we are obligated to obey. The subjective is the feelings and interpretations of that Word that we apply to our own lives. We must not overly promote the release of emotions without applying the Word of God to everyday life.

> **"The Holy Spirit abiding in us is not just some mystical force that is in the air."**

One of Brazil's leading authors, in his book *Revival Coming From the Throne*, states his concerns about revival in Brazil, and these concerns could be easily applied to revival here in the United States. He states: "The revival Latin American style overflows with emotion, but without impacting a profound change within the lives of those which attend its services. We are concentrating well on the laughter and the falling down. I too believe in these things. I am a Presbyterian who happens to also be deeply Pentecostal. But our challenge is not so much learning to fall in the Spirit, but learning to walk in the Spirit. Being slain in the Spirit is easy; to walk in the Spirit is a different matter altogether. Revival Latin American style likes to manipulate the power of God, but does not like to submit to the power of God's Word. This is a modern danger to play with and manipulate the power of the Spirit without submitting ourselves to the sword of the Spirit."

The Holy Spirit abiding in us is not just some mystical force that is in the air. The Holy Spirit is in people and in the Word of God. As we are bound to the Word of God and the Holy Spirit lives within us, we focus our leadership on those things that would positively affect people's lives.

WE MUST KEEP OUR FOCUS ON THE PURPOSE OF GOD

Our top focus as we lead in times of revival should be on the purpose of God. That purpose is to change the lives of people by the truth of Christ's redemptive work.

WE MUST MAINTAIN THE BIBLICAL PURPOSE OF CORPO-RATE GATHERINGS

The public service, which usually includes prayer, worship, and teaching and preaching of the Word of God, can be changed drastically with renewal or revival activity. Making room for Holy Spirit activity and for maintaining a biblical purpose in our gatherings must be our goal. But again, we need to have a sense of what the Bible teaches concerning the public worship service and what we ourselves see as the purpose of this worship service.

During revival seasons, some teach that we should just start the service and let it go, that we should not try to quench the Holy Spirit by structuring the service around the old programs and the old ways we used to have. So if the Holy Spirit moves during the worship service, just let it go—do not stop what the Holy Spirit is doing. If there is no preaching that day, so be it. If there is no announcements, baby dedications, or offerings, fine! What we want is the moving of the Holy Spirit.

We must continually balance these different elements in the doctrine of the corporate gathering. What should be limited and what should be encouraged? The real issue of the public service in 1 Corinthians 14 is not tongues or prophecy or the moving of the Spirit, per se, or even the different parts of the worship service. The real issue is the building up of the congregation, which can only be effected when preaching of the written Word of God and understandable utterances of prophecy are the primary edification gifts used in the public gathering. Manifestations and phenomena of any kind that become a public focus (before the whole congregation, that is) must fall under the teaching of 1 Corinthians 14 before they can be encouraged or allowed in public meetings.

The unity and the spiritual growth of the whole congregation is the goal, and this is what is at stake during revival and renewal settings. So the main questions that we should ask concerning these manifestations are, "Do we understand it?" and "Does it edify (to edify means to bring encouragement)?" We should also ask these questions: Can we explain it intelligently? Is it profitable? Does it teach us something concerning Christ and His Word? Does it motivate toward worship or prayer?

Of course, there are times when the Holy Spirit moves in such a sovereign atmosphere that we must flow with what He is doing and saying, and it changes the whole course of the service. I am not addressing the times when that happens, but what takes place week in and week out, fifty-two weeks a year, over the next three, five, ten, and fifteen years, as we flow in the Holy Spirit and build the church of Jesus Christ.

> "The unity and the spiritual growth of the whole congregation is the goal, and this is what is at stake during revival and renewal settings."

WE MUST HOLD BIBLICAL EXPERIENCES AS THE HIGHEST MODEL

To allow or encourage individuals to seek private discernment is not enough to fulfill true leadership responsibility. Biblical experiences involve being born again, repentance, water baptism, communion, body life, prayer, worship, evangelism, and fasting. There are emotions in these experiences, but we must never push or encourage people to experience things that are not plainly stated in the Bible. Now, people do experience things that are not clearly stated in the Bible. But these experiences must be judged by the clear and objective Scriptures. We understand that there are many things that we do that the Bible does not specifically list out or explain for us. There are things that people might do under the initial moving of the Holy Spirit upon their lives that are genuine, but that they may not need to do every time they feel the move of the Holy Spirit.

WE MUST UNDERSTAND THAT MANIFESTATIONS, SIGNS AND WONDERS MAY BE BIBLICAL, UNBIBLICAL OR EXTRA-BIBLICAL

We must not try to force the extra-biblical manifestations to confirm what is biblical. On the contrary, we must focus on the biblical and judge the fruit of the extra-biblical. For instance, no doctrine should be based on a prophetic interpretation of a particular manifestation (see Matthew 7:15-16, Acts 5:2-3, John 4:1-3). Fruit inspection goes beyond initial impressions or outward appearances. Fruit takes time to grow, and we need to see what something will become over time. Therefore, we need to be careful not to pronounce something good when, in fact, the fruit has not had a chance to grow.

WE MUST UNDERSTAND
THAT PEOPLE WILL REACT IMMATURELY

In the excitement of the infilling and empowering of the Holy Spirit, some people may do or say things that are fleshly and immature. Out of zeal, they may say things to people that are immature and could, in fact, be harmful. Saying things to people like "fall," "be delivered," "you're not receiving because . . ." "you're hard-hearted," "there's something wrong here," "God doesn't seem to be able to penetrate you," in the heat of the moment could be offensive, immature, and harmful to people. is not not that those who say these things are bad people or that they are being used by Satan when they say these things. They may mean well. They are simply immature or untaught.

> "...we must not allow the immature or fanatical people to say things that quench other people's hearts."

As leaders, we must be careful not to allow this to happen. As people seek God in prayer and open themselves to ministry to receive from the Holy Spirit, we must not allow the immature or fanatical people to say things that quench other people's hearts.

WE MUST NOT BECOME TOO RIGID IN OUR INTERPRETA-TIONS OF WHAT GOD MIGHT BE DOING BY HIS SPIRIT

Some seemingly strange or abnormal behavior should be expected during times of revival. As leaders, we must not unduly promote or restrict these things. We need wisdom and patience as we deal with people's responses to the Holy Spirit.

WE NEED TO RESPOND TO THE HOLY SPIRIT IN A SPIRIT OF FAITH

Instead of a spirit of fear, we must have faith that a revival atmosphere—with all of its abnormalities, mysteries, and mind-boggling events—still can be under the sovereign hand of God. We need to have faith in God's Word and God's principles. As leaders, we need to adjust as we go and as we grow. We must not allow the fear of disorder, deception, or imbalance to stagnate or paralyze us. We can handle what is going on by following the Word of God and by being sensitive and balanced.

WE MUST SEEK GOD'S PRESENCE, NOT MANIFESTATIONS

As leaders, we must take responsibility by restraining or even prohibiting certain unusual or bizarre manifestations if they hinder the moving of God's people in unity into His presence and the receiving of His ministry. This is not quenching the Spirit. It is pastoring the whole flock with wisdom. The Bible says to test the spirits without quenching the Spirit of God (see 1 Thessalonians 5:19-20; 1 John 4:1-3; 1 Corinthians 14:29).

FACTORS IN MISSING VISITATION

As leaders, we are responsible to believe God for the days of visitation and to enter into the visitation ourselves. Some leaders will miss the visitation during times of revival for many different reasons:

Factors in MISSING VISITATION

- By judging the present visitation by past visitations and not realizing God may be doing something new and wonderful.
- By not being open to accepting the Holy Spirit's moving in a fresh way because it is not according to our denominational or religous backgrounds.
- By not being open because it is illogical to the natural mind.
- By not moving in fresh, new truths because of fear that we may be identified with those who have misused or abused these same truths.
- By not preparing for the visitation and prayerfully anticipating it.
- By not recognizing that visitation may add new converts to the church and change believers slowly by God's presence, rather than a revival type outpouring, which comes suddenly and subsides quickly.
- By backing off from God doing something different in the church today.

A.W. Tozer, in one of his books, stated: "I want here boldly to assert that it is my happy belief that every Christian can have a copious outpouring of the Holy Spirit in a measure far beyond that received at conversion and, I might also say, far beyond that enjoyed by the rank and file of orthodox believers today."

As we lead our churches in renewal and in revival, we must have the spirit of A.W. Tozer. We must believe that God will pour out upon believers a copious amount of the Holy Spirit and that we can enjoy more of the Holy Spirit than we have ever had and more of God's presence than we have ever seen in the past. It is open for us now.

As leaders, we do not want to in any way resist, hinder, quench, or stop the Holy Spirit's moving in our lives or in the lives of the people the Lord has given us oversight of. For that reason, it is very important that we have hearts that are responsive to the things of God, yet not so gullible that we would encourage or allow things that would be hurtful, excessive experiences that would quench people's love for God or their walk with God.

PART 7

DISCERNING THE TIMES

Chapter 23

REVIVAL PRAYING

*T*here has always been a spirit of prayer and intercession associated with spiritual awakening, both in Scripture and in history. Revival is preceded by prayer, birthed through intercession, and sustained by fervent, persevering prayer. Prayer is the central living element to every spiritual awakening and every moving of the Holy Spirit.

The historical reformation of the 1500s was undoubtedly the result of fervent, godly intercessory prayer. Many of the reformers extending from the 1400s to later 1600s were men and women of intense prayer. They prayed, believing for revival, reformation, or spiritual awakening. Girolamo Savonarola, the fifteenth century Italian revivalist; Martin Luther, father of the Reformation; John Knox, who captured the purposes of God for Scotland and paid the price for it; and George Fox, the founder of the Quakers, all birthed something in prayer.

A spirit of revival or renewal in the hearts of true believers should always result in a renewed spirit of prayer. Fervent prayer is one of the first signs of revived spiritual life in an individual believer and in that of the church. Personal prayer is a prerequisite to corporate revival. First, we are personally renewed in and by prayer, and then we can become a prayer center to intercede for global revival.

Adam Clarke, the Methodist theologian of the late eighteenth and early nineteenth centuries, said: "Prayer is a pouring out of the soul unto God as a free-will offering, solemnly and eternally dedicated to Him, accompanied with the most earnest desire that it may know, love and serve Him alone." This is the spirit of revival: a renewed soul and a freshly inflamed heart.

Prayer is an awesomely powerful weapon in our spiritual war with the enemy. Dr. Paul Cedar, pastor of the world's largest congregational church, in Pasadena, California, said: "Satan laughs at our toiling and mocks our trying, but he shakes when he sees the weakest saint of God on his knees."

Prayer can be dynamic and exciting, or it can be dull and deadly. It is simple, yet complex. It is natural, yet a skill to be learned.

A praying church moves more deeply in strategic and consistent prayer. The church may be like be a well-designed machine with intricate parts of all sizes and shapes designed and assembled to work smoothly, yet without lubrication these parts will destroy each other. Prayer is God's oil of lubrication for His church.

There are several steps to moving into a time of revival-type prayer. Let us prepare to seek God and His awesome presence.

BREAKING UP THE FALLOW GROUND

Hosea 10:12 is one of the great revival Scriptures concerning prayer: "Sow for yourselves righteousness; reap in mercy; break up your fallow ground, for it is time to seek the Lord, till He comes and rains righteousness on you."

The first work of prayer in a believer's life is the work of breaking up the unplowed ground of the heart. To break up implies shattering, penetrating, splitting, dividing, or opening up that which has been closed. Job 16:12 states: "I was at ease, but He has shattered me . . ." In Psalm 31:12, David says: ". . . I am like a broken vessel." In Matthew 21:44, the Lord Jesus simply states: "Whoever falls on this stone will be broken; but on whomever it falls, it will grind him to powder."

Unproductive soil produces nothing. It is ground that has been fruitful in the past, but it is now unproductive. Revival comes to renew this ground so that it might bring forth thirty, sixty, and a hundred fold fruit once again.

Unplowed ground is destitute of the fruit it might produce because of neglect. It is the soil of the hearts of those whose affections, habits, and thoughts were once bearing a rich harvest for God, but whose hearts have become barren through temptation, neglect, and ignorance.

The fallow ground is unprofitable soil. It is the carnal natural man, and it must be broken up. The hard ground must be broken by the plow of the Word and the plow of the Spirit, which works on our hearts through prayer.

> "Unproductive soil produces nothing. It is ground that has been fruitful in the past, but it is now unproductive."

Hard, uncultivated earth that is covered with weeds, thistles, and thorns that have caused unfruitfulness needs to be opened to the sun, the dew, and the rain of God. Unless the ground is prepared, the rain will fall but not be absorbed. It will not penetrate the heart.

This breaking up is a labor for which the Lord Jesus Himself imparts strength and wisdom. It is a work of renovation in which the owner of the ground knows that the soil in its present state is unfit to produce any useful crop. When the weeds that have covered the ground and kept it from being productive are removed and the hardness of the ground is turned to softness, then that ground can bear good fruit.

In this kind of prayer, God deals deeply with us, breaking up the ground of our hearts and minds through repentance and confession. This kind of praying prepares the heart, mind, and spirit to bring forth fruit unto God. It is praying while recognizing that the heart must be cleansed of ingratitude, neglect, coldness, worldliness, pride, unforgiveness, slander, lying, jealousy, and temper.

DISCERNING THE HEART CONDITION

The first call to prepare for revival is the discerning of the heart condition. In the parable given by the Lord Jesus in Matthew 13, He describes the four different heart conditions. Matthew 13:1-9 gives the parable and verses 18-23 are the interpretation.

The Cluttered Heart

"Now he who received seed among the thorns is he who hears the word, and the cares of this world and the deceitfulness of riches choke the word, and he becomes unfruitful" (Matthew 13:22).

The cluttered or overcrowded heart has good potential, but is full of distractions, and the ground becomes thorny. This speaks of a person whose life is filled with the interests of this world. The materialistic ambitions choke out the convictions for the kingdom. It has too many other commitments that slowly choke the struggling plant, which will consequently never mature and bear fruit.

The competing thorns are summed up under two headings: works of life and deceitfulness of riches. These thorns are so subtle that one might not be aware they are choking the heart until it is too late. This person finds all the seemingly good effect has gone, leaving the soil covered with a thicket of thorns.

Cares, riches, lusts, and other things in life can all suffocate the moving of the Holy Spirit and the receiving of the word of God. The seeds of thorns are already in the ground.

The Wayside Heart

"When anyone hears the word of the kingdom, and does not understand it, then the wicked one comes and snatches away what was sown in his heart. This is he who received seed by the wayside" (Matthew 13:19).

The wayside heart is the indifferent heart, a heart that is hardened through busyness or preoccupation. The seeds fall on the path, but the path is hard because of all of the trampling and traffic. Therefore, the seed is not able to penetrate the ground, and is wasted.

> **"The materialistic ambitions choke out the convictions for the kingdom."**

The Shallow Heart

"But he who received the seed on stony places, this is he who hears the word and immediately receives it with joy" (Matthew 13:20).

The shallow heart is the heart of those who respond to God, but with little depth because of the rocky places where the seeds have landed. This heart has a hidden agenda and other priorities that prevent in-depth understanding. This heart receives the word in a superficial, thoughtless way and shows immediate signs of life and promise to bear the best crop. But external pressures, troubles, and persecutions reveal the shallowness of the soil. This heart produces only a temporary disciple with temporary growth. It has no roots, and when temptation or immediate offenses come, the seed is wasted.

The country in Galilee is typically made up of limestone. It is layered rock with a thin covering of soil over the rock. In terrain like this, seeds will shoot up at once, but the roots have no place to penetrate because they are immediately confronted with the limestone.

> "The shallow heart is the heart of those who respond to God, but with little depth because of the rocky places where the seeds have landed."

The Responsive Heart

"But he who received seed on the good ground is he who hears the word and understands it, who indeed bears fruit and produces: some a hundredfold, some sixty, some thirty" (Matthew 13:23).

The responsive or understanding heart is honest and open, grasping the word and the moving of the Holy Spirit. This heart welcomes the word. It hungers and thirsts after righteousness, and longs for the meaning of right purpose.

An understanding heart in the Hebrew has the basic idea of perceiving a message, of being very attentive to hearing and responding to that message with obedience. In 1 Kings 3:5-15, God appears to Solomon and tells him that he may receive anything he asks for. Solomon answered by simply asking for an understanding heart. God was so pleased with this response from Solomon that He promised him that all other things—power, wealth, and influence—would come with this gift of understanding.

The ability to receive God's revelation and uphold God's truth is one of the heart, not of the head. The ability to receive and search out God is a childlike quality. It implies innocence and simplicity. These are the conditions in which God reveals Himself to people. Without them, people cannot know God or receive or understand God. People perceive God by revelation, not by philosophy. It is not through hard, stern, strong, great reasoning that people get hold of God, but through big, soft, pure hearts. Healthy spiritual inner attitudes that receive and retain the things spoken of by the Spirit, whether directly or by the preached word, are the responsive hearts, the hearts that are sensitive to the Holy Spirit. God can fill an understanding heart with His own wisdom so that He can be the governor of that life. The seed of insight is in the heart that discerns the work and word of God.

> "The ability to receive God's revelation and uphold God's truth is one of the heart, not of the head."

DISCERNING THE TIME

Hosea 10:12 says, "Break up your fallow ground, for it is time to seek the Lord." All revivals have a special sovereign time table that God Himself understands and works upon. We need to pray in times of visitation that the set times and appointed times of God's seasons will be revealed to us so that we might intercede and enter into the moving of the Holy Spirit that God has ordained.

Breaking up the fallow ground and plowing the hardened heart is the first step in revival praying. The next step is understanding the times. Job 14:13 states: "That You would appoint me a set time." This is a set time to intercede, a set time to understand the times of God. In Romans 13:11, it says, "Now is the time!" Revival praying taps into the appointed times of God's purposes (also see Nehemiah 10:39, 13:31; Ezra 10:14; Esther 4:14; Exodus 9:5; Jeremiah 8:7; Genesis 17:21, 18:14).

Time is significant in both the Old Testament and the New Testament. Scripture allocates the significance of time outside of the individual experience. Time, like the rest of the environments in which human beings move, has been ordered and designed by God. It is marked by cycles and repetition, and yet flows from a beginning toward a culmination.

We all deal with cycles, days, weeks, months, seasons, and years. Time flows toward a determined future. An individual, a congregation, or a nation may find that personal experience intersects with appointed times when life is bathed in prayer. There are times when God acts in the stream of history to keep history on its appointed course. God moves and creates circumstances, raises up leaders, and deals with people as He seeks to fulfill appointed crossroads in history.

Experienced time is simply that span of time in which an individual or generation exists. Experienced time is time spent, but it is not necessarily spiritually profitable. Experienced time can intersect with appointed times, making time particularly opportune (Titus 1:3; 2 Peter 5:6). This is why prayer is so important. The difference between significant time and wasted time will be greatly determined through a person's prayer life.

As we pray and discern God's dealings—God's time clock—we may intersect with divine appointment. Our lives and times then become filled with purpose. These appointed times are in His hands and develop according to His plan. The personal experience time that God allots each one of us may, through prayer, intersect with God's appointed times.

CHRONOS TIME AND KAIROS TIME

There are two words in the New Testament for time: *chronos* and *kairos*. *Chronos*, where we get our English word chronology, simply designates a period or space of time. It is close in meaning to the rather scientific way in which westerners speak of time. it is the succession of time, a ration of seasons.

> "Experienced time is time spent, but it is not necessarily spiritually profitable."

Chronos expresses the duration of a period, but *kairos* stresses time as being marked by certain features. Kairos speaks of a moment of opportunity marked by hearing God's voice afresh and anew. It highlights the significance of that brief or extended moment that *chronos* time brings. *Kairos* characterizes the content and the quality of the time. It is a moment made significant by a divine encounter with God. The due measure, proportion, or fixed definite period or season may become an opportune or appointed season, based on our seeking God. A *kairos* time is a time where we see prophecy being fulfilled, a time when God's purposes are extended.

"And do this, knowing the time, that now it is high time to awake out of sleep; for now our salvation is nearer than when we first believed" (Romans 13:11).

The time in this verse is *kairos* time. It is a time when God Himself seeks to work in wonderful and powerful ways.

"It is time for You to act, O Lord, for they have regarded Your law as void" (Psalm 119:126).

"You will arise and have mercy on Zion; for the time to favor her, yes, the set time, has come" (Psalm 102:13).

"For He says: 'In an acceptable time I have heard you, and in the day of salvation I have helped you.' Behold, now is the accepted time; behold, now is the day of salvation" (2 Corinthians 6:2).

There are appointed and acceptable times in God's economy when He fulfills His appointed purposes. Revival can be seen as an appointed season, a time when God makes culture, history, and His kingdom interact and intersect for His appointed purposes on earth. As we pray in preparation for revival, we may be praying ourselves into a position to experience a *kairos* time, an opportune season where God is fulfilling His purposes in history, and we can be a part of it.

Prayerlessness is not just a sin that will ruin your spiritual life, but it may cause you to miss God's extended purposes and His appointed times.

Andrew Murray said: "The sin of prayerlessness is a proof that the life of God in the soul is in deadly sickness and weakness."

Samuel Chadwick stated: "It would seem as if the biggest thing in God's universe is a man who prays. There is only one thing more amazing. That is, that man, knowing this, should not pray!"

In a very real sense, preparing for revival is praying in faith, believing that the appointed season is upon us. It is praying in faith that we can discern God's time table. In the time of revival, we pray for more of God's Spirit. This is enjoying the appointed time within the experienced time. Revival praying includes an understanding that it is time to seek the Lord. These are special seasons that God has set aside that we might embrace His living presence and be able to minister that same presence to our needy culture.

SEEKING GOD WITH INTENSITY

> "In the time of revival, we pray for more of God's Spirit. This is enjoying the appointed time within the experienced time."

We have an invitation to seek God at all times, but there are times when we find Him more easily. God is serious in every season, but especially in the seasons of outpouring. These are turning-point times, appointed times.

"To seek" implies an intentional turning to God with intensity, and not just with routine praying. To seek means to search for carefully, to run after, to search diligently, to reach out so as to take hold of. In 2 Chronicles 15:1-12, we have the covenant of Asa, who made a pledge to seek the Lord and entered into that covenant with great results.

"But from there you will seek the Lord your God, and you will find Him if you seek Him with all your heart and with all your soul. When you are in distress, and all these things come upon you in the latter days, when you turn to the Lord your God and obey His voice." (Deuteronomy 4:29-30).

"As for you, my son Solomon, know the God of your father, and serve Him with a loyal heart and with a willing mind; for the Lord searches all hearts and understands all the intent of the thoughts. If you seek Him, He will be found by you; but if you forsake Him, He will cast you off forever" (1 Chronicles 28:9).

> " 'To seek' implies an intentional turning to God with intensity, and not just with routine praying."

PRAYING WITH PERSEVERANCE—"UNTIL"

Revival means understanding that now is the time to seek God and that we are the people. Only God can send rain, and we should seek God until He rains upon us. We can prepare for the rain—plow the ground and ask—but only God can revive His people. The word until, in the Hebrew, means a duration of set time or space, whether long or short, with the idea of how long. It implies praying with perseverance and faith, believing that God will eventually do what He says in Scripture.

"Then Jacob was left alone; and a Man wrestled with him until the breaking of day" (Genesis 32:24).

"The scepter shall not depart from Judah, nor a lawgiver from between his feet, until Shiloh comes; and to Him shall be the obedience of the people" (Genesis 49:10).

"Until the time that his word came to pass, the word of the Lord tested him" (Psalm 105:19).

"Whom heaven must receive until the times of restoration of all things, which God has spoken by the mouth of all His holy prophets since the world began" (Acts 3:21).

"So Cornelius said, 'Four days ago I was fasting until this hour; and at the ninth hour I prayed in my house, and behold, a man stood before me in bright clothing' " (Acts 10:30).

(Also see Deuteronomy 3:20; Psalm 110:1, 112:8; Romans 8:22; Galatians 4:2, 4:19; James 5:7.)

The word until implies prayer that does not stop short. This is prayer that believes there is a breaking of the day, an outpouring of the Spirit, an appointed time of the Father, and that there is something to wait patiently for and to pray fervently unto. Persistence is the word here. It is sticking to a purpose or aim, never giving up what one sets out to do, and refusing to be discouraged by obstacles or difficulties. This is the prayer spirit that endures. This is a prayer faith that grasps and holds onto what God has said, continuing steadily with courage and patience, refusing to stop or be changed. This is the kind of prayer that gives constant attention in spite of all obstacles.

> "This is prayer that believes there is a breaking of the day, an outpouring of the Spirit, an appointed time of the Father..."

"Praying always with all prayer and supplication in the Spirit, being watchful to this end with all perseverance and supplication for all the saints" (Ephesians 6:18).

"These all continued with one accord in prayer and supplication, with the women and Mary the mother of Jesus, and with His brothers" (Acts 1:14).

"Rejoicing in hope, patient in tribulation, continuing steadfastly in prayer" (Romans 12:12).

The parable in Luke 18:1-8 is one of perseverance in prayer. It tells how the widow continually cried out day and night until her prayer was answered. This is praying until something breaks, until something is poured out, until deliverance is seen.

In Luke 11:5-13, there is another parable of perseverance. It is about a man who goes out at midnight to ask a friend for bread. Even though the door is shut, the lights are out, and the friend inside says "do not trouble me," the man does not give up. He is persistent until the person inside arises and gives him what he needs. Jesus said: "Ask, and it will be given to you; seek, and you will find; knock, and it will be opened to you." Praying persistently is praying with a fervent faith that believes the door will be opened and that the bread will come.

"Ask the Lord for rain in the time of the latter rain. The Lord will make flashing clouds; he will give them showers of rain, grass in the field for everyone" (Zechariah 10:1).

"Then it came to pass the seventh time, that he said, 'There is a cloud, as small as a man's hand, rising out of the sea!' So he said, 'Go up, say to Ahab, "Prepare your chariot, and go down before the rain stops you" ' " (1 Kings 18:44).

Preparing for revival means praying in faith and believing that clouds will gather and that God will send rain. Revival praying is a praying that grabs hold of this vision and sees the outpouring of the Holy Spirit as reality, then prays with all of its might and strength toward this end. It is praying that fruitfulness and refreshing will once again be part of the lives of God's people. Revival praying is taking hold of God in such a way that we will not let go (see Isaiah 27:5, 64:7).

"For the earth which drinks in the rain that often comes upon it, and bears herbs useful for those by whom it is cultivated, receives blessing from God" (Hebrews 6:7).

THE TRANSFORMING POWER OF PRAYER

Revival praying changes a lukewarm Laodicean Church to an on-fire, Holy Spirit-filled church. A Laodicean Church, referred to in Revelation 3, is a church that is complacent and self-centered.

A complacent church is one that is at ease, careless, proud and arrogant, one that has no burden for the lost or for spiritual activity. It is a church that is lounging in its own carnal luxury. This church is at ease.

"Woe to you who are at ease in Zion, and trust in Mount Samaria, notable persons in the chief nation, to whom the house of Israel comes!" (Amos 6:1). (Also see Job 5:12; Isaiah 32:9-11, 66:8.)

A self-centered church is one that spends more time decorating or adorning itself than it does seeking God. It is a church that loves self, money, and pleasure more than the Word, the Spirit, and the harvest.

Revival praying comes to change a complacent, self-centered church into a fervent, hot, praying church. In Matthew 21:13-14, Jesus quoted from Isaiah 56:7-8 when He said, "My house shall be called a house of prayer." Revival praying restores the concept and spirit of the house of prayer.

> **"Revival praying changes a lukewarm Laodicean Church to an on-fire, Holy Spirit-filled church."**

FILLING UP OF THE TWO CUPS

The house of prayer becomes a house of incense. Psalm 141:1-2 describes prayer as ascending to God as incense and the lifting of hands as an evening sacrifice. In Luke 1:9-11, Zacharias, who was the priest of the temple, was to burn incense. It says in verse 10 that the people were praying outside during the time of incense. In Revelation 8:3-4, Christ, as the High Priest, is offering incense, which is the prayers of the saints, up to God, and these prayers are being put into a cup.

There are two cups to be filled in these days. One is the cup of sin and iniquity, and the other is the cup of righteousness and intercession. Both cups will be filled, and both cups will be poured out upon the earth. The principle of filling the cup and the revelation of knowing the cup will be poured out is a motivation for revival praying. As the ungodly fill the cup with sin, corruption, lawlessness, and filth, we should be prepared for the judgment, the wrath and anger of God, to be poured out double upon the earth. Both the eighth and fourteenth chapters of Revelation deal with the cup that will be filled. (Also see Psalm 75:8, 11:6, 73:10; Habakkuk 2:16; and Revelation 16:19, 17:4, 18:6.)

The following illustration will show what these Scriptures teach us:

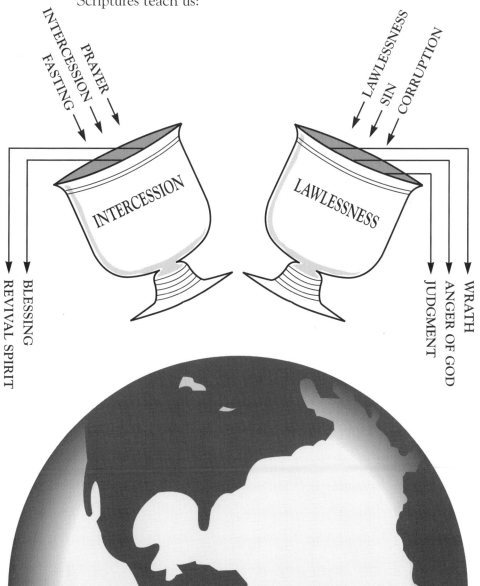

We will here draw one cup filled with sin, lawlessness, corruption, and filth. There will be another cup that is being tipped toward the right, as if to be poured out, and showing a pouring forth of the words judgment, wrath, and the anger of God.

Every person and nation is filling either the cup of lawlessness or the cup of prayer. The cup of righteousness and intercession is being filled by the people of God. In Revelation 8:3-4 are the golden censors, which were full of the prayers of the saints. This cup is being filled so that God can pour out upon the earth His blessing and His revival spirit (also see Psalm 23:5, 116:113; Job 36:27-30).

Here we have a picture of a cup that is being filled with intercession, faith, fasting, prayer, and righteousness. Then another cup being tilted and poured out which has blessing, honor, revival, joy, and Holy Spirit activity.

Two cups, two groups of people, two totally different contents in the cups, two results. There is a cup for every person, for every city, for every nation, and for the world. The smoke of the incense that comes up before the throne of God is the prayers of the saints that continually ascend up before the throne. This incense is to be sweet, pure, perpetual, and holy. This is the description of holy, fervent revival praying. (See 1 Thessalonians 5:16-17; Revelation 11:1; James 4:2-3; Ephesians 6:18-19.)

PRAYER HINDRANCES

Revival praying seeks to remove all hindrances to a powerful spirit of prayer that seeks to overtake the people of God.

Prayers can be hindered for several reasons. Here are just a few:

1. Prayer is hindered by sin and iniquity in our lives (Isaiah 59:1-2; Psalm 66:18).

2. Prayer is hindered by marital problems (2 Peter 3:7).

3. Prayer is hindered by willful, presumptuous, disobedience to God's Word (Proverbs 28:9).

4. Prayer is hindered by unforgiveness in our lives (Matthew 5:23-24, 6:9-13; Mark 11:2).

5. Prayer is hindered when we pray with selfish motives (James 4:3).

6. Prayer is hindered by idolatry in the heart (Ezekiel 14:3).

7. Prayer is hindered by selfishness or stinginess (Proverbs 21:13; Luke 6:38; 1 John 3:22; Philippians 4:19).

8. Prayer is hindered by unbelief (James 1:5-7).

9. Prayer is hindered by spiritual warfare or demonic powers (Daniel 10:10-14; Ephesians 6:11-12).

A PRAYER OF PURGING

St. Augustine spoke of the soul in these words: "Oh Lord, the house of my soul is narrow; enlarge it that You may enter it. It is ruinous, it displeases Your sight. I confess it, I know it, but who shall cleanse it? To Whom shall I cry out but to You? Cleanse me from my secret faults, Oh Lord, and spare Your servant from strange sins."

Revival reveals the smallness and the sickness of our souls so that we might cry unto God to change us. This prayer will lay the foundation for a spirit of revival in the midst of God's people. But we must first approach the throne of God and receive a coal off the altar so that our lips are purged. And then we can, through the fire of God, purge this generation.

Chapter 24

A PASSION FOR THE HARVEST

*A*while back, as I was preparing to pray for reaping the harvest in our city and to speak on that subject in the church I pastor, I jotted down a few thoughts that came to me out of my prayer time:

"I am overwhelmed with the multitude of lost souls around me in our city, our nation, and our world. At times, I feel overwhelmed with the burden of sin and eternity. I get caught up with life and really don't make room for true evangelism. I grow weary of the hype, the sensationalism, and the superficial gospelizing, and I am driven to withdraw from any tactics that smack of these things. Then I end up doing nothing at all because of my own reaction.

I am hungry for something fresh, something real and workable. I truly ache for more of the Holy Spirit's fire upon believers, which will result in true power evangelism and true soul winning. I understand our day and our culture and the absolute disintegration of godliness, church, Bible, family, and morality. I feel that we must break out and attack or be run over by secularism.

We need a Gideon spirit. I long, not only for evangelism, but for discipleship; not just winning souls, but keeping souls. The Bible is our only hope, the gospel, the book of evangelism. God, do something in me, now, today, for my generation."

TRUE REVIVAL IGNITES A PASSION FOR THE HARVEST

A revival spirit in the midst of the church should undoubtedly begin to nurture a spirit of passion for the harvest. Revival always arrives in God's sovereign time table to light the fires of evangelism once again in the hearts of His people. If there is any balancing statement that should be made about revival it is this: We should not seek revival for our own experience only. To see our own lives touched, changed, healed, and filled with more of the presence of God is only one aspect of God's intention for revival. The other aspect of revival is that after we are filled, healed, and have encountered the living presence of God, we are then to release what we have received to others.

> **"Revival was never meant to be an experience that we enjoy as we have a kingdom party."**

Revival was never meant to be an experience that we enjoy as we have a kingdom party. Of course, there are times when we will have spiritual refreshing when we soak in, enjoy, and are filled with God's presence. We must translate these times into intercessory prayer and strategies and plans to reach our cities for Christ.

We are to do the work of the kingdom of God, which is reaching the lost, seeing broken lives healed, and seeing our society penetrated by a clear message of the gospel of Jesus Christ.

PASSION IS BIRTHED BY REVIVAL

If we are to achieve God's best, it will require a wholehearted abandonment and a godly passion. All people who ever accomplished anything significant in life had a consuming zeal that enabled them to leap over all obstacles in pursuit of their goal. There was an element of passion in their area of accomplishment.

Positioning a church for evangelism goes far beyond implementing a program or hiring additional staff. Ultimately, it takes a corporate change of heart. Revival is simply a time when God comes in His power and by His Spirit to change the hearts of His people.

The church has historically been known as an institution that becomes ingrown with its own programs and needs as it ultimately loses touch with outside society and culture. Revival is a time when God comes and breathes back into the church a burden for the lost and the desire to reach back into society and be the salt and light it is called to be.

Passion can be defined as "Jesus Christ dying on the cross." Unlike secular thinking, passion in this context is not simply a joyful or lustful experience. When we speak of passion, we speak of intensity, emotion, and a heavy burden to find that which is lost. To be passionate means that you are stirred up, warm-blooded and awakened to the things of God. Revival comes to set people on fire. Revival comes to stir up, touch a cord, and go directly to our hearts. Revival should touch to the quick; it should go deep. Revival comes to turn our heads and sweep us off our feet toward the things of God.

The opposite of passion is passivity, which is to be inactive, untouched, unemotional, unstirred, indifferent, neutral, and sluggish. Obviously, we have not been called to be passive. We have been called to be passionate. We need to develop passionate affections, and we need to have a responsible, passionate concern for the harvest that is set before us in our generation.

The Scriptures speak of the Lord Jesus as being clothed with the cloak of zeal (Psalm 119:139; Isaiah 59:17). Being born in Christ and of Christ and having Him dwelling in our hearts by faith, we have that zeal living in our hearts also. We should, as God's people, be clothed with the cloak of zeal, as our Master and Lord was also clothed with zeal (1 Corinthians 14:12; 2 Corinthians 7:11; Galatians 4:18). We are not to be passive spectators or non-participants, quiet and neutral toward the moving of the Holy Spirit. We are to become fervent. Revival should keep us at the boiling point of the Holy Spirit (Romans 12:11; Exodus 35:21, 26; Matthew 3:11).

> "Revival spirit restores a passionate heart to the people of God."

PEOPLE OF PASSION

Revival spirit restores a passionate heart to the people of God. Lukewarmness goes, indifference is thrown aside, and the fire of God's Spirit burns deeply. Revival is a time when the Holy Spirit births a passionate spirit in all believers.

The Bible gives us several wonderful examples of the kind of passion we need to reach a lost world with the redemptive message of Jesus Christ.

Joshua had a passion and a dream for the land that God had set before him to possess. He had a passion that put faith in his mouth instead of unbelief, and a warrior's spirit in his heart instead of cowardice. "We are more than able to go up and take the land," said Joshua, because he had a spirit of warfare upon him and a vision and a passion that drove him into the land.

Caleb had a passion for the impossible. "Give me this mountain," was his cry. "Give me the giants."

Nehemiah had a passion to see the vision completed, to rebuild and restore the city of God. Others saw the rubble and the rebellion, but not Nehemiah. He saw with eyes of passion, the potential. He saw the city built. He looked beyond the work and saw the fruit of the labor.

David had a passion for God, a passion to love and do great things. He was a magnet. He drew others to himself because he was a passionate man. When the flames of passion died in his people, he lit them again with his own passion. Anyone who came close to David in the Cave of Adulum would arrive defeated, in bondage, and in debt, but they would not leave the same. They had been touched by the passionate spirit that rested upon David.

Paul had a passion to see the known world won to Christ. Nothing could stem his fire—not stretching, extension, suffering, or betrayal. A man of rare passion, he was able to channel and harness that passion and use it for the kingdom of God. He imparted passion to everyone who spent any time at all with him. He magnetized people. He taught them how to press toward the mark. He taught them zeal. He was a man who was so zealous that he would lay down his life for the passionate vision that he had for the harvest.

Jesus, who is our ultimate model, was a man of passion. He had a passion to fulfill the redemptive work that God had set before Him, to build His church and to defeat the gates of hell. He had a passion for people, a passion for the harvest. "The zeal of Thine house hath eaten me up," it says in the Gospel of John. Jesus knew that the house must be built in order for the harvest to be reaped.

In addition to these biblical examples of passion, there have been many, many people of God during church history who have demonstrated this kind of passion:

George Whitefield, the Great Awakening Evangelist, uttered these words: "Give me souls or I will die." This is a man driven by passion.

Henry Martyn, the Anglican missionary to India, cried out: "Now let me burn out for God," as he stood on Indian soil for the first time. These are words of passion.

As revival moves into our personal lives, our responsibility is to keep alive the flame of God's gracious gift and to fan that flame into a ministry that will reach out to others (2 Timothy 1:6). The words fervency, stirred, fire, awaken, arouse, and zealous are all biblical words that speak of people who have been revived and renewed in the Holy Spirit. (See Isaiah 51:9; Philippians 3:10-12.)

The church must contain an element of contagious intensity, an emotion and a spirit that has been set on fire by the Holy Spirit. A revived church has been set on fire with a passion for the harvest. The word harvest speaks of the season of gathering a crop, a time of reaping that which is mature and ripened. The Lord Jesus says that the harvest is ripe, but the laborers are few (Matthew 9:35-37).

We need a vision that sees the world as God's harvest field: the entire world—every city, every state, every nation, every continent. All unreached people groups in the world must be reached with the gospel of the kingdom. A people has been reached only when many of its members have become disciples of Christ and responsible members of His body. Until the church is well rooted in that society, it has not been reached. There are now approximately 17,000 unreached people groups within 3,000 different ethnic clusters of the world. A church for every people by the year 2000 can be a realistic goal for the people of God who are revived by the Holy Spirit and have received a new focus and mission for the harvest.

Oswald J. Smith, the great missiologist, spoke his burden when he said, "Why should anyone hear the gospel twice until everyone has heard it once?" D.L. Moody, the mighty evangelist, said, "It can be done. It must be done."

A VISION FOR THE HARVEST

The gospel of the kingdom of God must be preached to all the unsaved, to all those who have never heard the gospel and to those who have heard but have not yet made a decision. To have a vision for the harvest means we must go after those who have never called on the name of the Lord. These people are in every neighborhood, every city, every state, and every nation of the world.

We must be honest with our own evangelism status and our church growth. We need to nurture a philosophy that clearly understands and honestly evaluates all groups by asking these questions: Is it biological growth? Is it transfer growth? Is it conversion growth?

> "The church exists, not for herself, but for the world."

The church exists, not for herself, but for the world. She always has the two-fold task: winning people to Christ and taking people onto maturity in Him (Matthew 28:19-20). The church that reaps the harvest has a conviction and believes that as Christ's servants, we shall stand before His throne eternally saved but nonetheless accountable to answer for our stewardship of the gospel entrusted to us and for the souls committed to our care.

The Bible teaches and we should believe that at Christ's coming and the resurrection of the dead, each human being shall be committed to either heaven or hell, depending on each one's acceptance or rejection of Jesus Christ. There are now 4,000 unreached Muslim groups, 3,000 unreached tribal groups, 2,000 unreached Hindu groups, 1,000 unreached Han Chinese groups, 1,000 unreached Buddhist groups, and millions of Americans who have never called on the name of the Lord. We believe in the eternal value of the soul and that each one of these people who do not call upon the name of the Lord and are not born again will spend eternity in hell.

God loves every single soul. Every person is special to Him. Each human life is precious to Him. Yet every one of these precious people outside of Christ's salvation will be eternally lost. God desires that none be lost, but that all be saved. God has not predestined anyone to hell. Eternity is a choice. We all must choose, and God has given us Christ to persuade us toward that choice. Salvation has been freely given through the Lord Jesus Christ, and He is the only way to obtain forgiveness of sins and a seal of our eternal destiny.

DEDICATED TO THE HARVEST

For the church to reap the harvest in this generation, we need to have dedication. We need people who will dedicate and consecrate themselves to a divine plan and a sacred purpose. These are a people who give themselves wholly and completely to that purpose. Romans 12:1 says, "I beseech you, therefore brethren, by the mercies of God that you present your bodies a living sacrifice, holy, acceptable unto God which is your reasonable service."

Jim Elliot, the Auca Indian martyr, wrote "God, I pray, thee, light those idle sticks of my life that I may burn for thee. Consume my life, my God, for it is thine. I seek not a long life, but a full one, like you, Lord Jesus." God is not as concerned with your ability as your availability.

God has commissioned us to proclaim the message of salvation daily as His ambassadors. We are already more than qualified to do the work of evangelism. We already have the Holy Spirit to enable us to proclaim the gospel message by His power.

God working with us with supernatural signs following is a promise. He has promised to do so in every generation. We have prayed for renewal in this generation, and the Holy Spirit has responded. A revival spirit is being poured out upon us in a fresh and new way. God will give us the wisdom and power to reach our generation within our own unique culture. We can communicate the gospel message in a manner this generation will receive and respond to. God has a time and a space for every generation, and now can be that time.

> "We can communicate the gospel message in a manner this generation will receive and respond to."

We must affirm our commitment to reaping the harvest, to being God's sent messengers into this harvest, now, today. The Amsterdam Evangelism Conference affirmed this commitment by writing this statement: "We affirm our commitment to the Great Commission of our Lord and declare our willingness to go anywhere, do anything, sacrifice anything God requires of us in the fulfillment of that commission."

May all of us, as people of the living God, make that same commitment to reaping the harvest.

Revival comes to pour fresh oil upon the fire of our hearts. The fire of our zeal needs to burn brighter and stronger than ever. In the book *Pilgrim's Progress*, Christian saw the fire on the hearth in the Interpreter's house and saw one sprinkling it with water, yet the flame rose higher and higher. He marveled at this until he saw someone beyond the fire pouring oil on it.

It is the work of the Holy Spirit to constantly pour oil on the fire and keep our zeal at a boiling point. The devil will always try to pour water on our zeal and our passion for the harvest. But remember, revival season is the time to receive oil on the fire.

> "The devil will always try to pour water on our zeal and our passion for the harvest."

Alexander Whyte, the Scottish minister in the mid 1800s to the early 1900s, stated: "Yes, if you will, you can think and read and pray yourself into the possession of a heart as hot as Paul's heart. For the same Holy Spirit as gave Christ His hot heart and Paul his hot heart is given to you also."

EMPOWERING FOR REAPING

The purpose of revival is to empower the people of God to reap the harvest. God is like a wise farmer who sows seeds so he may reap a harvest. God wants the harvest. He is not pleased with a non-harvest, no-fruit mentality.

The Lord is not pleased with:

- Fishing without catching (Luke 5:4-11).
- Empty banqueting tables (Luke 14:15-23).
- Sowing without reaping (Matthew 13:3-9).
- Fig trees that bear no fruit (Luke 13:6-9).
- Lost sheep that are not brought into the fold (Matthew 18:11-14).
- The lost coin that is not sought and is not found (Luke 15:8-10).
- Ripe harvests that are not reaped (Matthew 9:36).
- Proclamation without response (Matthew 10:14).

Proverbs 10:5 reads, "He who gathers in summer is a wise son; he who sleeps in harvest is a son who causes shame." The church cannot be a son who brings shame to the name of the Lord Jesus Christ. We are not a son who sleeps in harvest, who closes his eyes and turns over in bed and ignores the ripened fields that are crying out to have someone thrust in their sickle. We are ordinary people going into ordinary places to reap extraordinary harvest.

We need to develop a conviction and a harvest philosophy that can be adopted by all people, one that will excite the people of God into the harvest fields. Revival occurs to bring this kind of passion, this kind of a stirring.

A HARVEST PHILOSOPHY

Bill Bright, founder of Campus Crusade for Christ, when asked what motivated him for evangelizing the world, responded: "The filling of the Holy Spirit and knowledge that the harvest is not forever. It will soon be past." We need to develop a harvest philosophy that excites believers into sharpening their sickles and preparing for the greatest harvest ever reaped in all of history.

A Harvest Philosophy Results in a Church that Becomes a Force in the Earth

A harvest philosophy tells us that the church is a place of growth, power, and excitement. God is not pleased with evangelistic and missionary work that does not result in church growth and church harvest. We need 100,000 new missionaries and 12,000 new church-plant teams each year. There are 70 million evangelical Christians in America between the ages of 18 and 35, and we only need one half of 1 percent of those to fulfill the need in evangelizing the world. There are now more than 2,000 plans operating with the goal of reaching the entire world for Christ. Ninety-two of these plans are minutely detailed blueprints.

A Harvest Philosophy Results in a Spirit of Intercessory Prayer

Hudson Taylor, the great missionary to China, stated "We have given too much attention to methods and to machinery and to resources and too little to the source of power, the filling with the Holy Spirit." The Holy Spirit is poured out in a more powerful way during revival times. As the Holy Spirit touches the hearts of people and enlarges their vision for the harvest, it should result in a spirit of intercessory prayer and a willingness to be involved in reaping the harvest.

A Harvest Philosophy Faces a Negative Society with a Positive Faith

A harvest philosophy propagates a positive approach to a negative society. It can give us a positive attitude of faith because the answer is found in Christ, and He is committed to the harvest. People with a harvest passion believe that every generation in every culture deserves to receive the communication of the gospel in a manner maximizing the likelihood of a positive, soul-saving response.

The church of the Lord Jesus Christ is to be filled with new souls every day, every week, every month, and every year. The ultimate victory and triumph of the church is God's last instrument to use in His eternal plan and purpose and is the foundation to a person who has a passion for the harvest.

A harvest philosophy makes bringing people into a living relationship with Jesus Christ the priority.

When we have a harvest mentality, we believe that God has assigned the highest priority to bringing people into a living relationship with Jesus Christ. We may define our mission narrowly as an enterprise devoted to proclaiming the good news of Jesus Christ and to persuade men to become His disciples and dependable members of His church.

John Wimber, in his book *Power Encounter and Power Evangelism* states: "It is the Holy Spirit, the go-between to God, who holds the key to power encounters. Our openness and availability to His direction and enabling, anointing and power are the catalyst to fulfilling the Great Commission."[2]

CHRIST'S MISSION

In Luke 10, we have the first biblical account of Christ appointing, training, and sending ordinary people to do the work of evangelism. This is the first mission outside of the twelve apostles. These instructions were probably repeated often by Jesus and the apostles. These are the instructions to those unnamed workers, the vast army of unknown Christian workers, no-names who were honored in heaven.

Here, Jesus commissioned seventy people—thirty-five pairs of committed harvesters. He sent these men as advance messengers along the route He intended to follow along the southern board of Galilee and down the eastern side of the Jordan through Perea. This was new territory where He Himself was about to go. Luke 10 is the account of the "Mission Seventy," the appointing and sending of ordinary people into ordinary places of society to reap an extraordinary harvest of people for Christ.

In context, Luke 9 and 10 are the closing days of Jesus' ministry. Ahead was the cross with its agony and passion. As the time was drawing near for His death, resurrection, and ascension, Jesus steadfastly set His face to go to Jerusalem. He never lost sight of the cross. The destiny that God had given Him was set before His eyes. His face was set like a flint. This implied His determined, fixed purpose. He was born to die. Christ knew that He must taste death for every man and destroy the works of darkness. Christ, with perfect clearness, saw His life being shot like an arrow into history, into the inevitable and purposed end: the cross.

THE SPIRIT OF THE "MISSION SEVENTY"

Jesus sent messengers to prepare the cities where He would stop on His way to His final destiny. First, He sent the apostles and then the seventy ordinary people. In Luke 9:55, the messengers were rejected as they preached the gospel in particular cities. Jesus turned and rebuked them for their spirits and their attitudes.

The messengers' experience of rejection exposed their faulty concepts of the ministry of Christ. They asked, "Do You want us to call fire down from heaven to consume them?" That was certainly the wrong attitude. "There is much pride and passion and personal revenge underneath your pretended zeal for Me" were His words. He rebuked their intolerance, their vindicative spirits, and their false zeal, which all turned to be misdirected enthusiasm. They did not understand the lostness of people's souls. They did not understand that people in darkness would respond this way, and that they were not to be destroyed because of their ignorance and hard-hearted response. They were to be prayed for. The harvest was to be reaped, not burned up. They did not know what spirit they were of. They were of the spirit of fire and brimstone.

THE SPIRIT OF CHRIST

Jesus again clearly articulates His mission in Luke 9:56: "For the Son of Man did not come to destroy men's life but to save them."

"For God sent His Son into the world not to condemn the world, but in order that the world might be saved through Him" (John 3:17).

"I did not come in order to judge the world but in order to save the world" (John 12:47).

"For the Son of Man came to seek and to save what was lost" (Luke 19:10).

Christ's mission, the mission that brought Him from heaven to earth, was to save and rescue people from sin and damnation and to place them in permanent safety. His spirit was one of grace and mercy. It was a spirit that loved and labored so earnestly, so perseveringly, and so patiently that He would set the example for all evangelism. Christ's mission, His whole work, was to bring salvation. His miracles were those of healing. His teaching was for the saving of souls.

> "Ordinary people must become witnesses of the power of the kingdom of God to a dying world."

The disciples were unacquainted with the infirmities of their spirits and not aware of the principles and motives by which their present conduct was influenced. They needed to begin to see the harvest the way Christ saw the harvest. They needed to feel deeply toward the harvest the way He did.

Christ's mission was to open up a new era under a release of unbounded mercy. He came to be a destroyer and our savior. He came to destroy the works of darkness and to save us from the sin that would only devour our lives.

Jesus appointed the seventy, and He was the Lord, the master, the king, the supreme ruler, the One with the authority to do and to say as He would wish. The servants were to obey without question. Jesus would appoint, that is designate, and give them their divine mission in life. The Lord appointed those who had experienced firsthand the kingdom of God and those who had become disciples and would go forth with utmost obedience into the harvest.

Ordinary people must become witnesses of the power of the kingdom of God to a dying world. A witness is a person who tells others of something that is real to him or her. This is the foundation of true preparation for evangelism. A witness talks about what he has seen, felt, and experienced. Ordinary people witness about Christ working in their lives. They witness about how Christ changes their lives, changes their marriage, alters their vocabulary, gives them power to forgive, gives them a new sense of purpose and meaning, and delivers them from destructive habits that were previously in their lives.

Christ's evangelistic strategy is not programs to reach the multitudes. It is people chosen, equipped, and sent into society. People are His method of winning the world. We are His people and this is our mission.

NOTES

1. *Pilgrims Progress*.

2. John Wimber, *Power Encounters and Power Evangelism*.

Chapter 25

THE PERMANENCE OF REVIVAL

*R*evival seasons are times of intensified Holy Spirit activity that reinforce the need to practice the spiritual principles found in the Word of God.

The word renew speaks of going back to something in the past and reestablishing it. To renew means there must be something there to revive in the first place. The Holy Spirit seeks to revive the church in all areas of truth and practice as seen in the New Testament, especially the Book of Acts. Revival redesigns us with the power and presence that could and should be the norm for a church functioning in the Spirit with the same power of the early church.

The church today should walk in that level of New Testament Christianity, whether in revival or out of revival. These permanence principles are to be established before revival, during revival, and after revival.

Revival seasons renew powerful praying, God-filled worship, signs and wonders, evangelism, and Holy Spirit-anointed preaching and teaching. Revival may occur to renew or recover these truths, or to rediscover or discover them for the first time. Revival alone does not build great churches or great people. Revival must be absorbed into truth. Without this, we will be forced into fabricating a revival atmosphere.

If the church responds to and receives the true purpose of revival, it will establish permanent principles of Holy Spirit activity. The church does not need to choose between spiritual death or spiritual life, or between revival and church-as-normal deadness. The church is called to walk in the Spirit, to sustain the life power of Christ's presence all the time, in revival season and out of revival season. If we fail to grasp this truth, we will seek to go from revival season to revival season, and with long intervals of spiritual dryness in between.

Truths and principles of permanence will allow the church to enjoy revival seasons because they intensify the permanent principles and truths already being cherished by the people of God. We must relish the seasons when the Lord "stirs the water" (John 5:14), but prepare ourselves to walk in the seasons when there are no stirrings (John 5:35). We need to remember that the water is always available. Revival seasons come and go, but the Word of God stands forever (2 Timothy 4:2).

> **"Truths and principles of permanence will allow the church to enjoy revival seasons..."**

As the rain of the Holy Spirit falls upon the ready soil during seasons of revival, we must make sure there is plenty of seed in the ground. Without seeds, or permanent truths and principles, present in the soil, the rain will only soften the ground for a period of time with no longstanding spiritual growth. Truth must be in the ground of people's hearts so that revival rains can nurture these truths, causing new growth and new fruit.

Church With No Permanent Principle Truths

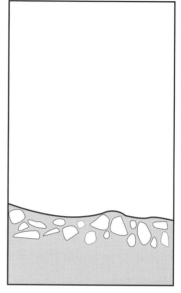

This soil will be softened for the moment, it will look better, feel better, appear to have great potential for productivity but it doesn't have the seeds of permanent principle truths in the soil and will in time bear little or no fruit after revival showers cease.

The soil has now returned to its former condition - a piece of ground without the power to produce life. The problem here is that it will become worse than it was before it received the revival shower.

"...revival intensifies what is already present in the church at the time of spiritual outpouring..."

Revival may or may not correct a church's weaknesses in the important areas of permanent truth. In most cases, revival intensifies what is already present in the church at the time of spiritual outpouring, and if a church is weak in vision, revival may not change this. Worse yet, the church might make revival its purpose and vision. If a church is weak in the systematic teaching of the Word of God, revival may further weaken this permanent building truth, allowing revival experiences, emotions, and subjective blessings of God—all of which are wonderful—to replace strong Bible teaching. When the church allows that to happen, it will struggle to retain spiritual life and flow.

Revival spirit cooperates with biblical truth, which sustains the life flow of the Holy Spirit. A healthy church that has established the unmistakable permanent truths clearly laid out for us in Scripture will receive more from a revival season than a non-prepared church. Permanent truth and principles sustain the precious revival spirit that brings life, fire, and love. Seasons of revival should position the church to walk in the power and truth revealed and inspired during these times.

Church With Permanent Principle Truths

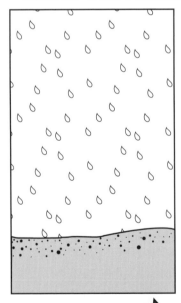

REVIVAL SEASON

REVIVAL SEASON PASSES

The soil is filled with permanent truth seed. Revival showers water the seeds; this soil will be productive and greatly empowered by the revival showers.

After revival showers cease there is still the fruitful growth of permanent truths. These truths continue to bear fruit in season and out of season.

PERMANENCE PRINCIPLES THAT SUSTAIN SPIRITUAL LIFE AND POWER

1. The permanence principle truth of a vision for a glorious church.
2. The permanence principle truth of a biblically governed church—leadership plurality.
3. The permanence principle truth of a unified purpose and mission statement for the church.
4. The permanence principle truth of a committed membership.
5. The permanence principle truth of a Holy Spirit-empowered church.
6. The permanence principle truth of a Word-governed and Word-fed church.
7. The permanence principle truth of dynamic corporate gatherings with biblical principles with presence prayer, worship, gifts, word, response, edification, exhortation, and comfort.
8. The permanence principle truth of seeking God with fasting and prayer.
9. The permanence principle truth of anointed power praise and worship.
10. The permanence principle truth of building strong families.
11. The permanence principle truth of the Great Commission.
12. The permanence principle truth of the many membered body of Christ.

WALKING IN TRUTH

"Then the churches throughout all Judea, Galilee, and Samaria had peace and were edified. And walking in the fear of the Lord and in the comfort of the Holy Spirit, they were multiplied" (Acts 9:31).

The walking church is a church that has experienced exhilarating Holy Spirit seasons and has learned how to translate them into a consistent walk of truth. The walking church understands, respects, and assimilates the permanence truth principles.

"I rejoiced greatly that I have found some of your children walking in truth, as we received commandment from the Father" (2 John 4).

"But those who wait on the Lord shall renew their strength; they shall mount up with wings like eagles, they shall run and not be weary, they shall walk and not faint" (Isaiah 40:31).

This verse refers to the spirit of renewal, the power of God to revive spiritual life by His grace and power. This kind of renewal results in a mounting up, like an eagle soaring into the heavenlies. Revival is a time for spiritual soaring, for mounting up on the wings of the Spirit. We greatly need these seasons of renewal for the lifting of our souls out of the humdrum of life, for lifting us above the hassles of the enemy, and for revealing to us a new glimpse of God's power, love, and mercy. Vision is renewed during revival. Our spirits takes on new dimensions of grace and wisdom.

This renewing releases a new energy, a new spiritual grace to run in the Spirit and to pursue things with passion and a mission. But after the soaring and running, we must have a time to walk. It is not as exciting, and it seems at first a letdown. We may ask, "Where are the days of hot passion and swift moving of God's Spirit? Have we missed something? Did we do something wrong? Why aren't we soaring and running?"

We can only soar when God lifts us into the realm of spiritual activity. The eagle cannot create the wind, but can only cooperate with and make use of the stormy gusts or the quite breezes. Let us be like the eagle and be as content with the still breezes that slow us down as we are with the stormy gusts that lift us into new realms.

Walking in the Spirit is the key to long-lasting fruitfulness and maturity. Let us not fabricate a perpetual soaring, running atmosphere. Revival seasons are to be enjoyed, not manipulated.

> "Revival is a time for spiritual soaring, for mounting up on the wings of the Spirit."

What is experienced during seasons of revival usually takes on certain forms of physical behavior, program planning, and unique church service schedules and activities. Revival seasons can mean intensified church schedules, more meetings and prayer times, longer sessions at the altar, and more personal ministry. But when the season changes, these same structures may need to be altered in order to accommodate a new season of walking in the things of God. This may mean the implementing of a new children's ministry or a new Christian education program that fits this new season. It may mean adapting the worship service to long-term body life without losing the power of God's presence.

We must not try to sustain certain unique or even strange behavior that occurs during revival season. We cannot—or should not—try to sustain the church service styles from seasons of revival. We have all probably witnessed at one time or another groups that have retained past quirks or oddness of behavior from previous revival seasons. It was probably embarrassing or puzzling.

Every revival has its own time of encountering God with genuine responses such as shaking, trembling, crying, laughing, jerking, lying on the floor, shouting, or screaming. This is not fabricated or learned. It is real and from God. But we should not seek to sustain these things forever. These things are not truths to establish and pass on to the next generation. There is nothing that will drive the next generation away from God more than dead, learned spiritual behavior.

A new season does not mean we must lose what has been gained during revival. It simply means we must sustain what has been gained by new application. In a new season of walking, the schedule will undoubtedly need to reflect the realities of life: work, raising children, making and keeping friends, taking time for relatives and family, and pursuing personal spiritual development. Again, this is not going backward or losing the fire of revival. It is sustaining the work of revival.

What has begun in the Spirit must be sustained through the Word. Spiritual deliverances, breakthroughs, and life-changing encounters with God must be secured through the proper disciplines of the Word of God, of serving others, and of the deepening of character.

Revival seasons come and go, as we can verify from history. No spiritual awakening lasts forever—twenty, thirty, or forty years, maybe—but the truths discovered and the spiritual life released can be sustained forever.

Let us sustain the truth, not our responses to truth. Let us sustain the truth that God's Holy Spirit is available to move in every generation in His own unique way. As seasons come and go let us be quick to discern our season and walk in the purposes of God.

"To every thing there is a *season* and a *time* for every matter or *purpose* under heaven" (Ecclesiastes 3:1).